The Pashtun Tahafuz Movement

Forced Disappearances, Military Courts Violation of Fair Trials and War Crimes in Waziristan

The Pashtun Tahafuz Movement

Forced Disappearances, Military Courts Violation of Fair Trials and War Crimes in Waziristan

Musa Khan Jalalzai

Imal Katswal

Vij Books

New Delhi (India)

Published by

Vij Books
(An imprint of Vij Books India Pvt Ltd)

(Publishers, Distributors & Importers)
4836/24, Ansari Road
Delhi – 110 002
Phone: 91-11-43596460
Mobile: 98110 94883
e-mail: contact@vijpublishing.com
www.vijbooks.in

Contents

Introduction

The emergence of the Pashtun Tahafuz Movement in 2018 has generated aspiration, hope and ambition among Pashtun communities across the Durand Line that now the organization will generate awareness in young generations to unite against Pakistan's army, which kills innocent women and children in Waziristan, Khyber Pakhtunkhwa and Balochistan. The army and its paramilitary forces, including intelligence agencies, pick, kidnap, torture and disappear young Pashtun students from colleges and universities. Former Army Chief, General Raheel Sharif protected terrorists and accommodated them in guest houses, ordered the killing and kidnapping of young men, women and children, and used sophisticated weapons in the region. He never allowed maimed, disabled and mutilated children to treat their wounds, or leave the region safely. Extrajudicial killings in FATA and Waziristan by his forces caused permanent consternation and schizophrenic diseases in North Waziristan. More than 1,000 women and girls were kidnapped, and 2,000 tribal leaders have been disappeared by the intelligence agencies and the army in Khyber Pakhtunkhwa and Waziristan since 2004. Reftworld in its recent report highlighted cases of torture, humiliation, ill-treatment and unlawful arrest and detention in Pakistan: "Irrespective of the "war on terror", the people of Pakistan suffer widespread violations of their civil and political rights. In Pakistan, torture and ill-treatment are endemic; arbitrary and unlawful arrest and detention are a growing problem; extrajudicial executions of criminal suspects are frequent; well over 7,000 people are on death row and there has recently been a wave of executions".

Domestic and foreign media, intellectuals, think tanks, and literary forums are critical of the unconstitutional operations and actions of Pakistan's armed forces and the ISI in North Waziristan, Khyber Pakhtunkhwa and Balochistan. The army and ISI treat residents of Waziristan and Baluchistan like enemies, kill and arrest them with impunity, their houses are being destroyed and set on fire and their businesses are looted and plundered. Newspapers reported the army spokesman's announcement of controlling Miranshah town, while he didn't disclose war crimes of rogue military units there. Journalist M. Ilyas Khan confirmed atrocities of Pakistan army in his BBC News report: "In May 2016, for example, an attack on a military post in the Teti Madakhel area of North Waziristan triggered a manhunt by troops who rounded up the entire population of a village. An eyewitness who watched the operation from a wheat field nearby and whose brother was among those detained told the BBC that the soldiers beat everyone with batons and threw mud in children's mouths when they cried. A pregnant woman was one of two people who died during torture, her son said in video testimony.

This business of killing and torture of the rogue army and its sarcastic agencies is expanding when they illegally enter houses and rape helpless women as they did in Bangladesh in 1971. The TTP Leader, Manzoor Ahmad Pashteen's family was forced to flee Waziristan for IDP refugee camps in Dera Ismail Khan District. In 2007, his family once more fled their home town in 2007 and returned to his home town in 2008. In 2009, due to the military operation of Rah-e-Nijat, his family was forced to flee South Waziristan for the fourth time. The Pashtun Tahafuz Movement was frequently stopped by the army and its supporters were incarcerated. Hostile attitude of the failing Pakistani state and its corrupt institutions towards the people of Waziristan and Balochistan has prompted alienation and unending insurgencies, which brought more destruction and wrecking to the nation. The war against Pashtuns has entered a crucial phase where the Pakistan army receives dead bodies on daily bases, and one day this unjust war will enter Punjab and will repeat history of the past. The military agencies in Pakistan also kidnap family members of Pakistani social media activists to surrender their account credentials to take control of their accounts, delete posts critical of the 'government' and peddle propaganda and disinformation from the accounts. The Pakistani 'government' previously banned Tweeter in February 2024. The ban continues to be in place by the day. The PTM activist, Gulalai Ismail was also accused of treason, but human rights defenders said allegations were bogus and she was being targeted for highlighting abuses committed by Pakistan's military.

Notwithstanding her arrival in New York, she still lives in consternation. She was arrested and harassed by intelligence agencies to change her opinion on the war crimes of the army in FATA and Waziristan, but she strongly refused to become reticent. In his New York Times article, Jeffrey Gettleman (19 September, 2019) reported that Gulalai Ismail had been advocating the rights of raped women, kidnapped and tortured Pashtuns,

Punjabis and Balochs since years: "Her account of being chased out of the country does not help the government's efforts to win diplomatic support at a time when the economy is tanking and Pakistan is begging the world to censure India for its recent moves on Kashmir, a disputed territory claimed by both Pakistan and India. It has taken Ms. Ismail some time to feel safe even in New York, she said, but she has begun to meet with prominent human rights defenders and the staff of congressional leaders. "The PTM EU chapter has also been playing a significant role in promoting the narrative of the organization. Expert and political worker, Mr. Imal Katswal is an active member of PTM in Douai, France, contributing his professional experience, intellectual tips-off and ideas to make PTM members vigilant and updated. He worked and supported Pashtun's rights movements in Belgium from 2009-2013, before shifting to France. However, he participated in PTM protests and rallies in Europe to draw the attention of the international community towards the forced disappearances and torture of its workers and leaders by the agencies.

The PTM has become a powerful civil and human rights organization that shacked military establishment and political culture of Pakistan by arranging protests against the brutalities and torture of the army and governments. In Khyber Pakhtunkhwa and Balochistan provinces, the PTM has gained a good support of communities. Experts and writers, Dr. Sudha Ramachandran, Hamsini Hariharan and Shibani Mehta in their research paper (Impact of the Pashtun Tahafuz Movement on Pakistan's Political Landscape, Takshashila Strategic Assessment, 2018-03. June 20, 2018. Takshashila Institution) have noted mobilization of PTM supporters in all provinces of Pakistan: "The PTM rallies have captured the attention of international media and have brought the Pashtun identity into the consciousness of the Pakistani people and exposed the atrocities faced by the Pashtuns to a global audience. Mobilization against the army could have a demonstration effect on other ethno-nationalist groups like the Balochis and Sindhis. These are groups that have traditionally felt excluded from the mainstream to come out in the open to raise their own grievances which could possibly contain anti-state and anti-military sentiments and demands. Each of these sub-nationalist groups possesses a different view of their place in Pakistan and different social orders- which could make Pakistan nationalism all the more complex. It is too early to predict whether the PTM will evolve into a viable nationalist movement, the kind seen in the past when the Pashtunistan movement was at its height. The Pashtuns remain fragmented along tribal, sub-tribal and ideological lines.

Such divisions have traditionally been utilized by the army (and earlier by the British) to stop the Pashtuns from coalescing in the past".

In 2019, PTM leader Arman Loni was killed by the police in Loralai. In 2019, following the Kharqamar incident, a clash between the army and PTM workers left 13 dead. On 27 January 2020, Manzoor Pashteen was arrested by Peshawar police on allegation of sedition. On 28 March 2021, Manzoor Pashteen was arrested in Kohat, while Mohsin Dawar was arrested in Karak. On 07 December, Islamabad High court granted seven days remand for Manzoor. The leader of the Pashtun Tahafuz Movement (PTM), Manzoor Ahmad Pashteen then called for a large gathering of Pashtuns on 11 October 2024 to draw attention of the international community towards the policies, attitude and so-called military operations of Pakistani army in Waziristan, and other areas of Khyber Pakhtunkhwa and Balochistan provinces. In the last several years, the Military carried out several operations in South and North Waziristan, Dir, Swat, Malakand and Khyber Agency, which resulted in the killing of thousands, men, women, children and destruction of infrastructure. In January 2018, Pashtun March reached Islamabad, which was a mass mobilization to exhibit its strength and present its demands to the Federal administration. This mobilization, later on, resulted in forming an organization of the Pashtun Tahafuz Movement.

On 11 February, 2019, in his New York Times article, PTM leader Manzoor Pashteen gave an account of his struggle for the recovery of kidnapped Pashtun activists by Pakistan's military establishment: "The government ignored us when these militants terrorized and murdered the residents. Pakistan's military operations against the militants brought further misery: civilian killings, displacements, enforced disappearances, humiliation and the destruction of our livelihoods and way of life. No journalists were allowed into the tribal areas while the military operations were going on. Pashtuns who fled the region in hopes of rebuilding their lives in Pakistani cities were greeted with suspicion and hostility. We were stereotyped as terrorist sympathizers. The Pakistan military was always criminal, but what it transformed under General Bajwa and now under General Asim Munir is unprecedented. Pashtun Tahafuz Movement (PTM) is a political-non-violent organization that has been challenging Pakistan's terrorist army since 2014.

The Pakistan army is facing a robust wave of violence across the country due to its failed strategies and policies. The Pashtun Tahafuz Movement didn't emerge abruptly, it emerged as a result of state hate and brutalities against

Pashtuns and Baloch people. The PTM adopted a culture of non-violence against the failing state. However, the Taliban takeover of Afghanistan in 2021 caused many problems; including Pakistan's deep political, and military interference, intelligence war of different Asian and European agencies, famine and torture of civilians by the Taliban terrorist militia across the country. Lashing, beating, stoning, corporal punishment and the death penalty under the Taliban militia forced three millions Afghans to flee the country. Prominent research scholar and expert of Afghanistan, Kate Clark (AAN, 08 May 2023) in her paper highlighted torture and corporal punishment of Taliban regime: "A new United Nations report on capital and corporal punishment has detailed the widespread use of corporal punishment delivered ad hoc by non-judicial authorities, such as the police and 'Vice and Virtue' officials. It also documents a rise in corporal punishment ordered by judges since November 2022 when the Taliban's Supreme Leader encouraged the use of such measures where they are considered divinely mandated".

The British newspaper, the Guardian (Annie Kelly and Zahra Joya for Rukhshana Media 26 August 2024) noted the new law of the Taliban that banned women from speaking or showing their faces outside their homes was condemned by the UN and met with horror by human rights groups. "The Taliban published a host of new "vice and virtue" laws, approved by their supreme leader Hibatullah Akhundzada, which state that women must completely veil their bodies –including their faces–in thick clothing at all times in public to avoid leading men into temptation and vice. Women's voices are also deemed to be potential instruments of vice and so will not be allowed to be heard in public under the new restrictions. Women must also not be heard singing or reading aloud, even from inside their houses. "Whenever an adult woman leaves her home out of necessity, she is obliged to conceal her voice, face, and body," the new laws state. Men will also be required to cover their bodies from their navels to their knees when they are outside their homes." The Guardian reported. The international community strongly condemned the Taliban's treatment of women. The so-called Islamic Emirate's supreme leader, Mullah Hibatullah Akhundzada issued a new law laying out the duties, powers and punishments available to the enforcers of the Ministry for Promoting Virtue and Preventing Vice.

The law orders women to cover their bodies and faces entirely and not speak or sing loud enough for non-family members to hear them. Men must dress so as to cover their bodies from navel to knee. Professor in Conflict and Humanitarian Studies at Qatar Foundation's Hamad Bin

Khalifa University and an Honorary Professor of the University of York, Sultan Barakat in his commentary (Taliban ban on girls' education defies both worldly and religious logic: The ban stands against the core principles of Islam and hinders the Taliban's efforts to gain international recognition. Al Jazeera 01 April 20241 Apr 2024) has argued that Taliban shouldn't teach world leaders and religious clerics: "The Taliban's stance on this issue defies both worldly and religious logic. Afghanistan, a post-conflict nation that has just emerged from the jaws of multiple protracted armed conflicts spanning four decades, needs all hands on deck to work towards getting the country out of the economic abyss that it finds itself in. The Taliban takeover of Kabul in 2021 and the ensuing uncertainty precipitated the exodus of a vast number of Afghan professionals, leading to a brain drain at a very precarious time. The last thing that the nation needed was its new leaders to handicap it further and jettison any prospects of recovery by excluding half the population from participating in education, and thus the recovery efforts.....From the religious perspective, too, the Taliban leaders must realize that they are accountable before Allah SWT for thrusting ignorance upon a generation of girls just so they can claim a perceived localized victory of tradition".

No country can make aggrandizement when half of its population is left behind," the United Nations' children's agency noted the ban on girls attending school became 1,000 days old. Since their return to power, Taliban have started persecuting and prosecuting Afghan women and girls and forcing them to marry their illiterate fighters, leaders and military commanders. Expert, Ehsan Qaane (Gender Persecution in Afghanistan: Could it come under the ICC's Afghanistan investigation? AAN, 26 May 2023) has noted brutalities of Taliban against Afghan women: "Since the Taliban regained power in Afghanistan in August 2021, they have imposed multiple orders and regulations on Afghan women and girls that do not apply to men and boys. Two United Nations independent experts, Special Rapporteur on the Situation of Human Rights in Afghanistan, Richard Bennet and Chair of the Working Group on Discrimination against Women and Girls, Dorothy Estrada-Tanck, have concluded that these restrictions, which they say are "violating girls' and women's rights to education, work, freedom of movement, health, bodily autonomy and decision-making, freedom of peaceful assembly and association, and access to justice," amount to "gender persecution." This book focuses attention on the struggle of Pashtun Tahafuz Movement in Pakistan against the brutalities and genocide of armed forces in Waziristan and Balochistan. I hope this book will generate awareness among educated Pakistani and Afghans in colleges and universities in Pakistan and Afghanistan. The book also highlights the atrocities of the Taliban government in Afghanistan and its ban on girl's education.

Musa Khan Jalalzai London

September 2024

Summary

Operations Zarb-e-Azb, Rah-e-Nijat, Azm-e-Istehkam and Raddul Fassad, Enforced Disappearances and Failure of Security Agencies to Counter Extremism and Talibanization in Pakistan

The unending war of Pakistan's military establishment against the Pashtun population in Waziristan, Swat, Sararogha and Khwazakhela began on 25 October 2007. The failure of the Pakistan army to settle ethnic and sectarian issues resulted in the citizens' alienation from the state. The TNSM and TTP challenged the credibility and integrity of clean-shaved Qazi appointed by the government.[1] In 2008, Operation Zelzala was launched to eliminate Baitullah Mesud's control over Sararogha Fort in South Waziristan agency. The army focused on retaking the fort and requested tribal leaders to cooperate with armed forces, but they refused. The armed forces controlled several villages and towns including Spinkai, the stronghold of Mehsud, but Mehsud militia strongly resisted the army. On 24 October 2008, 3,000 strong Pakistani soldiers and officers arrived in Swat to confront the Taliban militia. The army was deployed on hill-top and heavy fighting started with suicide bombing that killed 17 soldiers and 13 civilians. On 31 October, 2008, the military reported up to 130 militant fighters killed, however, the next day about 700 militants overran a police position on a hill in Khwazakhela. The police surrendered and the police station was handed to the Taliban militia. Taliban controlled Swat district, established sharia courts and their own local governors in Tehsil Kabal, Matta and Khwazakhela. The Pakistan Army's military operations in the Swat Valley, particularly from 2007 to 2009, were launched to combat militant groups, including the Pakistani Taliban (TTP) that had gained control of the region.

There were claims of extrajudicial killings of suspected militants or their supporters. Many individuals went missing during the military operations, leading to accusations of enforced disappearances, use of Heavy Force. The use of artillery, airstrikes, and heavy weaponry in populated areas led to civilian casualties and widespread destruction, detention and Torture.

Some detainees, including alleged militants and suspected supporters, were reportedly subjected to torture and ill-treatment. While the Pakistan Army denied these accusations and maintained that they took measures to avoid civilian harm, human rights groups have called for investigations into these claims. However, there has been little official accountability for any alleged war crimes, and independent investigations into these incidents have been limited. The Tehrik Taliban Pakistan (TTP) was established in December 2007 to further support Baitullah Mehsud's operation against the Pakistan army in Waziristan. The TTP sought to replace the secular state with a regional Islamic State. Its presence in Afghanistan has been strongly supported, where thousands of its forces were receiving military training. In 2007, a provincial government signed a peace deal with the father-in-law of Mullah Fazlullah, leader of the TTP's faction in the restive Swat valley. Pakistan army launched several military operations to fight the exponentially growing militancy in Waziristan and Khyber Pakhtunkhwa province.

These operation were given names like operation Sirat-i-Mustaqeem in Khyber Agency (2008), operation Sherdil in Bajaur Agency (2008), operation Rah-i-Haq-III in Swat valley and Shangla (2009), operation Black Thunderstorm in Buner, Lower Dir and Shangla district (2009), operation Brekhna in Mohmand Agency (2009), operation Rah-i-Rast, commonly known as Swat Operation, (2009), and operation Rah-i-Nijat in South Waziristan (2009) in which Pakistan army committed war crimes by killing women and children with impunity. Doctoral student at the Fletcher School of Law and Diplomacy, expert Rabia Zafar in her paper (Development and the Battle for Swat, The Fletcher School–al Nakhlah– Tufts University Journal of Academic and Social Research, 2018 Vol.1) argued that in early 2009, the army and Taliban fighting in Sway valley diverted attention of international community towards challenges of the army and civilian government: "In the early summer of 2009, world attention focused on Pakistan as Taliban militants gained a foothold just 70 miles outside of the nation's capital, Islamabad, challenging the country's nascent civilian government. The government responded with a strong show of military force, pummeling the Swat Valley and surrounding areas with tanks, heavy artillery, and helicopter gunships. In the process, some 2 million people were internally displaced leaving Pakistan on the brink of a large-scale humanitarian crisis. By late June, however, the military operation had started yielding results and the government claimed that the Malakand Division, including Swat, had been cleared of the Taliban.[1] Most of the displaced civilians began returning to the area and international observers seemed satisfied that this story had come to an end. Yet, this battle, with its seemingly existential consequences and high-level human drama, Thus, the Taliban–in one form or another–and the government have battled for years over the control of Swat's legal, judicial, enforcement and structures".[2]

However, on 28 November 2022, TTP cancelled a five-month truce with Pakistan due to the attitude of the army generals. The TTP accused the army for not fulfilling the deal because it did not meet all its demands, notably the release of key TTP members. The proxy militia (Afghan Taliban) of US-Pakistan in Kabul abruptly announced they don't recognize the Durand Line. Thus challenges of the army become multiple. The Afghan Taliban militias had to deal with insurgencies across Afghanistan. North Waziristan has experienced the wrath of the Pakistan army and its war crimes from 2014 to 2024. Landmines, drone attacks, bombs and plunder of resources, homes and shops wrecked the lives of poor people in Khyber Pakhtunkhwa and Waziristan, while house-to-house search operations by the army added more fuel to the pain of citizens. Most of Pakistan's counterterrorism operations between 2003 and 2014 were linked to the U.S.-led global war on terrorism. In some parts of the bazaar most of the shops were half open, with saleable goods still on display as if the shopkeepers had just gone for prayers or a short break'. BBC noted. According to the Al Jazeera report (15 July 2014), "The weeks-long air and ground operation, named Zarb-e-Azb, caused the exodus of tens of thousands of people, with some fleeing into neighbouring Afghanistan. Officials have told Al Jazeera that at least 787,888 men, women, and children were registered as Internally Displaced Person (IDPs), but their number was higher.[3]

Miran Shah, the regional capital, was nearly deserted, as most people fled to Bannu in neighbouring Khyber Pakhtunkhwa province to escape the bombing." Expert, Lt General V.K. Kapoor (Retd) in his analysis, (Pakistani Army Operations in North Waziristan. Land Forces, Issue 04, 2014) has noted criticism of expert forums on military operation in North Waziristan on the behest of the United States. Now the country's army failed to control large swathes of Pakistan: "Today the state of Pakistan is not in control of fairly large swathes of territory. The jihadi terror groups pay no heed to any instructions passed by the government. They are a law unto themselves and find support among the local population. The youth of Pakistan have been radicalized to a large extent. Quite a few are offering their services to various terror groups fighting in Syria, Sudan and Iraq. The Pakistan military has also been radicalized. May 2011, the attack against the Karachi Naval base which saw six Taliban militants hold off security forces for more than 16 hours and kill a dozen naval personnel, had caused particular alarm. One naval officer said that the attackers knew the base "inside out" and were likely to have received intelligence on the US-supplied aircraft and the presence of US and Chinese technicians."[4] In this fake war against militants, Army Chief General Raheel Sharif committed war crimes. He ordered the killing of Pashtuns in North Waziristan and kidnapped more than one thousand women. The rogue army on the behest of the US army decided to launch another war (Azm-e-Istehkam Operation) against the people of Waziristan to further destroy houses of Pashtuns.

Since 2007, this is the twelfth schedule of the army organizing a carnage of innocent civilians, while Operation Rahi Nijat killed many children. Operation Rah-e-Nijat was a major military offensive conducted by the Pakistan Army in South Waziristan, a region in the Federally Administered Tribal Areas (FATA) of Pakistan, starting in June 2009. The operation aimed to eliminate the Tehrik-i-Taliban Pakistan (TTP) and other militant groups that had established strongholds in the region, but failed. Expert and writer Sushant Sareen (Azm-e-Istehkam: China's wish is Pakistan's command, Jun 24, 2024) has noted some major operations of Pakistan army: "Most of the earlier operations were of a tactical nature, focusing on a particular area that had become particularly troublesome. Sareen has argued that the Operation Rah-e-Rast and Rah-e-Haq were in Swat region, Sherdil was in Bajaur and Rah-e-Nijaat was in South Waziristan agency. He also noted the two big operations on a much broader front were the Zarb-e-Azb, which started in North Waziristan and then was extended to other regions, followed by Radd-ul-Fassad which was more an intelligence based operation to strike at terrorist networks which had spread throughout Pakistan". The new operation Azm-e-Istehkaam, according to Sareen, "is aimed at curbing the Islamist terror networks which have resurfaced with renewed vigour and virulence after the Afghan Taliban shattered the "shackles of slavery" of US and its allies, ironically enough with Pakistan's assiduous assistance".[5]

The Radd-ul-Fasaad operation was a counter-terrorism initiative launched by the Pakistan military in 2017, following the controversial operation of Zarb-e-Azb. While it killed innocent women and children but never reduced the operational capacity of terrorist groups, several factors contributed to its inability to completely undermine the network of terrorist organizations in Pakistan. The terrorist organizations in Pakistan, such as Tehrik-i-Taliban Pakistan (TTP) and various sectarian groups, operate through complex and decentralized networks. These groups are highly adaptable, often relocating and reconstituting after military offensives. This adaptability makes it challenging to completely dismantle them through conventional military operations, geographic and Tribal Challenges. Additionally, the close-knit tribal systems often provide protection to militants, either out of loyalty or fear, cross-border Militancy. Pakistan shares a porous border with Afghanistan, where many of these terrorist groups have safe havens. Despite efforts to improve border security, militants have been able to retreat across the border, regroup, and then re-enter Pakistan.

Some political factions have historically had ties with militant groups, and there has been ambivalence or even support from certain segments of society towards these organizations. This socio-political complexity hinders comprehensive action against all terrorist networks. The Azm-e-Istehkam military operations in Waziristan, Pakistan, were part of the larger military efforts by the Pakistan Army aimed at combating militancy and terrorism in the region. These operations came after earlier campaigns like Operation Zarb-e-Azb (2014) and Operation Radd-ul-Fasaad (2017), which were launched to root out terrorist groups, particularly in the Federally Administered Tribal Areas (FATA), including North and South Waziristan, but the army rooted out Pashtun families and destroyed their houses. The Azm-e-Istehkam operations also claimed to counter militant insurgency in Waziristan. Waziristan had long been a hub for militant groups, including the Tehrik-i-Taliban Pakistan (TTP), al-Qaeda, and other extremist organizations. After the success of Operation Zarb-e-Azb, many militant leaders and fighters were eliminated or fled the region. However, remnants of these groups and their networks continued to operate in a more covert manner. The Azm-e-Istehkam (which translates to "Resolve for Stabilization") aimed to consolidate the gains made in earlier operations like Zarb-e-Azb and ensure long-term stability in the region.

The military sought to prevent militants from regrouping and re-establishing their presence, particularly after they had been weakened by previous campaigns. Border Security and Cross-Border Threats. As Afghanistan experienced instability, especially after the U.S. withdrawal, securing the border and preventing infiltration by militants became a priority for Pakistan's military. Another goal of the Azm-e-Istehkam operations was to ensure that development projects could be carried out in Waziristan and surrounding tribal areas. These projects included building infrastructure, roads, schools, and healthcare facilities. Stabilizing the region was seen as crucial to integrating the tribal areas into the broader national fabric and addressing the underlying socio-economic grievances that contributed to extremism. Counterinsurgency. The Azm-e-Istehkam continued Pakistan's broader counterinsurgency strategy to eliminate sleeper cells, militant hideouts, and disrupt their financial and logistical networks. The military sought to win the "hearts and minds" of the local population by providing security and fostering development, thereby reducing local support for militants. Pakistan's fight against militancy has been a key component of its national security policy.

The country was under considerable international pressure, particularly from the United States and neighbouring Afghanistan, to continue its efforts to eliminate terrorism. The military operations were part of Pakistan's commitment to counterterrorism and ensuring the region would not be used for terrorist activities that could affect international security. Now, the Azm-e-Istehkam operation is expectedly to ensure the stability and security of the region, but this will further destabilize the region. The Pakistan army is not countering terrorism and extremism, it is countering Pashtun communities in Waziristan and Khyber Pakhtunkhwa province. Its counterinsurgency operations are a pretext to receive more money from the United States. Pakistan's counterinsurgency operations have faced significant challenges and shortcomings in the past, leading to some failures. Pakistan's insurgencies, especially in the tribal regions like the Federally Administered Tribal Areas (FATA) and Khyber Pakhtunkhwa (KPK), have deep-rooted causes tied to complex tribal structures, ethnic tensions, and political marginalization. Counterinsurgency operations often failed to fully understand or address these dynamics, leading to ineffective engagement with local communities. Pakistan's counterinsurgency efforts have often been led by the military, with little integration of civilian governance and developmental efforts. Militant groups operating in Pakistan had access to sanctuaries both within Pakistan's remote regions and across the border in Afghanistan. This provided insurgents with places to regroup, resupply, and continue their operations.

Intelligence sharing and coordination between Pakistan's military, intelligence agencies (ISI), and local law enforcement was often insufficient, leading to operational failures. Poor intelligence gathering and analysis allowed insurgents to exploit gaps and continue their operations. Economic and Social Underdevelopment. The regions most affected by insurgency, like FATA and parts of Balochistan, were economically and socially underdeveloped, with weak infrastructure, limited education, and few economic opportunities. Expert and writer, Manuel Lamela has noted (Pakistan's Inter-Services Intelligence and its ties with radical groups. Universidad de Navarra. https://www.unav.edu/en/web/global-affairs/detalle/-/blogs/pakistan-s-inter-services-intelligence-and-its-ties-with-radical-groups) the ISI links with militant and radicalized groups and was involved in radicalizing the Rohingya Muslim groups in Bangladesh: "Pakistan's Inter-Services Intelligence (ISI) has been accused on many occasions of being closely linked to various radical groups; for example, they have recently been involved with the radicalization of the Rohingya refugees in Bangladesh. Although Islamabad continues strongly denying such accusations, reality shows us that cooperation between the ISI and various terrorist organizations has been fundamental to their proliferation and settlement both on national territory and in the neighbouring states of India and Afghanistan. The West has not been able to fully understand the nature of this relationship and its link to terrorism. The various complaints to the ISI have been loaded with different arguments of different kinds, lacking in unity and coherence. Unlike popular opinion, this analysis will point to the confused and undefined Pakistani nationalism as the main cause of this close relationship".[6]

The Directorate for Inter-Services Intelligence, together with the Intelligence Bureau and the Military Intelligence, constitute the intelligence services of the Pakistani State, the most important of which is the ISI. The ISI can be described as the intellectual core and center of gravity of the army. Its broad functions are the protection of Pakistan's national security and the promotion and defence of Pakistan's interests abroad. BBC in its news story (Pakistan's shadowy secret service, the ISI. On 03 May 2011. https://www.bbc.co.uk/news/world-south-asia) uncovered a double game of the ISI in the Afghan war by secretly supporting the Afghan Taliban against the US forces in Afghanistan. Experts were confused to find whether Osama bin Laden was living in Islamabad under the nose of ISI. Some experts knew that ISI had a link with his hiding in Islamabad: "Pakistan's directorate for Inter-Services Intelligence, or ISI, is once again facing accusations of double-standards over its role in the fight against al-Qaeda and the Taliban. Many observers find it hard to believe the organization had no idea that Osama Bin Laden had been living under the nose of the Pakistani military until his death. As to the US Special Forces raid that killed the al-Qaeda leader, questions abound about what the ISI knew and when it knew it. Similar Western doubts over the ISI's loyalties have been a recurring theme in recent years. The truth will no doubt always be murky - because like many other military intelligence organizations, the shadowy ISI zealously guards its secrets and evidence against it is sketchy. What is not in doubt however is that the agency is a central organ of Pakistan's military machine and has played a major - often dominant - role in the country's volatile politics? BBC noted.[7]

The Inter-Services Intelligence (ISI), Pakistan's premier intelligence agency, has often been accused by Western politicians, military experts, and analysts of being complicit or collaborative in terrorism, especially in Pakistan and Afghanistan. These allegations stem from a variety of incidents and geopolitical dynamics. One of the most consistent accusations against the ISI is its alleged support for the Afghan Taliban. Western politicians, especially from the U.S. and NATO countries, claim that the ISI has provided sanctuary, training, and logistical support to Taliban leaders, particularly the Quetta Shura (the Taliban's leadership council based in Pakistan). The ISI is thought to view the Taliban as a strategic asset to counter Indian influence in Afghanistan. By supporting a friendly government in Kabul, Pakistan could maintain a buffer against India. The ISI has also been accused of supporting militant groups operating in the Kashmir region, which has long been a flashpoint between India and Pakistan. Groups like Lashkar-e-Taiba (LeT), responsible for attacks such as the 2008 Mumbai attacks, have been linked to the ISI. The discovery of Osama bin Laden in Abbottabad, a military town in Pakistan, in 2011 raised serious suspicions about whether elements within the ISI were harbouring the al-Qaeda leader. The proximity of bin Laden's hideout to military facilities, and the fact that he lived there undetected for years, fueled these accusations. In addition to Afghanistan and Kashmir, the ISI has also been accused of using jihadist groups domestically to further its political aims within Pakistan. Groups like the Pakistani Taliban (Tehrik-i-Taliban Pakistan, or TTP) have attacked both the Pakistani state and Western targets, but there are claims that the ISI maintains selective relationships with certain factions for its own purposes.

The allegations of ISI complicity in terrorism have significantly influenced Western foreign policy, particularly the U.S.'s relationship with Pakistan. Periodically, aid to Pakistan has been suspended or reduced, and trust has been strained. However, Pakistan's strategic importance, particularly its geographic proximity to Afghanistan and role in counterterrorism, has led to a pragmatic continuation of U.S. engagement with the country. Expert and writer, Manuel Lamela (Pakistan's Inter-Services Intelligence and its ties

with radical groups. Universidad de Navarra. https://www.unav.edu/en/
web/global-affairs/detalle/-/blogs/pakistan-s-inter-services-intelligence-
and-its-ties-with-radical-groups) argued that the two Taliban groups were
different in their way of radicalization and extremism. The TTP carried
out attacks against the army school in Peshawar, which caused confusion
in society about their objectives: "The attack carried out by the Tehrik-
i-Taliban Pakistan (TTP) in the Army Public School in Peshawar in the
year 2014 generated a great stir in society, turning it against these radical
groups. This duality marks Pakistan's strategy in dealing with terrorism
both globally and internationally. While acting as an accomplice and
protector of these groups in Afghanistan, he pursues his counterparts on
their territory. We have to say that the operations carried out by the armed
forces have been effective, especially the Zarb-e-Azb operation carried out
in 2014 in North Waziristan, where the ISI played a fundamental role in
identifying and classifying the different objectives. The position of the TTP
in the region has been decimated, leaving it quite weakened. As can be
seen in this scenario, there is no support at the institutional level from the
ISI, as they are involved in the fight against these radical organizations.
However, on an individual level if these informal links appear. This
informal network is favored by the tribal character of Pakistani society, it
can appear in different forms but often draw on ties of Kinship, friendship
or social obligation".[8]

Pakistan's intelligence agencies, especially the Inter-Services Intelligence
(ISI), have been repeatedly accused of orchestrating enforced
disappearances. These agencies often operate with limited transparency
and oversight, making it difficult to hold them accountable for violations.
Their role in counterinsurgency and anti-terrorism operations has further
complicated efforts to ensure they respect human rights. The lack of
transparency and accountability within Pakistan's intelligence agencies
adds to the mistrust. Enforced disappearances in Pakistan are a deeply
troubling issue that has been ongoing for several decades, particularly
since the 2000s. These disappearances typically involve the abduction of
individuals by state agencies or groups with state connections, followed
by a refusal to acknowledge the person's detention or provide information
on their whereabouts. The rise of militancy and terrorism in Pakistan,
particularly after 9/11, has led to an aggressive crackdown by the state.
Security agencies, such as the military and intelligence services, have been
accused of detaining individuals suspected of being involved in extremist
groups or activities. Research Scholar at the JNU Special Centre for
National Security Studies, Wankhede Rahul Bhojraj, in one of his book

reviews (The Defense Horizon Journal, 15 August, 2023) has argued that the 1970s and 1990s were significant years that shaped the ISI's intelligence culture in Pakistan:

"From the 1970s till the 1990s, the "critical years" played a significant role in shaping the ISI's intelligence culture, as it gained strategic experience training the mujahideen against the Soviets and later the Taliban against the U.S. This period was marked by the ISI's expansion into neighbouring countries like Nepal, which were then used as bases to launch attacks on India. Said expansion marginalized other intelligence agencies in Pakistan, granting the ISI dominance. Although Western spy agencies consider the ISI superior to its Indian counterpart, the Research and Analysis Wing, the ISI does not possess the professionalism found in organizations like the CIA or Britain's MI6. It suffers from the same inefficiencies and corruption prevalent in the rest of the Pakistani state. The ISI has repeatedly lost control over its most dangerous assets. Additionally, its analytical capabilities have been questioned, including its tendency to interpret information based on predetermined ideological biases. Pakistan's internal political situation, highlighting Baloch nationalism, the rise of the Tehreek-e-Taliban Pakistan, and other social movements. Despite the current internal turmoil in Pakistan, the ISI and the Pakistan Army maintain control, ensuring the country remains intact. The ISI's functioning, overseen by influential generals and army officers, remains unchecked, while civilian oversight remains superficial".[9]

Many individuals have been taken into custody without formal charges, often as part of counterterrorism operations. Enforced disappearances are often used as a tool to silence political dissent and suppress opposition. Human rights activists, journalists, and critics of the government, military, or intelligence services have been targets. These agencies often operate with significant autonomy and power, making it difficult for the civilian government or judiciary to hold them accountable. There is often a lack of sustained political will to address the issue. Governments, both civilian and military, have historically been reluctant to confront powerful security agencies. This hesitance is exacerbated by fears of political backlash, especially in a country where the military holds significant influence over national security and foreign policy. The Majeed Brigade was formed to fight the Pakistan army and its proxy groups in Balochistan. The Majeed Brigade is a specialized wing of the Balochistan Liberation Army (BLA), a separatist militant group operating in the Balochistan region of Pakistan. The BLA, which seeks independence for Balochistan, has been engaged in an insurgency against the Pakistani state for decades, citing grievances related to political marginalization, economic exploitation, and human rights abuses against the Baloch people. The Majeed Brigade, named after Abdul Majeed Baloch, a prominent figure in Baloch resistance history, is particularly notorious for its use of suicide attacks and other forms of high-profile, violent operations.

Unlike the broader BLA, which typically focuses on guerrilla-style attacks on Pakistani military and infrastructure, the Majeed Brigade is known for carrying out suicide bombings, targeted assassinations, and attacks on high-value targets, such as military installations, Chinese nationals, and infrastructure projects linked to the China-Pakistan Economic Corridor (CPEC). The BLA, including the Majeed Brigade, has been declared a terrorist organization by Pakistan and several other countries, including the UK and the U.S. Despite this, the insurgency continues, driven by deep-rooted political and socio-economic issues in the region. Relationship of the Pakistan army with the Taliban is complex and shaped by a variety of historical, geopolitical, and security factors. While Pakistan officially denies supporting the Taliban's violent activities, especially their suicide campaigns, there are several key reasons behind the perception that Pakistan has backed the Taliban, particularly in Afghanistan. Pakistan has long sought to maintain influence in Afghanistan for strategic reasons. Pakistan's rivalry with India plays a crucial role in its Afghanistan policy. Pakistan fears that a strong, independent, or pro-India government in Afghanistan could encircle it, threatening its security from both its western and eastern borders. The Taliban, in contrast to the Afghan governments that were closer to India, are seen as more aligned with Pakistan's interests in counterbalancing India's influence in the region. With the Taliban's return to power in 2021 after the U.S. withdrawal, Pakistan's influence over the group has been put to the test.

The Hindu newspaper on August 31, 2024 reported former US National Security Advisor, General MacMaster's revelations that Pakistan's ISI has been complicit with terrorists. During his office, the White House faced resistance from the state department and Pentagon over providing security aid to Islamabad. "There is an "undeniable complicity" of Pakistan's Inter-Services Intelligence (ISI) with terrorist groups, he said. Lt. Gen McMaster in his book 'At War with Ourselves' noted that his duty in the white house, General Jim Mattis was adamant to provide a military aid package to Islamabad that included over $150 million worth of armoured vehicles but the aid was stopped with his intervention, General McMaster noted in his book. "I started by noting that the president (Trump) had been very clear on multiple occasions to suspend aid to the Pakistanis until they halted support for terrorist organizations that were killing Afghans, Americans, and coalition members in Afghanistan...We had all heard Trump say, 'I do not want any money going to Pakistan,'" the General noted.[10]

Expert and writer, Senior fellow at the Wilson Center, affiliated with the South Asia Institute, and a visiting fellow at the Hoover Institution at Stanford University, Nader Nadery in his analysis of Pakistan's interference in Afghanistan and its national security challenges (Unraveling Deception: Pakistan's Dilemma after Decades of Promoting Militancy in Afghanistan and beyond. Wilson center September 26, 2023) noted that the country has grappled with powerful operations of militant groups based in Balochistan and Afghanistan: "Inside Pakistan's biggest corridor of power, General Asim Munir, Pakistan's Chief of Army Staff, is grappling with an unsettling rise in terrorist attacks. These deadly assaults, often claimed by groups like the Tehrik-i-Taliban Pakistan (TTP) and more recently the Islamic State of Khorasan (ISK), have taken a toll on both military and civilian targets. Disturbingly, Pakistan's security apparatus has pointed fingers at Afghan nationals for some of the most recent attacks, deepening the country's complex predicament." The ISI trained the Taliban in various skills, including crafting explosive devices and orchestrating intricate suicide attacks. The arsenal included materials like ammonium nitrate and military-grade explosives. Tragically, these skills were turned against Afghans and international partners, causing significant harm to civilians".[11]

Chapter 1

The Pashtun Tahafuz Movement (PTM) and its Fight for Justice in Pakistan

The Mehsud Tahafuz Movement was established in 2014, immediately after the Pakistan army commenced operations against the people of Waziristan.[1] Eight university students, including Manzoor Ahmad Pashteen, demanded the removal of landmines from the area. In 2018, protests against the illegal killing of Naqeebullah Mehsud in Karachi city by a Punjabi police officer. There is an immense misunderstanding in Pakistan and Europe that Mr. Mazoor Ahmad Pashteen is not a greatly educated leader, but according to my authenticated information, he received his primary education from his village in South Waziristan. When the army sowed the seeds of breaching social contract in 2005 by kicking off an operation against militants, Manzoor's family was forced to flee Waziristan for IDP refugee camps in Dera Ismail Khan District.[2] In 2007, his family once more fled their home town in 2007 and returned in 2008.[3] In 2009, due to the military operation Rah-e-Nijat, his family was forced to flee South Waziristan for the fourth time. Later on, he completed secondary education in Bannu's army public school and high school in Karak. In 2016, he received his degree in Veterinary Medicine from Gomal University, Dera Ismail Khan.[4] The Pashtun Tahafuz Movement was frequently stopped by the army and its supporters were incarcerated. The PTM war was totally ignored by Pakistani media accusing its leaders of furthering foreign agenda.[5]

Operation Rah-e-Nijat ("Path to Salvation") was a major military offensive conducted by the Pakistan Army in South Waziristan, a region in the Federally Administered Tribal Areas (FATA) of Pakistan, starting in June 2009.[6] The operation aimed to eliminate the Tehrik-i-Taliban Pakistan (TTP) and other militant groups that had established strongholds in the region. Operation Rah-e-Nijat was a military operation by the Pakistan Armed Forces against the Tehrik-i-Taliban Pakistan (TTP) and their allies in South Waziristan, Pakistan. The operation began on June 19, 2009.[7] On

October 2, 2009, the preparations for the operation were made after a top civic-military meeting took place in Islamabad which led to the revival and starting of Navy's reconnaissance and surveillance air operations to monitor the troop rotations of Taliban forces.[8]

South Waziristan had become a hub for militants, including the TTP, led by Baitullah Mehsud, and foreign fighters affiliated with Al-Qaeda. The militants were involved in numerous terrorist attacks across Pakistan, and the region served as a launching pad for these operations. The primary objective was to dismantle the TTP's infrastructure, including its command and control centers, training camps, and supply lines. The operation also aimed to restore the writ of the state and bring stability to the region. The operation was launched in October 2009, following months of aerial bombardments and preparatory strikes by the Pakistan Air Force. The Pakistan Army deployed around 28,000 troops, including regular army units and paramilitary forces, to South Waziristan. The operation involved a combination of ground assaults, air strikes, and intelligence-led operations. By December 2009, the Pakistan Army had successfully captured most of the major militant strongholds in South Waziristan. Baitullah Mehsud was killed in a drone strike in August 2009, and the TTP's organizational structure was severely disrupted. The operation significantly weakened the TTP, forcing its leadership to flee to other areas, including North Waziristan and across the border into Afghanistan.

The operation was followed by a series of smaller, targeted operations in other parts of FATA to prevent the regrouping of militants. Despite the military success, challenges remained in terms of reconstruction, rehabilitation of displaced civilians, and ensuring long-term stability in the region. The operation was a precursor to later military actions, including Operation Zarb-e-Azb in North Waziristan in 2014, which targeted the remaining militant sanctuaries. Operation Rah-e-Nijat was a crucial step in Pakistan's broader counterinsurgency campaign, contributing to the disruption of militant networks in the tribal areas, though the long-term success required continued military and developmental efforts. The Radd-ul-Fasaad operation, also known as "Operation Radd-ul-Fasaad" or "Operation Rahi Nijat," was a counter-terrorism initiative launched by the Pakistan military in 2017, following the success of Operation Zarb-e-Azb. While it made significant strides in reducing the operational capacity of terrorist groups, several factors contributed to its inability to completely undermine the network of terrorist organizations in Pakistan: The terrorist organizations in Pakistan, such as Tehrik-i-Taliban Pakistan

(TTP) and various sectarian groups, operate through complex and decentralized networks. These groups are highly adaptable, often relocating and reconstituting after military offensives. This adaptability makes it challenging to completely dismantle them through conventional military operations.

The tribal areas in Pakistan, particularly the Federally Administered Tribal Areas (FATA), present significant challenges. The rugged terrain and the historical autonomy of these regions make it difficult for military forces to maintain long-term control. Additionally, the close-knit tribal systems often provide protection to militants, either out of loyalty or fear. Cross-border Militancy: Pakistan shares a porous border with Afghanistan, where many of these terrorist groups have safe havens. Despite efforts to improve border security, militants have been able to retreat across the border, regroup, and then re-enter Pakistan. The cross-border dimension of militancy complicates the effectiveness of unilateral military operations. Internal Political and Societal Factors: There are deep-seated political, religious, and societal issues within Pakistan that contribute to the persistence of extremism. Some political factions have historically had ties with militant groups, and there has been ambivalence or even support from certain segments of society towards these organizations. This socio-political complexity hinders comprehensive action against all terrorist networks. While military operations target the physical infrastructure and leadership of terrorist groups, they often do not address the ideological roots of extremism. The spread of radical ideology through madrassas, online platforms, and local communities continues to fuel recruitment and support for terrorist organizations. Without a parallel focus on countering extremist narratives and ideology, military operations alone cannot fully eradicate the threat.

The PTM is fighting for the rights of Pashtun communities peacefully. The PTM became popular in 2018, when it started a justice campaign.[9] On 13 January 2018, Naqibullah Mehsud was kidnapped and killed in a fake police encounter in Karachi.[10] The Pashtun Tahafuz Movement is the only well-branded together movement that created awareness within the Pashtun communities about the atrocities and war crimes of the Pakistani army in Khyber Pakhtunkhwa.[11] The PTM's EU chapter has been playing a significant role in promoting the narrative of the organization. Expert and political worker, Imal Katswal, is an active member of PTM in Douai, France who contributed his professional experience, intellectual tips-off and ideas to make PTM members vigilant and updated.[12] He worked and supported Pashtuns right movements in Belgium from 2009-2013, before shifting to France.[13] However, he participated in PTM protests and rallies in Europe to draw the attention of international community towards the forced disappearances and torture of its workers and leaders by the agencies.[14] The PTM used social media as a bridge of communication in the EU and demanded the release of missing persons and an end to extra-judicial killings of Pashtuns, stopping humiliation of passengers at security checkpoints, and removal of landmines. Dr. Madiha Afzal (07 February 2020) interviewed leaders of PTM for her book in Lahore, and highlighted the PTM demand in her book and noted that the movement noted grave human rights violations by Pakistani military against Pashtuns in Pakistan.[15] The PTM is the latest manifestation of decades of Pashtun protest against state brutalities. Its origin can be traced back to 2014 when student leaders of Gomal University in the Khyber Pakhtunkhwa (KP) province were propelled into activism to protect the rights of Pashtuns.[16]

The PTM presented its demands during the Pashtun Long March in 2018 including the arrest of Rao Anwar who killed Naqeebullah, establishment of Truth and Reconciliation Commission, interception of forced disappearances, and removal of landmine from Pashtun regions.[17] All these points, Muhammad Irfan Mahsud (02 April, 2024) has noted in his research paper (The emergence of nonviolent nationalist movement among the tribes of Waziristan in Pakistan) 'contributes to defend the Pashtun identity and rights. According to the PTM narrative, (The emergence of nonviolent nationalist movement among the tribes of Waziristan in Pakistan. Muhammad Irfan Mahsud (02 April, 2024) with the help of religious political parties in the 1980, President Zia relied on tribesmen's religious feeling to launch jihad against the Soviet Union in Afghanistan. For PTM this decision of Zia-ul-Haq damaged social and political stratification of Waziristan.[18]

In 2019, PTM leader Arman Loni was killed by the police in Loralai.[19] In 2019, following the Kharqamar incident, a clash between the army and PTM workers left 13 dead. On 27 January 2020, Manzoor Pashteen was arrested by Peshawar police on allegation of sedition.[20] On 28 March 2021, Manzoor Pashteen was again arrested in Kohat, while Mohsin Dawar was arrested in Karak. On 07 December, Islamabad High court granted seven days remand for Manzoor.[21] The leader of the Pashtun Tahafuz Movement (PTM), Manzoor Ahmad Pashteen has called for a large gathering of Pashtuns on 11 October 2024 to generate awareness among Pashtuns of Pakistan and Afghanistan and draw attention of the international community towards the policies, attitude and so-called military operations of Pakistani army in Waziristan, and other areas of Khyber Pakhtunkhwa and Balochistan provinces.[22]In the last several years (mostly between 2007 and 2017), the Military carried out several operations in South and North Waziristan, Dir, Swat, Malakand and Khyber Agency, which resulted in the killing of thousands, men, women and children and destruction of infrastructure.[23]

In January 2018, Pashtun March reached Islamabad, which was a mass mobilization to exhibit its strength and present its demands to the Federal administration. This mobilization, later on, resulted in the formation of an organization of Pashtun rights protection (Pashtun Tahafuz Movement). The PTM was established in response to the genocidal tactics and enforced disappearance in FATA and Waziristan.[24] Operation Zarb-e-Azb was a military operation in Pakistan's North Waziristan Agency that began in June 2014. The operation's goals were to remove militants and evacuate civilians.[25] The operation was part of a series of operations Pakistan has conducted to counter terrorism. Up to 30,000 Pakistani soldiers were involved in the operation. In 2014, when Pakistan army commandos killed 130 innocent students in army public school and established military courts to further prosecute Pashtun leaders, General Raheel Sharif was commander of the rogue army who killed thousands of men, women, children and tribal elders and demolished business Markets and shops of Pashtuns in Miran Shah District.[26] General Raheel Sharif killed the children of Pashtun in their houses, shops and markets with impunity, which breached human rights of citizens of the state. Expert and writer, Sana Hamid in her Modern Diplomacy article (The Crisis of Pashtun Tahaffuz Movement in Pakistan, Modern diplomacy June 25, 2023) noted military operation against Manzoor Pashteen, Ali Wazir, and Mohsin Dawar in Waziristan and Khyber Pakhtunkhwa regions:

"PTM came into being in its contemporary form in 2018. Before that, it existed as Mehsud Tahafuz Movement since 2014. As a Pashtun rights movement, its demands ranged from reducing number of check posts in east-while FATA, de-mining of the region to the issue of forced disappearances-issues that were concomitant of Pakistan joining USA block in Global war on Terrorism as well as state's anti-terrorism efforts and operations that followed. Ex-FATA, due to its staggering lack of development and literacy rate became the foremost fallout of the war Pakistan forced itself into with the subsequent state's inconsideration giving power to such hostile elements as that of PTM. While their demands are legitimate, the modus operandi of PTM casts serious aspersions on their ambitions and intentions towards states. It would have been more effective if PTM had channeled its demands through diplomatic means-as two among its foremost leadership are MNAs from South and North Waziristan in the parliament. But rather than working for the sequestered socio-economic problems grappling ex-FATA, it implicated negative tendencies by enforcing upon the vulnerable Pashtun masses that such social upheavals represent state's systemic prejudice against the entire Pashtun population of the country".[27]

An Anti-Terrorism Court in Karachi had charged Ali Wazir and Pashtun Tahafuz Movement chief Manzoor Pashteen as offenders in a sedition case.[28]In 2020, more than 500,000 Pashtuns were displaced from North Waziristan and Khyber Pakhtunkhwa by the military commanders. Expert and writer, Osama Ahmad in his article (Nonviolence: the most effective counter-terrorism tool-May 12, 2023) has noted the struggle of Pashtun Tahafuz Movement against the terrorist army: "As the state continues to neglect Pashtuns, the Pashtun Tahafuz Movement (PTM) has emerged to advocate for their rights. A grassroots civil rights movement of Pashtuns from the ex-FATA region, PTM has come out against both the state army and Taliban for the atrocities they commit against members of the minority group, and has demanded lasting peace. The counterterrorism strategy employed by PTM is characterized by nonviolent tactics such as organizing mass sit-ins and demonstrations, which stand in contrast to the state's violent approaches".[29]

The violent crackdown of Pakistan army against the Pashtuns in all parts of the country enraged political parties of the country that the terrorist army follows the footprints of the Hitler policy of genocide. Now, the army occupies the land of Pashtuns. Writers and experts, Seth Uzman and Snehal Shingavi (Solidarity with the Pashtun Tahafuz Movement) have established the fact that 'the military establishment lubricates state violence with the most absurd of misinformation campaigns. Claims that the popular movement provoked state violence on 26 May come after months of media silence – maintained at the behest of the Pakistani military establishment – on the peaceful protests led by the PTM'.[30] The Pashtun Tahafuz Movement emerged once again in Islamabad protests. There was a large gathering in the city which pressured the military establishment to halt military operations in the Waziristan region. Expert, Zalmay Azad (Pashtun Tahafuz Movement's Great Disconnect: Zalmay Azad asks the existential question about PTM: why has it struggled to establish a meaningful connection with the broader Pashtun populace?), The Friday Times. September 05,

2023) has argued that the emergence of PTM in Islamabad protests was a significant development:

"The Pashtun Tahafuz Movement (PTM) has once again emerged under the spotlight following its recent political gathering (Jalsa) in Islamabad. The event was notable for the large gathering in the federal capital and the fiery speeches from PTM's leadership, with particular emphasis on the oration by Manzoor Pashteen. But for the general public, the significance and intentions behind this gathering remain puzzling, as does the question of why the PTM does not enjoy greater support outside of its native South Waziristan. The timing of the rally is quite significant. One is forced to ask why the PTM chose to spontaneously convene this assembly in Islamabad at this point? Adding to the curiosity was the choice of the rally's venue: Islamabad. A majority of the rally attendees hailed from South Waziristan. At the same time, several accounts indicated the substantial presence of Afghan refugees at the rally. The incendiary speeches by PTM's leadership were a curious choice as well. It carried echoes of the secessionist mantra reminiscent of Tehrik-e-Taliban Pakistan's (TTP) Mufti Noor Wali as the speakers asserted that the erstwhile federally administered tribal areas (FATA) belong to Afghanistan and can only be emancipated through coercion".[31]

On 14 March 2022, the inaugural meeting of Jirga was held in Bannu, a city in Khyber Pakhtunkhwa. The Jirga of political leaders in Khyber Pakhtunkhwa on 26 June 2024 also condemned the new so-called military operation. On 04 December 2023, Manzoor Pashteen was attacked and arrested by the Pakistani army.[32] When Gilaman Wazir was attacked in broad daylight in Islamabad and later died in hospital on 10 July 2024, Pashtuns in the whole world were alerted by the killings and torture policies of the army. Dr. Fazal Rahman Afridi, a known human rights activist and member of PTM Europe authenticated the destruction of 200,000 homes and 25,000 commercial sites in a single operation which resulted in the displacement of more than six millions people.[33]

The mass killing of innocent students at a school in Peshawar on 16 December 2014 by commandos of the Pakistan army and the army operation to attack North and South Waziristan and several other areas along the Durand line uncovered the real face of corrupt Generals. War criminal General Raheel Sharif wanted to kill innocent women and children in Waziristan, and he was killed. Later on, the army established their own courts to execute their darling militants.[34] Nawaz Sharif and General Raheel forged a consensus to come down hard on the Pashtuns through a concerted national effort, and later on, it was changed into a so-called twenty-point National Action Plan (NAP) approved by Parliament on 24 December 2014. Pakistani military courts challenged the authority of the country's judicial system, and awarded death sentences to people in their custody. On 24 November 2015, the President amended the army act, and allowed intelligence agencies to detain civilians even before the passing of the 21st Amendment. The army was authorized to detain, kill, and torture suspects, and try them in military courts where no human rights organizations or journalists were allowed to cover the court proceedings. Dr. Muhammad Zubair, (28 January 2019) in his article noted the changing shape of the Army Act that authorized military courts to hold in-camera proceedings and keep identities of individuals associated with the cases secret.[35]

The military courts also became a part of Pakistan's National Action Plan (NAP); along with the Zarb-e-Azb, these three were seen as Pakistan's primary counter-terrorism strategy. While the Army is still continuing with the Zarb-e-Azb, the achievements and failures of the NAP have become a political issue during the recent months, whereas the military courts technically came to an end on 07 January 2017.[36] According to media reports, close to 270 cases were tried by the military courts; the majority of whom (approximately 160) were sentenced to death and the rest to prison. On 12 January 2019, Mehdi Hasan, Chairperson of the Human Rights Commission of Pakistan (HRCP), expressed grave concern at the government's decision to table a bill in favour of extending the tenure of military courts, which were otherwise due to end their term. In the aftermath of the December 16 Peshawar school attack, Pakistan also lifted a seven-year-long moratorium on death penalties. The military, responding to public anger over the Peshawar killings, was moving fast. The military promised that it will not abuse its new powers by prosecuting politicians, journalists or rights activists, as happened in the 1980s. The mandate of the new courts was set to expire after two years, and the trials were subjected to civilian oversight. Journalist Imad Zafar once argued that the political system has been the target of the military establishment propaganda machine.[37]

Former army chief, General Bajwa, exhibited special interest in the incarceration of PTM leader Ali Wazir. He was incarcerated on December 31, 2020 in several fake cases that accused him of hate speech, sedition and inciting the public against the state. In November 2021, Pakistan's Supreme Court granted Wazir post-arrest bail in one of these cases, but in view of the other cases against him, he remained incarcerated. The ISI tried to eliminate Manzoor Pashteen but due to fear of mass mobilization of Pashtun across the country, the plan was procrastinated. The point is that the Inter-Service Intelligence (ISI) lacked adequate intelligence information collection experience from remote areas of Balochistan, Sindh and Khyber Pakhtunkhwa, while lacked trained manpower, failed to understand modern technology, it lacked proper intelligence sharing approach with policymakers, and lacked a technique of actionable intelligence. The PTM contributed significantly to change the narrative of these agencies.[38]

Torture and sexual abuse policies of Pakistan's intelligence agencies, military establishment and police in large parts of Khyber Pakhtunkhwa have become an unwritten law, where thousands of innocent and powerless PTM workers and their families have lost their lives. Human Rights Watch (HRW) called on Pakistani lawmakers to speed up the adoption of a bill that criminalizes the use of torture; a practice that the rights group said was widespread in Pakistan.[39] In view of this illegal business, the ISI and the army lost their professional capabilities and remained hanging in the air. The ISI lost public confidence and its roots were emaciated in civil society. All civilian and military agencies have a specific mind set, their sectarian affiliation and dearth of electronically trained manpower, lack of professional surveillance approach, and the absence of a proper intelligence-sharing culture raised serious questions about their credibility. The Pakistani military establishment and its secret agencies have been using jihadists in Waziristan to achieve their strategic goal since years. The lack of credibility of ISI and Military Intelligence has been a longstanding concern in civilian circles. Gilaman Wazir, Poet, and PTM Activist, died in Hospital. Wazir was attacked by unknown people in Islamabad. That attack sparked a wave of reactions both inside and outside of Pakistan. Manzoor Pashteen, leader of the Pashtun Tahafuz Movement (PTM), confirmed Gilaman Wazir's death, stating that if the Pakistani police do not identify the perpetrators of this attack, it will indicate that the government of Pakistan was involved in the attack. Manzoor Pashteen said: "It is very difficult for me to say that Gilaman Pashteen is no longer among us."[40]

Known research scholar and journalist, Daud Khattak (Foreign Policy, 30 April 2019) in his well-written analysis of PTM noted important aspects of PTM's challenges in demanding justice for families whose relatives were kidnapped by the army. However, BBC journalist, M. Ilyas Khan (Uncovering Pakistan's secret human rights abuses, M Ilyas Khan, BBC News, Dera Ismail Khan, 02 June 2019) authenticated atrocities of Pakistani army: "In May 2016, an attack on a military post in the Teti Madakhel area of North Waziristan triggered a manhunt by troops who rounded up the entire population of a village.[41] An eyewitness who watched the operation from a wheat field nearby and whose brother was among those detained, told the BBC that the soldiers beat everyone with batons and threw mud in children's mouths when they cried.[8] However, Maj General Asif Ghafoor's irresponsible tweets, comments and conferences against the Pashtun nation left a black contemptuousness blot on the face of Pakistani army that the army only represents a club of Punjabi Generals. Gen Asif Ghafoor acted like a vandal and warlord that put the army in ordeal by challenging the Pushtun nation of Pakistan. His resentment against Pashtuns, and his toxic statements issued from the platform of ISPR could not attract civil society in Pakistan.[42]

Chapter 2

The Pashtun Tahafuz Movement, Forced Disappearances and Violence in Khyber Pakhtunkhwa Province

The Pashtun Tahafuz Movement is the only well-branded together movement that created awareness within the Pashtun communities about the atrocities and war crimes of the Pakistan army in Khyber Pakhtunkhwa and Waziristan. However, it started long marches and rallies to divert the attention of the international community towards the forced disappearances of its workers and leaders by the agencies. Frequently, they used social media as a bridge of communication. Originally, its demands included the release of missing persons and an end to extra-judicial killings of Pashtuns, stopping humiliation of passengers at security checkpoints, and removal of landmines in FATA. On 13 January 2018, Naqeebullah Mehsud was killed in a fake police encounter in Karachi.[1] The PTM is the latest manifestation of decades of Pashtun protest against state brutalities. Its origin can be traced back to 2014 when student leaders of Gomal University in the Khyber Pakhtunkhwa (KP) province were propelled into activism to protect the rights of Pashtuns. The PTM is a nonviolent movement led by Manzoor Pashteen against the alleged enforced disappearances, extra-judicial killings, as well as the mistreatment of the Pakhtun community by security forces. Madiha Afzal (07 February 2020) interviewed leaders of PTM for her book in Lahore, highlighted the PTM demand in her book:

"The movement alleges grave human rights violations by Pakistan's military against Pashtuns in the country's northwest. It says that Pashtuns have been the target of violence at the hands of both the Taliban and the Pakistani military for two decades. The movement claims that the military has killed innocent civilians in its operations against the Pakistani Taliban, and that it needs to answer for "missing persons." It also contends that Pashtuns are regularly harassed at checkpoints and treated with suspicion, and that landmines continue to make their lives insecure. These complaints festered for years before the movement was officially created in 2018. In 2015, while conducting interviews for my book, I met Pashtun students in Lahore who told me that the army's ongoing, multi-year military operation—Zarb-e-Azb—was not what it seemed from outside the tribal areas. The PTM demands a truth and reconciliation commission to address claims of extrajudicial killings and missing persons. The movement also claims that the military supported Pakistani Taliban (also known as Tehreek-e-Taliban Pakistan, or TTP) militants, and its leaders have said—most explosively — that after the military claims to have decimated the Pakistani Taliban in Zarb-e-Azb, "the Taliban are being allowed to return" to the tribal areas in a "secret deal with the military."[2]

The Pashtun Tahafuz Movement (PTM) was established in Pakistan to advocate the rights and protection of the Pashtun people, particularly in the context of their treatment by the Pakistani state and military. The movement emerged in response to a long history of violence, discrimination, and human rights abuses experienced by Pashtuns, especially in the aftermath of the War on Terror and the military operations conducted in Pakistan's tribal areas. Key objectives of the PTM was the end to extrajudicial killings, enforced disappearances, and other human rights abuses that have disproportionately affected Pashtuns, particularly in regions like the Federally Administered Tribal Areas (FATA) and Khyber Pakhtunkhwa (KP). The movement seeks accountability for military operations that have led to civilian casualties, displacement, and the destruction of property. PTM calls for the demining of areas where military operations have left unexploded ordnance, posing ongoing threats to civilians. Restoration of Civil Rights: PTM advocates for the restoration of civil rights for Pashtuns, including the freedom of speech, assembly, and movement. The movement has criticized the curtailment of these rights in the name of national security.

The PTM calls for an end to the racial profiling and discrimination against Pashtuns, who are often unfairly targeted as being sympathetic to or supportive of terrorist groups. Justice for Victims of Violence: The movement seeks justice for the victims of violence, including those killed or injured in incidents like the Army Public School attack in Peshawar, as well as other acts of terrorism and military action. Overall, the PTM aims to bring attention to the plight of the Pashtun people and to seek justice and equality for them within Pakistan's legal and political systems. The Pakistan Army has faced significant challenges related to violence and unrest in various regions of the country. These challenges are often linked to complex socio-political factors, including perceptions of discriminatory practices against certain ethnic and religious groups, historical grievances, and economic disparities.[3]

Pakistan is home to diverse ethnic groups, including Punjabis, Sindhis, Baloch, Pashtuns, and Mohajirs, among others. There have been longstanding grievances among some of these groups, particularly in Balochistan and Khyber Pakhtunkhwa, where accusations of political and economic marginalization by the central government and military have fueled unrest. The Baloch insurgency, for instance, has been driven by demands for greater autonomy and control over natural resources, with many Baloch people feeling that the central government, backed by the military, has prioritized the interests of Punjab at the expense of their region. Sectarian tensions, particularly between Sunni and Shia Muslims, have also contributed to violence. Some critics argue that the state and its institutions, including the military, have not done enough to curb extremist groups that target religious minorities. In some cases, there have been allegations that certain elements within the state apparatus have tacitly supported Sunni militant groups as part of a broader strategic calculus, which has exacerbated sectarian divisions.

The Pakistan Army's extensive role in governance and security, especially in regions like Balochistan and the former Federally Administered Tribal Areas (FATA), has led to accusations of heavy-handedness. Operations aimed at countering insurgency and terrorism have sometimes been criticized for their impact on civilian populations, including allegations of extrajudicial killings, enforced disappearances, and other human rights abuses. These actions have, in some cases, deepened local resentment and contributed to cycles of violence. The military's perceived interference in political processes, including support for or against particular political parties, has also been a source of contention. This has led to accusations that the military undermines democratic institutions and perpetuates instability by fostering political polarization. While the Pakistan Army has conducted extensive counterterrorism operations, particularly against groups like the Tehrik-i-Taliban Pakistan (TTP), these efforts have sometimes led to a backlash, including retaliatory attacks against security forces and civilians.

The complex relationship between the state and various militant groups, some of which have been seen as strategic assets in the region, has further complicated the security landscape. The Pakistan Army's role in addressing violence across the country is deeply intertwined with broader issues of governance, ethnic and sectarian divides, and regional geopolitics. Perceptions of discriminatory practices by the military have, in some cases, exacerbated tensions, making it difficult to achieve lasting peace and stability. Addressing these challenges requires not only military action but also comprehensive political, economic, and social reforms that address the root causes of unrest. The Pashtun Tahafuz Movement (PTM) is a social movement in Pakistan that advocates for the rights of the Pashtun people. It emerged around 2018, though its roots go back earlier to various issues faced by the Pashtun community, particularly in the wake of the War on Terror and military operations in the tribal areas of Pakistan. The PTM highlighted the issue of enforced disappearances, where many Pashtuns have allegedly gone missing, reportedly detained by security forces without any legal process. The movement also raises concerns about extrajudicial killings of Pashtuns during counter-terrorism operations in Pakistan's tribal regions. The PTM criticizes the presence of numerous military checkpoints in the tribal areas, which they argue infringe on the everyday freedoms and rights of Pashtuns.

The movement is led by figures such as Manzoor Pashteen, a young activist who became the face of PTM. His leadership and the movement's peaceful protests have attracted significant support, especially among young Pashtuns. The Pakistani government and military have responded with suspicion, often labelling PTM as anti-state or influenced by foreign powers. This has led to a tense relationship between the movement and the state, with PTM leaders and activists frequently facing arrests, censorship, and other forms of repression. PTM has gained considerable attention both domestically and internationally, as it highlights the plight of the Pashtun community in a country where ethnic issues are often sensitive and politicized. The movement, however, remains non-violent and continues to call for the rights and dignity of Pashtuns within the framework of the Pakistani state. The Pashtun Tahafuz Movement (PTM) was established in Pakistan to advocate for the rights and protection of the Pashtun people, particularly in the context of their treatment by the Pakistani state and military. The movement emerged in response to a long history of violence, discrimination, and human rights abuses experienced by Pashtuns, especially in the aftermath of the War on Terror and the military operations conducted in Pakistan's tribal areas. Key objectives of the PTM included addressing extrajudicial killings and enforced disappearances.

The PTM demands an end to extrajudicial killings, enforced disappearances, and other human rights abuses that have disproportionately affected

Pashtuns, particularly in regions like the Federally Administered Tribal Areas (FATA) and Khyber Pakhtunkhwa (KP). The movement seeks accountability for military operations that have led to civilian casualties, displacement, and the destruction of property. PTM calls for the demining of areas where military operations have left unexploded ordnance, posing ongoing threats to civilians. PTM advocates for the restoration of civil rights for Pashtuns, including the freedom of speech, assembly, and movement. The movement has criticized the curtailment of these rights in the name of national security. The PTM calls for an end to the racial profiling and discrimination against Pashtuns, who are often unfairly targeted as being sympathetic to or supportive of terrorist groups. The movement seeks justice for the victims of violence, including those killed or injured in incidents like the Army Public School attack in Peshawar, as well as other acts of terrorism and military action.

The situation in Waziristan, where Pashtuns have historically faced significant challenges, has been complex and fraught with tension, particularly involving the Pakistani military's operations. Waziristan, part of the Federally Administered Tribal Areas (FATA) in Pakistan, has been a focal point for military operations against various militant groups, especially after the rise of terrorism post-9/11. It's important to note that the Pakistani government and military often justify their actions in Waziristan as necessary for national security and combating terrorism. However, the situation remains deeply controversial, with ongoing debates about the balance between security measures and the rights of the local population. Given the sensitivity and complexity of the issue, the narratives around the targeting of Pashtuns by the army are highly contested and depend significantly on the perspective from which the situation is viewed. The military operation "Rahi Najat" took place in North Waziristan, a region in Pakistan's Federally Administered Tribal Areas (FATA), as part of Pakistan's broader efforts to combat militancy and terrorism, particularly against groups like the Tehrik-i-Taliban Pakistan (TTP) and other militant factions operating in the area. This operation was one of several that the Pakistan military launched over the years to regain control of tribal areas from militant groups.

Operation Zarb-e-Azb, launched by the Pakistan Army in June 2014, was a major military offensive aimed at rooting out militant groups, including the Tehrik-i-Taliban Pakistan (TTP), in North Waziristan. The operation targeted various militant strongholds, including the town of Miranshah, which was a key base for insurgent activities. As a result of the operation, a significant portion of the local population, including traders and business owners, were displaced, and their properties were damaged or destroyed. The demand for uniformity of compensation by traders in Miranshah reflects ongoing grievances regarding the distribution of compensation and support for those affected by the operation. Many traders and residents feel that the compensation provided has been inconsistent, with some receiving more or less than others, or facing delays in receiving the promised amounts. These concerns have led to calls for a more equitable and transparent compensation process. The demand for uniformity underscores the broader challenges in post-conflict recovery, including ensuring that all affected individuals and communities receive fair treatment and the necessary support to rebuild their lives and businesses. The issue also highlights the difficulties in balancing security objectives with the needs of the local population, who often bear the brunt of the consequences of such military operations. Addressing these concerns is crucial for fostering long-term stability and rebuilding trust between the government and the local communities in regions like Miranshah. This includes the controversial removal of the former Prime Minister Imran Khan, perceived interference in politics, and the subsequent civil unrest. Public support is crucial for counterterrorism operations, as it fosters cooperation and intelligence-sharing between civilians and security forces. Without this support, military operations become more challenging and less effective. Torture and humiliation in Waziristan couldn't undermine Talibanization, extremism, and terrorism, it alienate citizens from the state. Manzoor never targeted the Pakistan army, and never killed a single soldier of security forces; he is fighting for the fundamental rights of the residents of Waziristan and FATA regions.

On 11 February 2019, in his New York Times article, PTM leader Manzoor Pashteen gave an account of his struggle for the recovery of kidnapped Pashtun activists by Pakistan's military establishment: "The government ignored us when these militants terrorized and murdered the residents. Pakistan's military operations against the militants brought further misery: civilian killings, displacements, enforced disappearances, humiliation and the destruction of our livelihoods and way of life. No journalists were allowed into the tribal areas while the military operations were going on. Pashtuns who fled the region in hopes of rebuilding their lives in Pakistani cities were greeted with suspicion and hostility. We were stereotyped as terrorist sympathizers. I was studying to become a veterinarian, but the plight of my people forced me and several friends to become activists. In January 2018, Naqeebullah Mehsud, an aspiring model and businessman from Waziristan who was working in Karachi was killed by a police team led by a notorious officer named Rao Anwar. Mr. Anwar, who is accused of more than 400 extrajudicial murders, was granted bail and roamed free. Along with 20 friends, I set out on a protest march from Dera Ismail Khan to Islamabad, the capital. Word spread, and by the time we reached Islamabad, several thousand people had joined the protest. We called our movement the Pashtun Tahafuz Movement or the Pashtun Protection Movement".[4]

Mr. Manzoor Pashteen holds Pakistan army responsible for the disinformation campaign against his movement, and complained that agencies also concocted stories of the involvement of RAW and NDS in his campaign for the recovery of kidnapped men, women and children from the custody of the police and agencies. He, however, accused the army and police for the killing of his workers. PTM leader also lamented military establishment and the police for the harassment of social media activist, and the arrest of Alamzaib Khan Mehsud, (an activist who was gathering data and advocating on behalf of victims of landmines and enforced disappearances), activist Hayat Preghal, and Gulalai Ismail:"The military unleashed thousands of trolls to run a disinformation campaign against the P.T.M., accusing us of starting a "hybrid war." Almost every day they accuse us of conspiring with Indian, Afghan or American intelligence services. Most of our activists, especially women, face relentless online harassment. A social media post expressing support for our campaign leads to a knock from the intelligence services. Scores of our supporters have been fired from their jobs. Many activists are held under terrorism laws. Alamzaib Khan Mehsud, an activist who was gathering data and advocating on behalf of victims of landmines and enforced disappearances, was arrested in January. Hayat Preghal, was imprisoned for months for expressing support for our movement on social media. He was released in October but barred from leaving the country and lost his pharmacist job in Dubai, his sole source of income. Gulalai Ismail, a celebrated activist, has been barred from leaving Pakistan. On Feb. 5, while protesting against the death of Mr. Luni, the college teacher and P.T.M. leader, she was detained and held incommunicado in an unknown place for 30 hours before being released. Seventeen other activists are still being detained in Islamabad".[5]

On 17 February 2020, the Print published a yell of Gul Bukhari against the ISI wing of the Pakistan Embassy in the UK. Gul Bukhari complained that the ISI wing was sniffing for her home address in London. "I am at a loss, I can't understand what is it about me that fascinates the Pakistani government or makes it obsess over me so much. I left Pakistan in December 2018 and am leading a quiet life in the UK. Yet, the establishment hasn't stopped hounding me. Just a few days ago, a friend sent me some screenshots of Pakistani media channel ARY and asked what the case against me was, and what 'dehshatgardi' I had done. I was stunned. I asked around if these were fake screenshots. "No, Gul, this is breaking news on ARY right now," I was told. According to the news, Pakistan's Federal Investigation Agency (FIA) had sent a notice, asking me to appear before it and explain myself. And if I fail to do so, I would be slapped with charges under cybercrime and anti-terror laws, my properties in Pakistan would be seized, and I would be extradited via the Interpol". Gul said.[6]

Gul Bukhari also kicked up the fuss that the PTI government requested the UK government to expel her from London as soon as possible. The PTI government wrote directly to the government in the UK, hoping that action will be taken against her here, but the UK government does not prosecute asylum seekers, and the PTI government cannot force the UK government in any case because Gul Bukhari is a human rights activist: "The Pakistan Tehreek-e-Insaf (PTI) government wants the UK to take action against me under the country's hate speech and anti-terrorism laws. And the Pakistani establishment, according to journalist Ali Shah, has sent this letter to 10 Downing Street, the Foreign Office, the Home Office, and to the local police. It was another shock to me. As reported by the journalist, the language used in the letter (which I haven't seen yet) contained typical fauji terms like "inimical activities", and seeks an investigation into my "lifestyle". Having realized it may not be successful in bringing me back to Pakistan via the FIA, the Imran Khan Regime wrote directly to the government in the UK, hoping that action will be taken against me here. She said[7]

"I am wondering if those in power in Pakistan think the UK government is as big a duffer as they are. Yes, we have Boris Johnson at the helm here but he is not the one and all. Murtaza spat out his Coke laughing while reading the letter, but the serious concerns are these: they are hounding me; slapping me with made-up charges or trying to get that done by the UK government; the Inter-Services Intelligence (ISI) wing of the Pakistan embassy in the UK is trying to sniff out my residential address. They are trying anything and everything.........I was in their safe house and under their control in 2018 when they asked me if I would toe their line if they put me on prime time TV. I said no. Then they asked me again in the car (when they were taking me back home after my abduction) and also threatened me with my son's life, "Aitchison jata hai na (he goes to Aitchison, doesn't he?)", they said, referring to his school. "Uss ko kuchh ho gaya toh hum se na gila karna (if something happens to him, then don't complain to us)." I replied, "No, you must be out of your mind." They literally threatened to kill my son" Gul Bukhari grumbled, Newspaper reported.[8]

Having commented on her tearful complaints against Pakistan Embassy in London, prominent journalist Aurang Zeb Khan Zalmay (17-02-2020) in his Facebook account criticized agencies for their campaign against Pakistani human rights activists in Britain and Europe: "The Pakistani monster is constantly following and intimidating journalists and human-rights activists across Europe and Middle East. This project to hound rights-activists was launched by Gen. Bajwa on his official visit to Pakistan High Commission in London in Jun 2019. Since that day the Pakistan's embassies in Europe and their spies and stooges have been active to stop voices of the voiceless.[9] hey attacked one of our friends in Rotterdam in front of his home. They can't intimidate us with their cowardice and cheap tactics, they are in self-deception, and we will never give up our peaceful rights activism". The PTM activist, Gulalai Ismail was also accused of treason, but human rights defenders said allegations were bogus and she was being targeted for highlighting abuses committed by Pakistan's military. Notwithstanding her arrival in New York, she still lives in consternation. She was arrested and harassed by intelligence agencies to change her opinion on the war crimes of the army in FATA and Waziristan, but she strongly refused to become reticent. In his New York Times article, Jeffrey Gettleman (19 September, 2019) reported that Gulalai Ismail had been advocating the rights of raped women, kidnapped and tortured Pashtuns, Punjabis and Balochs since years:

"Her account of being chased out of the country does not help the government's efforts to win diplomatic support at a time when the economy is tanking and Pakistan is begging the world to censure India for its recent moves on Kashmir, a disputed territory claimed by both Pakistan and India. It has taken Ms. Ismail some time to feel safe even in New York, she said, but she has begun to meet with prominent human rights defenders and the staff of congressional leaders. "I will do everything I can to support Gulalai's asylum request," said Senator Charles Schumer, Democrat of New York. "It is clear that her life would be in danger if she were to return to Pakistan." Pakistani security officials said they had suspected for some time that Ms. Ismail had slipped through their fingers. "Our guys have been after her, by all means, but she is not traceable," said a Pakistani intelligence agent who spoke on the condition of anonymity, citing intelligence protocols. "She has gone to a place beyond our reach."......Ever since she was, Ms. Ismail has been speaking out about human rights abuses, focusing on the plight of Pakistani women and girls who suffer all kinds of horrors including forced marriages and honor killings. In January, she aired accusations, on Facebook and Twitter, that government soldiers had raped or sexually abused many Pakistani women. She has also joined protests led by an ethnic Pashtun movement that Pakistan's military has tried to crush. Pakistani officials have accused Ms. Ismail of sedition, inciting treason and defaming state institutions".[10] The CIVICUS analysis of Gulalai's struggle to save lives of innocent women and children noted her pain and industrious struggle. Some newspapers also published stories about her zeal and pluckiness. Gulalai led a protest in Islamabad against police brutality and misconduct and spoke up about sexual harassment of women and girls of tribal areas.[12] Due to her activism, the government brought two criminal cases against Gulalai for attending gatherings of the PTM, but these were quashed by the courts: "Gulalai visited an area named Khaisoor along with a group of women human rights activists. Women and girls shared their stories about sexual harassment by army personnel. Gulalai assured them that she would highlight their situation and work on the issue of sexual harassment of women and girls in conflict areas.[13]

Chapter 3

The Pashtun Tahafuz Movement and War Crimes of Military Establishment in Waziristan

Manzoor Pashteen, the leader of the Pashtun Tahafuz Movement (PTM), has been targeted by the Pakistani state, particularly its military, due to several factors related to the PTM's activism, despite the movement's nonviolent stance. The PTM calls attention to human rights violations committed by the Pakistani military in the tribal areas, especially during operations against militants. Pashteen and PTM have criticized extrajudicial killings, enforced disappearances, and the destruction of property during these military operations. By directly confronting the military, which holds significant power in Pakistan, PTM challenges the state's official narrative on counterterrorism. Mr. Manzoor demands accountability for the military's actions, which is sensitive in a country where the army plays a dominant role in both security and politics. The military sees PTM's demands for truth and justice, such as the return of missing persons and the removal of landmines from conflict zones, as a threat to its authority and public image. The army and government have repeatedly accused PTM and its leaders, including Manzoor Pashteen, of having links with foreign intelligence agencies, particularly from Afghanistan and India, but they couldn't prove it. These allegations are used to discredit the movement domestically, even though PTM has denied such links and maintains that its struggle is focused on the rights and dignity of the Pashtun people.

The PTM's base is primarily among Pashtuns, an ethnic group that has historically been marginalized in Pakistan. The movement has highlighted the grievances of Pashtuns, especially those living in the tribal areas and Khyber Pakhtunkhwa, which were deeply affected by the war on terror. The state likely fears that PTM's activism could fuel broader ethnic mobilization, which could destabilize the country's already complex ethnic landscape. The Pashteen's rise as a grassroots leader who speaks about the hardships faced by Pashtuns has gained him widespread popularity, particularly in

40

areas where the state has struggled to provide security and justice. This grassroots popularity can be perceived as a challenge to state authority, as it creates an alternative narrative to that promoted by the government and military. MNA Mr. Ali Wazir, a prominent Pakistani politician and member of the Pashtun Tahafuz Movement (PTM), has been repeatedly arrested due to his outspoken stance against state policies, particularly regarding the treatment of Pakistan's Pashtun population. His arrests often stem from allegations of incitement against state institutions, inflammatory speeches, and accusations of treason. Ali Wazir, along with other PTM leaders, has been vocal in criticizing Pakistan's military establishment, particularly over its handling of counterinsurgency operations in tribal areas.

He has accused the military of human rights abuses, enforced disappearances, and mistreatment of the Pashtun population. As a leader of the PTM, Ali Wazir has been part of a movement that demands justice for the victims of violence in the tribal regions, particularly in the aftermath of military operations. The PTM has organized large rallies and protests, which have drawn significant attention but also brought the movement into conflict with the state, which views it as a potential threat to national unity and security. Wazir has faced charges of sedition and incitement for his speeches, where he allegedly accused state institutions of wrongdoing. In many cases, the government has taken these statements as an attack on the integrity of the state, leading to his arrests. Many of Wazir's supporters and human rights organizations claim that his repeated arrests are politically motivated and an attempt to silence dissent. Given his influence among the Pashtun community and his ability to mobilize people for the PTM cause, some argue that the state views him as a political threat.

Wazir's family has a history of political activism, and many of his relatives have been killed or targeted, possibly due to their opposition to state policies in the tribal areas. This has further entrenched his position as a key figure of resistance. The issue of Pashtun political parties' support is of great importance, such as the Awami National Party (ANP) and other regional parties, who have complex reasons for their cautious or limited support for the Pashtun Tahafuz Movement (PTM). They may not fully support the PTM to maintain their own political influence in the region. Pashtun political parties operate within the formal political system in Pakistan and face pressure from the state to distance themselves from groups seen as disruptive or critical of national security policies. Pashtun political parties, particularly those with nationalist leanings, tend to have broader agendas that encompass economic development, political autonomy, and cultural rights. On 08 September 2024, Tehreek-e-Taliban Pakistan (TTP) ordered its militants to launch suicide attacks against the Pakistan Army, escalating an already tense conflict. This development followed by the breakdown of ceasefire talks between the TTP and the government. The TTP's actions appear to be a direct challenge to the state, threatening to intensify violence across the country. This escalation could trigger a broader conflict, with Pakistan possibly retaliating more aggressively. Political persecution in Pakistan, especially of politicians by the army and governments in power, stems from a complex mix of historical, institutional, and political factors.

Pakistan's political history is marked by recurring tensions between civilian governments and the military. Civilian leaders who attempt to assert control over defence, foreign policy, or other domains traditionally managed by the military often face pushback. Politicians perceived as opposing military interests or challenging its dominance are frequently targeted through legal cases, intimidation, or even forced exile. Pakistan's democratic institutions, including the judiciary, parliament, and political parties, have often been fragile. The military's influence over the judiciary and bureaucracy allows it to manipulate legal and administrative processes to undermine political leaders it perceives as a threat. Politicians are frequently arrested, charged with corruption, or disqualified from holding office. The use of the judiciary and accountability institutions like the National Accountability Bureau (NAB) to target political opponents is a common practice. Corruption charges, which are sometimes valid but often politically motivated, are used to discredit politicians and neutralize opposition. Pakistan's strategic importance, particularly in the context of regional politics (e.g., Afghanistan, India) and its relationship with countries like the U.S., China, and Saudi Arabia, means that external factors sometimes influence domestic political dynamics. Politicians perceived to be aligning against the military's preferred foreign policy stance may face persecution.

In May 2019, a nine-year-old girl whose parents had been internally displaced from tribal areas was raped and killed in Islamabad, the capital of Pakistan. The police refused to file a first information report (FIR) of the incident, and instead abused and harassed the father and brother of the child in the police station. Gulalai led a protest in Islamabad against police brutality and misconduct and spoke up about sexual harassment of women and girls in tribal areas and of the internally displaced population from tribal areas. Due to her activism, the government brought two criminal cases against Gulalai for attending gatherings of the PTM, but these were quashed by the courts. On 12 October 2018, Gulalai was arrested at Islamabad Airport by the Federal Investigation Agency (FIA) on her arrival from London and her name was put on the Exit Control List (ECL), which banned her from travelling outside the country.[1] In February 2019, Gulalai was picked by security agencies at the Islamabad Press Club while she was attending a protest for the release of PTM activists, but her name was not on the list of people arrested and she went missing for 36 hours. She was produced and released by the Pakistani army after the Prime Minister of Pakistan interceded". PTM was helped by social media in circulating its message across the globe. Without the help of the social media and international press, information about the military operation in Waziristan was inaccessible. Known scholar and journalist Daud Khattak (Foreign Policy, 30 April 2019) in his well-written analysis of Pashtun Tahafuz Movement (PTM), has noted some aspects of PTM's challenges in demanding justice for families whose relatives were kidnapped by the army:

"Pashtun Protection Movement came to prominence in early 2018 in Waziristan, a remote outpost along Pakistan's rugged border with Afghanistan. Although the grievances PTM tapped into—discrimination against tribal people, violence by the Taliban, and military presence in the area—were long-standing, the trigger for the group's recent explosion was the extrajudicial killing of an aspiring model and artist from Waziristan in the city of Karachi in January 2018. Despite a media blackout—the major news channels have refrained from covering PTM gatherings or running interviews with its leadership, allegedly because of bullying and arrests by the intelligence agencies—Pashteen's protest is gaining ground. In February 2018, the PTM staged a sit-in in Islamabad, which was followed by more protests against the military in all major Pakistani cities. In February this year, for example, hundreds of young men and women marched in Lahore, the country's second-largest city, to demand freedom of expression, respect for the country's constitution, and civil rights. The name of their rally— Shehri Tahafuz March, or Citizen Protection March—was homage to PTM. And in April, tens of thousands of people demonstrated under the PTM banner in the North Waziristan city of Miran Shah".[2] The agencies intercepted all newspapers and electronic media from reporting PTM's protests across Pakistan. Tehreek Insaf's government has a turbulent relationship with the media under Imran Khan, elected as Prime Minister with strong backing from the military. Journalists were living in a climate of consternation and suppression.

Scholar and journalist Daud Khattak also noted some incidents of kidnapping of PTM leaders and workers by Pakistani intelligence agencies. He also noted the statement of General Ghafoor, in which he accused PTM leadership of getting money from Indian and Afghan intelligence agencies: "In early February, for example, Ammar Ali Jan, a college teacher and PTM supporter, was picked up by law enforcement agencies from his house in Lahore in the middle of the night on charges of supporting the PTM. In response, dozens of Punjab-based activists launched a social media campaign for his release. A few days after his release, Jan explained his ordeal in an op-ed. He clarified that he is not an ethnic Pashtun but has supported the PTM in its broader struggle against human rights violations. Facing widespread protest, the Pakistani military has resorted to its old playbook and condemned the PTM and other emerging movements as "fifth-generation warfare"—that is, hybrid warfare against the state. Meanwhile, the military has also linked Pashteen and others to foreign governments and intelligence agencies. Addressing a news conference on April 29, Pakistani military spokesman Maj. Gen. Asif Ghafoor accused the PTM leadership of getting money from Indian and Afghan intelligence. "But tell us how much money did you get from the NDS [Afghan National Directorate of Security] to run your campaign?" he asked. "How much money did RAW [India's Research and Analysis Wing] give you for the first dharna [sit-in] in Islamabad?"[3]

General Raheel Sharif protected terrorists, and accommodated them in guest houses, and ordered the killing and kidnapping of young men, women and children in Waziristan, and used sophisticated weapons in the region. He never allowed maimed, disabled and mutilated children to treat their wounds, or leave the region safely. Extrajudicial killings in FATA and Waziristan by his forces and illegal torture of children and women by his cronies caused permanent consternation and schizophrenic diseases in North Waziristan. More than 1,000 women and girls were kidnapped, and 2,000 tribal leaders have been disappeared by the army in FATA and Waziristan since 2004. Reftworld in its recent report highlighted cases of torture, humiliation, ill-treatment and unlawful arrest and detention in Pakistan: "The fate of some of the victims of arbitrary arrest, detention and enforced disappearance has been disclosed – some have been charged with criminal offences unrelated to terrorism, others have been released without charge, reportedly after being warned to keep quiet about their experience, while some have been found dead".[4]

Human Rights Commission of Pakistan in its report "State of Human Rights in 2018" noted the scourge of enforced disappearances in Pakistan and reported the statement of Sardar Akhtar Mengal of the BNP-M, who warned that the situation in Naya Pakistan didn't changed as 235 people, including nine women gone missing from Balochistan: "Families had received 45 dead bodies during the period from 25 July to 30 October 2018 and as many as 5,000 people are still reportedly missing from Balochistan. According to him, people were afraid to register FIRs if any of their family went missing because, if they did, they received threats from law enforcement agencies. Sardar Akhtar claimed that human rights activists, nationalists, and anyone who raised the issue of enforced disappearances on social media were also picked up by intelligence agencies. In their Bi-annual Report for 2018, The State of Baluchistan's Human Rights, the Baloch Human Rights Organization and Human Rights Council of Balochistan said they had received 'partial reports' of 541 cases of enforced disappearances in the first half of the year. In the majority of cases 'the persons were picked up by security forces from their homes, in front of the entire families and villagers'. According to Amnesty International in March, the UN Working Group on Enforced or Involuntary Disappearances had more than 700 pending cases from Pakistan. Addressing a press conference at the Quetta Press Club in April, Hamida Baloch, sister of missing Saghir Baloch, appealed to the government of Pakistan, the Supreme Court, the Human Rights Commission of Pakistan, and civil society to raise their voice for the safe recovery of her brother. Saghir, a student of BS Political Science at the University of Karachi, went missing on 20 November 2017.[5]

In April 2019, Al Jazeera reported Pakistan army allegations against PTM leaders that they received funds from foreign intelligence services, warning its leaders that "their time is up". Major General Asif Ghafoor, speaking at a press conference at the military's headquarters in Rawalpindi levelled allegations that the Pashtun Tahafuz Movement (PTM) had been funded by RAW and NDS: "The way they are playing into the hands of others, their time is up," he said. "No one will be hurt and nothing illegal will be done. Everything will be done according to the law. Whatever liberties you could take, you have taken." General Ghafoor said. PTM leaders denied the charges, saying they were ready to present the group's accounts before parliament or other accountability bodies to be examined. "These accusations are being levelled against us only because we are demanding accountability," said Mohsin Dawar, a PTM leader and Member of Parliament, on the floor of Pakistan's National Assembly hours after Ghafoor's press conference. "We want accountability for targeted killings, for extrajudicial killings, for missing persons, people who have been held without charge or crime by the government. Whenever anyone speaks of these issues, they are accused of being foreign funded, "he said.[6]

However, the Pakistani army attacked PTM workers near the border of Afghanistan, leaving at least three people dead and scores wounded. Leaders of the Pashtun movement said they exercised their right to protest peacefully, but the military saw the movement as being propped up by foes of the state and accused neighboring Afghanistan and India of trying to stir up unrest with support of the movement in areas straddling the Afghan border. "You have enjoyed all the liberty that you wanted to," Maj. Gen. Asif Ghafoor, the military spokesman, warned P.T.M. leaders in a news conference. However, on 01 May 2019, Zahid Hussain noted General Ghafoor warning and the army bitterness against Pashtuns: "Notwithstanding the conscious efforts of some elements to turn to chauvinism, the movement has so far remained peaceful, and there have not been incidents of any violence in its protest rallies, which is quite a rare phenomenon in Pakistani politics. The move to turn it into an anti-state movement can only be criticized, and the use of force would fuel negative propaganda. The allegation of foreign funding is very serious and no state can tolerate foreign meddling in its internal matters. There is an urgent need to investigate the matter and action must be taken if the charges are substantiated. More important, however, is that the blackout of the PTM should be lifted. The Senate committee has done the right thing by hearing the PTM leaders. This kind of dialogue must continue. A rational dialogue is the only way out of the problem".[7]

The Pakistan army needs to adopt a new strategy of counterinsurgency, instead of killing and kidnapping innocent people in Pakistan. This policy of oppression and humiliation will turn the region into an endless war, and foreign involvement will also challenge the authority of the state. On 30 May 2019, Human Rights Watch demanded the investigation of the North Waziristan atrocities: "Pakistan authorities should impartially investigate the deaths of at least three people during violence between Pashtun activists and the army in North Waziristan on May 26, 2019, Human Rights Watch said. Both the army and supporters of the Pashtun Tahaffuz Movement (PTM), which campaigns for the rights of ethnic Pashtuns in the former tribal areas bordering Afghanistan, accuse the other of initiating a clash at a military checkpoint at Khar Kamar. In addition to the deaths, several people, including soldiers, were injured. "The uncertainty surrounding the deaths at Khar Kamar requires a prompt, transparent, and impartial investigation by Pakistani authorities," said Brad Adams, Asia director. "Upholding the rule of law is critical for maintaining security and protecting human rights in North Waziristan." The incident arose during a protest at the checkpoint by local residents following the arrest of two men after a military search operation. The search operation was in response to two attacks on army personnel, on May 6 and May 24, that killed one soldier and injured three others. A key PTM leader, Mohsin Dawar, told the media that as the group's elected representative, he and his supporters had gone to meet the demonstrators at the checkpoint. Dawar said that while he was meeting with the protesters, soldiers opened fire without provocation. After the incident, the army issued a statement that a group led by Dawar and Ali Wazir, another leader of the Pashtun group attacked the military checkpoint to force the release of a suspected terrorist facilitator. "In exchange of fire," the statement said, "three individuals who attacked the post lost their lives and 10 got injured." The prime minister's office endorsed the military's statement. The authorities registered a criminal case against Wazir and eight other PTM members who have been arrested. On May 27, the army issued a statement that five more bodies were found close to the area where the clash occurred"[8]

Pakistan's Armed Forces have been implicated in torture and other ill-treatment cases of individuals detained over the last decade of so called counter-insurgency operations in Waziristan and FATA. As the state practices have moved away from traditional counterinsurgency operations to sporadic clashes with local population since 2014, security and law and order situation is consecutively deteriorating in the region. With this shift in focus, Amnesty International became increasingly concerned about the treatment of detainees. Charles Pierson in his Wall Street Journal article noted the killing of 20 truck drivers by the Pakistan army: "Only three months ago, the Journal reported on an army massacre of unarmed civilians. This earlier story quoted local residents, three of them named, who told how an army unit ordered more than 20 men out of a restaurant in North Waziristan and then killed them execution style. No trial, no jury. The restaurant owner said that the men killed were truck drivers".[9]Raheel Sharif inflicted huge fatalities on civilian population in North Waziristan. His army kidnapped women and children, and humiliated tribal leaders.

On 02 May 2019, Kunwar Khuldune Shahid in his analysis noted the resentment of Gen Ghafoor and the army against Pashtuns: "Pakistan Army's spokesperson, Major General Asif Ghafoor, has warned the leadership of the Pashtun Tahaffuz Movement (PTM) that their "time is up." Ghafoor dedicated most of his press conference on April 29 to the PTM–a nationalist movement dedicated to safeguarding the rights of the Pashtun community–accusing the group of receiving funds from Indian and Afghan intelligence agencies. While Ghafoor failed to substantiate his allegations, he laid the onus of disproving the Army's claims against the PTM on the movement's leadership. He put forth a questionnaire for the PTM, demanding answers regarding the group's responsibilities in the tribal areas, their overseas activities, collaborators in Kabul and New Delhi, narrative against the military, and income sources. At the same time, Ghafoor categorically told the media not to invite the movement's leadership on their channels to answer his own questions, amid the continued blanket ban on covering the PTM. In the same press conference, the spokesperson had earlier said with a straight face that the Army does not tell the media what to air and what not to air. When Member of the National Assembly (MNA) Mohsin Dawar, a PTM leader, tried to respond to the Army spokesperson's questions, his speech was cut short by the NA speaker. But there was enough time for Dawar to express his readiness for accountability, asking the military establishment if it could similarly come clean".[10]

The army strived to undermine the leadership of Pashtuns in Waziristan but failed, and clefts appeared within the army ranks. Jaibans Singh in his analysis of the Pashtun Tahafuz Movement noted responses of Pashtun leaders and activists to the former ISPR Chief tweets: "DG-ISPR's comments, especially on the missing persons, created a twitter storm. "The whole presser was horrendous. Screenshot of Pakistani Journalist Gul Bukhari's tweet in response to DG-ISPR Maj. Gen. Asif Ghafoor's admission that Pakistan Army has been responsible for missing Pakistani citizens. Gulali Ismail, a well-known Human Rights Activist from Khyber Pakhtunkhwa tweeted, "I consider this Press Conference not an attack on PTM, but an attack on the Parliament of Pakistan, an attack on the Democracy of Pakistan and an attack on the Constitution of Pakistan PTM Zindabad." In fact, there are thousands of tweets on the same line with PTM Zindabad which, by now, must be giving nightmares to the Pakistan Army. They are also generating debates on the role of social media across the country. It will not come as a surprise if the DG-ISPR is soon transferred from the post. It is now apparent that the PTM and its leadership are not going to be cowed down by the usual pressure tactics of the Pakistan Army based on rising of anti-National, anti-Islam bogeys. These calls for accountability of the actions taken by the Army are going to increase and also envelope other trouble torn areas of the country like Balochistan and Pakistan Occupied Kashmir (POK)".[11]

On 14 January 2020, the News International reported leaders of Pakistan's political parties to work with Pashtun Tahafuz Movement (PTM) for the protection of the rights of Pashtuns. PTM chief Manzoor Pashteen at a public rally in Bannu announced the formation of a jirga to convince Pashtun leaders to collectively work for Pashtuns rights. Jamaat-e-Islami (JI) leader Senator Mushtaq Ahmad Khan told The News that he had raised the problems being faced by Pashtuns at the highest forum in the country. "Pashtuns rights are being violated at every level in Pakistan, adding that their undisputed rights provided in the Constitution were made disputed," he added. He said that all parties' conference would be convened on January 29, 2020.[12] Senator Mushtaq Ahmad Khan also said that he had raised the issues of net hydel profit, gas and others. He said Khyber Pakhtunkhwa was denied the rights to use its gas resource, which had been ensured in article 158. "They are making their own interpretation of this article to deny our rights," Mushtaq said. Jamiat Ulema-e-Islam-Fazl (JUI-F) leader Maulana Attaur Rehman said that they could respond on the possibility of cooperation after the PTM leaders present their demands. "The party leaders could take a decision on whether or not to work with PTM when we meet them and know their position, "he added.[13] PTM held the public gathering in Bannu after a break of seven months and reiterated its demand of de-mining of the erstwhile FATA, end to enforced disappearances and constitution of truth and reconciliation commission.[14]

However, Mohsin Dawar, a leading member of Pashtun Tahafuz Movement (PTM) and Pakistani parliamentarian, termed the PTM rally in Bannu as a bigger success, adding that participation of thousands of Pashtuns in the rally showed that Pashtuns want their rights and could not remain silent. Mohsin Dawar said that since the start of the PTM, a number of issues faced by Pashtun in Pakistan have been resolved: "Cases of forced disappearances as well as violence in tribal districts reduced and PTM is getting more attention. However, he added, When the pressure is reduced they (Security forces) will yet again resort to their old ways".[15] Talking to Radio Ashna, Dawar added that the Bannu meeting was according to their expectations. Other political parties have not organized such a huge gathering in the region.[16]"Our issues would automatically be resolved if they properly implement the constitution of the Pakistan," Dawar argued, and said: "We would continue our non-violent protests and would keep pressurizing the government to accept the PTMs' demands," He said. Before the Banu

PTM conference, on 22 Fabruary 2019, Senator Farhatullah Babar in his Friday Times analysis argued that the military culture of torture must be undermined. He also noted that new legislation will limit the right of free trial, and the army will be operating with impunity:

"Due to conflict zones in Balochistan and erstwhile tribal areas, new legislation limiting the right to free trial, opaque detention centers under control of the military and increasing reliance on so called 'doctrine of exceptionalism' has blurred focus on the culture of impunity of torture in Pakistan. However, two recent developments should help return our focus on this issue and can serve as a catalyst for criminalizing torture and ending the widespread impunity of the crime in the country. First, a recent Peshawar High Court verdict overturning scores of convictions awarded by military courts on grounds that suggested questionable ways of confessions extracted possibly under torture. Second, a report jointly prepared by the National Commission of Human Rights (NCHR) and Justice Project of Pakistan (JPP) on systematic torture by police in Faisalabad over a seven-year period covering three different administrations. Although Pakistan signed the Convention against Torture (CAT) in 2008 and also ratified it in 2010, it has still not made domestic legislation that defines and criminalizes torture. Pakistan's official report to the third Universal Periodic Review (UPR) in 2017 of its human rights record, referring to articles of the Constitution and penal laws, claimed that torture had already been eliminated and no one was tortured in the country. Referring to the Extradition Act, the official report claimed fool proof guarantees against handing over suspects to other parties who could subject them to torture. 1,424 cases of torture and other forms of cruel, inhuman and degrading treatment by the police were documented. No official inquiry was launched by any government body into any of these cases."[17]

However, Maj General Asif Ghafoor's irresponsible tweets, comments and conferences against the Pashtun nation left a black contemptuousness blot on the face of Pakistan army that the army only represents a club of Punjabi Generals. Gen Asif Ghafoor acted like a vandal and warlord that put the army in ordeal by challenging the Pushtun nation of Pakistan. The fact is, his resentment against Pashtuns, and his immature statement issued from the flatform of ISPR couldn't attract civil society in Pakistan. His past history and loose character show that he has often been swimming in contaminated water where he adopted an abusive language. A man of shameless character created numerous controversies while his childlike statements and tweets caused misunderstanding between the Pakistan army and the Pashtun population across the border. On 15 January 2020, he shamelessly warned the Pashtun nation that the Pakistan army would butcher their children again. These and other artless statements and tweets forced GHQ to replace him by Maj General Babar Iftikhar.[18]

Domestic and foreign media, intellectuals, think tanks, and literary forums are critical of the unconstitutional operations and actions of Pakistan's armed forces and the ISI in North Waziristan, Khyber Pakhtunkhwa and Balochistan. Pakistan army and ISI treat residents of Waziristan and Baluchistan like enemies, kill and arrest them with impunity. Their houses are being destroyed, and set to fire and their businesses are looted and plundered. Newspapers reported the army spokesman's announcement of controlling Miranshah town, while he didn't disclose war crimes of rogue military units who killed thousands, kidnapped women and girls and looted their businesses. On 08 September 2016, Daily Times reported: "All North Waziristan Petroleum Owners Association President, Sirajuddin, Vice President, Property Association of Miran Shah and Mir Ali along with owners of petrol pumps, representatives of various trade bodies, and tribal elders gathered for a news conference at press club. Thousands of protesters attended anti-military protests overnight in northwestern Pakistan after activists from a rights group were killed when soldiers fired at their demonstration. According to Radio Free Europe, members of the Pashtun Tahafuz Movement (PTM) representing ethnic Pashtuns protested in major cities across the region late on May 27, chanting slogans against the army and demanding the release of their leaders.[19] The Pakistan Army launched several operations to regain control of the Miran Shah, most notably Operation Zarb-e-Azb in June 2014, aimed at eliminating terrorist safe havens. During these military operations, the Miran Shah market was destroyed because it was believed to be a center for the militant activity, with some parts of the market reportedly used for storing weapons, explosives, and other supplies for the insurgents. The destruction of the market was part of a broader effort by the military to dismantle the infrastructure that supported militant operations. However, the destruction of the market also had significant consequences for the local population, particularly the poor Pashtuns who depended on the market for their livelihoods.

Many local residents and human rights organizations criticized the operation for the extensive damage to civilian infrastructure and the displacement of thousands of people, arguing that it exacerbated the economic and social hardships faced by the already marginalized communities in North Waziristan. On 15 August, 2015, the Pakistani Minister resigned after alleging the former head of ISI encouraged violent street demonstrations to unseat the government. The comments of Mushahidullah Khan once again exposed the fragile balance between civilian government and military. He alleged that a civilian intelligence agency (IB) had recorded former Inter-Services Intelligence (ISI) chief Lieutenant-General Zaheer-ul-Islam instructing protesters to cause chaos. The tape had been played to the prime minister and chief of army staff, Khan said. He said he had not personally heard it. The ISI, driven by the Pakistan Armed Forces, (Ehsan Sehgal-19 September, 2017) ignores the supreme constitutional rule of a democratic head of the state, under which even the Armed Forces themselves fall. This is not only a violation of the constitution, but also a rejection of the civilian leadership.

Pakistan's interference in Afghanistan causes pain and consternation and its financial and military support to the Taliban terrorist group prompted destruction, poverty, and displacement. According to a detailed comment of Daily Outlook Afghanistan newspaper: (08 June, 2021) "Taliban occupy residential houses in order to fight against Afghan security forces. There the locals, mainly Pashtuns, have complained against the Taliban militant fighters. According to them, the Taliban insurgents occupy their houses as well as schools.[20] The newspaper noted destruction of their houses and death of their family members are not significant for the militants. That is, the Taliban use locals as human shields. In case the Afghan soldiers attack residential areas, which could lead to civilian casualties, the Taliban will say out loud that Afghan soldiers do not respect humanitarian law and kill ordinary people".[21] On 07 June 2021, Afghanistan Times in its editorial page noted atrocities of Taliban and the ISI supported groups: "The Taliban are not irresolute even to carry out car bomb attacks and the government is trying to overplay the collapse of the districts as a tactical retreat of the Afghan security forces. What is more worrisome is that the militants have been gaining territorial gains around the country. Meanwhile, there is no doubt that the Afghan National Defense and Security Forces are the cornerstone of a durable peace, and it's imperative to stand in their support. They are rendering sacrifices on a daily basis to protect from an independent Afghanistan. We, the Afghan people must do everything in their support and we can overcome the difficult time only to come up to the fore with a full support to the Afghan security forces and our unity can defeat militant networks". Moreover, politicians in Afghanistan noted the issue of Pakistan's strategic depth. "Many Afghan leaders had repeatedly said that the key to peace in Afghanistan is in the hands of the U.S. and Pakistan. If the policy is changed, there should be some practical actions, like the Pakistani authorities should force the Taliban to engage in meaningful talks with Afghan peace members, and also agree to a comprehensive ceasefire". Afghanistan Times noted.[22]

Pakistan army and the ISI has been torturing and consternating people of North Waziristan, Khyber Pakhtunkhwa and Balochistan. Everyone who raises his voice against the ISI atrocious campaign of kidnapping and disappearance, he/she is arrested and killed. Newspapers in Pakistan are not allowed to publish news of enforced disappearances, and electronic media is banned to talk about the grievances and pain of Waziristan and Baluchistan. Journalist and analyst, F.M. Shakil (30 October 2020) in his article documented pain in the neck and resentment of families and relatives of missing persons in Waziristan and Baluchistan, and noted rallies of Pakistan Democratic Movement (PDM) in Punjab, Sindh and Balochistan: "Mass Pakistan Democratic Movement (PDM) rallies in Punjab, Sindh and Balochistan demonstrated significant popular support for the opposition's pro-democracy rally cry, a potent call in a country plagued by a long history of coups, political engineering and electoral manipulation.....Nawaz's apparent aim is to cut off the "transgressing generals" from the lower tiers of the army establishment and thus drive a wedge between the military's leadership and rank and file....The PDM's broad demands have been outlined in a 26-point declaration, which, among other things, calls for an end of the "establishment's" interference in politics, new free and fair elections after election reforms with no role of armed forces and intelligence agencies, the release of political prisoners, implementation of a national action plan against terrorism, and across the board accountability under a new accountability law"[23]

Pakistani and international media have reported numerous cases of forced disappearance in Punjab, Sindh, Balochistan and Khyber Pakhtunkhwa. Writers, bloggers, journalists, politicians, and members of parliament have been kidnapped and disappeared by intelligence agencies since 2001. Amnesty international (Pakistan: Enduring Enforced Disappearances-27 March 2019) in its report noted challenges faced by journalists, bloggers and activists: "In April 2017, Hidayatullah Lohar, school teacher (headmaster), blacksmith and political Sindhi activist was forcibly disappeared from the school where he taught. He was taken away in a "double-cabin grey coloured" vehicle by men in police uniform and civilian clothes. Since then the authorities have refused to disclose his whereabouts. Despite the presence of eye-witnesses, his family had to petition the Larkana High Court to order the area police station to register the First Information

Report. Hidayatullah Lohar is one of Sindh's "missing persons". His family have been patiently seeking truth and justice through the courts and on the streets of Pakistan since his disappearance.....Enforced disappearances have long been a stain on Pakistan's human rights record. Despite the pledges of successive governments to criminalize the practice, there has been slow movement on legislation while people continue to be forcibly disappeared with impunity......The groups and individuals targeted in enforced disappearances in Pakistan include people from Sindhi, Baloch, Pashtun ethnicities, the Shia community, political activists, human rights defenders, members and supporters of religious and nationalist groups, suspected members of armed groups, and proscribed religious and political organizations in Pakistan"[24]

Families of disappeared people have been threatened with dire consequences by spy agencies and Rangers in all four provinces. Amnesty international (Pakistan: Enduring Enforced Disappearances-27 March 2019) in its report documented maroon's mothers and daughters of incarcerated Pakistanis: "While marching against enforced disappearances, Sasui and SorathLohar have spent Eids in hunger strike camps outside the Karachi Press Club with other families of the "missing persons", as the victims of enforced disappearance are commonly referred to in Pakistan. In May 2018, during a violent dispersal of the protest they were part of in Sindh, Sasui says she was assaulted by a law enforcement officer. In November 2018, a peaceful march of the missing persons of Sindh was interrupted repeatedly by the Sindh Rangers and by officials in plain clothes – who are thought to be from the intelligence agencies. On 12 January 2019, Sindh Rangers attempted to detain one of Lohar's sons, Sanghaar Lohar, without search warrants from his mobile shop in Karachi. The sisters and mother resisted and raised enough noise to gather neighbours and managed to halt the detention. The video evidence of the entire incident shows men in uniform claiming that their brother was involved in wrongdoing, without specifying any allegations or charges".[25]

Relatives of all disappeared people are in pain and trouble. There sons and daughter have kidnapped by intelligence agencies, and they are not allowed to meet in secret prisons: "Associate Asia Director, Patricia Gossman (End Pakistan's Enforced Disappearances: Prime Minister Imran Khan Should Back Promises with Accountability-Human Rights watch 22 March 2021) in her analysis noted the grievances of disappeared families: International human rights law strictly prohibits enforced disappearances, the detention of an individual in which the state denies holding the person or refuses to provide information on their fate or whereabouts. In addition to the grave harm to the person, enforced disappearances prompt continuing suffering for family members. In January, the Islamabad High Court, after hearing a petition on a disappearance case from 2015, ruled that the prime minister and his cabinet were responsible for the state's failure to protect its citizens "because the buck stops at the top." The court called enforced disappearances "the most heinous crime and intolerable."[26]

Pakistan's rogue army and political establishment of Nawaz-Zardari parties, and their collaboration with ISI and the army corrupt General have put the lives of Pashtun and Baluch nations at risk by allowing intelligence agencies to kill, torture, kidnap and disappear men, women and children in Balochistan and Khyber Pakhtukhawa province. Private terrorist Militia of notorious Chief Minister of Balochistan Mir Sarfraz Bugti who has established secret torture cells across Balochistan, where Baloch and Pashtuns are being humiliated, raped and tortured. According to Jamal Baloch, Mir Sarfraz Bugti is running a death squad under the supervision of Pakistan rogue Army; involved in abductions, torture of political activists in Balochistan. The US State Department in its report noted arbitrary or unlawful killings by the Pakistan army. 'Security forces reportedly committed extrajudicial killings in connection with conflicts in Punjab, Balochistan, FATA, Sindh, and KP. Physical abuse while in official custody allegedly caused the death of some criminal suspects. Lengthy trial delays and failure to discipline and prosecute those responsible for killings contributed to a culture of impunity'. The Report noted.[27] On 16 November 2023, Balochistan Post reported appointment of warlord Sarfaraz Bugti as the head of a new committee on enforced disappearances by the government sparked controversy and criticism in Balochistan.[28]

Sammi Deen Baloch, General Secretary of Voice for Baloch Missing Persons (VBMP) and daughter of the missing Dr. Deen Mohammad, (Appointment of Sarfaraz Bugti as head of missing persons committee draw criticism 16 November 2023, The Balochistan Post) expressed skepticism about the committee's effectiveness. 'She referred to the unsuccessful outcomes of similar past commissions, including COIOED and a commission led by Sardar Akhtar Jan Mengal appointed by the Islamabad High Court. Baloch accused the government of toying with the emotions of the families of missing persons by appointing Bugti, who she claims downplays the severity of enforced disappearances. The Post reported.[29] Balochistan National Party President and former chief minister of Balochistan Sardar Akhtar Mengal has alleged that Caretaker Interior Minister Sarfraz Bugti was running death squads under the patronage of the state. The Balochistan Express Akhter Mengal accuses Interior Minister Sarfraz Bugti of running a death squad. October 20, 2023) reported. "Everybody knows how many people have been killed and abducted by this death squad. At the moment, rockets fell near where I am right now," he said in an exclusive interview on" Spot Light "with Munizae Jahangir. He alleged that two of his employees were hurt in firing on his house. "My house was hit with bullets fired from heavy weapons and rockets. People fear for their lives in Wash."Express noted.[29]

The PTM's nonviolent struggle against the rogue army atrocities and genocide in Waziristan and Khyber Pakhtunkhwa has intensifies by calling Pashtun Judicial Council meeting in October 2024. Expert and writer, Col. Harsh Vardhan Singh, in his article (Pashtun Tahafuz Movement (PTM): Achilles Heel of Pak Army, March 26, 2021) documented policies of the deep state in Pakistan: "PTM's protests during the past year have seen the first cracks in such a narrative. Punjabi insensitivity towards sub-nationalism resulted in the military's propensity of interpreting the lack of consensus to accept a singular and centralized national identity or state narrative as disloyalty and treason. Pakistan Punjab has always stayed quarantined from the calamitous effect of terrorism until the arrival of Pashtun refugees from FATA and KPK who have been ghettoized in large metros like Lahore. Every time an atrocity is committed by Pakistan Army in the Wild West, a consequent terrorist attack in Punjab by the Pashtun in Punjabi heartland further drives a chasm between the Pashtuns and Punjabis which would eventually impact the cohesion of Pakistan Armed Forces....Pakistan's military has always guarded itself against accountability, and in recent months, Pakistan's civil-military scales have tipped further in favor of the military. The real question is: How far will the Pakistan Army go to repress this movement? The cause for concern is the potential for the confrontation to turn violent and effects it would generate on the PDM that wants to cash on this military intervention of Pakistan's fragile democracy".[30]

Chapter 4

The Military Establishment, Inter-Services Intelligence (ISI) and Tehrik-Taliban Pakistan (TTP)

Insurgency, or war of destruction by Pakistan army against the Pashtuns of Swat, Buner, Mohmand and Shangla districts became an uncontrollable genocide that resulted in huge destruction and killing of innocent women and children in order to satisfy the United States and Britain that the army can do anything in return for money. The army received money, scholarships for their children in the US and Britain, and internally displaced one million Pashtun from their motherland. The war in North-West Pakistan or Pakistan's war on Pashtuns, received little support from Punjab and Sindh provinces. The TTP, Jundallah, Lashkar-e-Islam, TNSM, al-Qaeda, and their Central Asian allies such as the SK Khorasan terrorist group, Islamic Movement of Uzbekistan, East Turkestan Movement, Emirate of Chechnya, and Punjabi Taliban collectively responded to the army unwanted operation in KPK. War on the Pashtun land began in 2004. That war was for the US dollars, but some terrorist groups fled Afghanistan in order to reorganize their infrastructure. The Pervez Musharraf administration launched operations with the Battle of Wanna to hunt down al-Qaeda fighters, but failed to achieve the results. Later on, the war of the Pakistani state against its own citizens became complicated when madrassa students Sieged building of Lal Masjid in Islamabad city. The TTP declared Pakistan Army as a proxy of US army and started campaigns of suicide bombings to force the army to retreat the region. Due to the above-mentioned wrong policies of the military established, former Prime Minister Benazir Bhutto was killed.[1]

Experts, Nazim Rahim, Hashmat Ali and Muhammad Javed in their research paper (Analysis of Social Impacts of Terrorism and Military Operations in Pakistan in Swat. Pakistan Languages and Humanities Review June 2019, Vol. 3, No. 1) have reviewed development of the Mullah

Sufi Muhammad struggle against the army by visiting towns and villages to win the support of local leadership: "Mullah Sufi Muhammad started his activities in 1990. He visited many villages and addressed huge gatherings. His main slogans were the imposition of Islamic Laws and speedy justice. In the beginning, he failed to attract people but the order of the Supreme Court to declare PATA null and ultra vires paved the way for him. He exploited the situation very well because he was a very good orator. He established Tehrik-e-Nefaz-e-Shariat-e-Muhammadi (TNSM). With time TNSM became stronger and extended its activities to other parts of KPK and FATA. It was very interesting to note that Mullah Sufi Muhammad belonged to Dir district but he was interested in implementing Sharia in Swat. He established Swat as the center of his activities. He established his movement in Swat (Roggio, 2009). The movement got popularity in 1994 when the activists of the movement started the black turban movement. They forced the government to bow to their demands and the governor signed the Nezam e Sharia Regulation Act.[2]

The Operation Black Thunderstorm of the army was launched on 26 April 2009, which resulted in the forced displacement of hundred thousand people. Mullah Sufi Muhammad travelled to Swat to discuss a peace plan with Mullah Fazllullah. The TTP supported the ceasefire agreement but the government in power was not prepared. Experts and writers, Manzoor Khan Afridi1, Musab Yousuf in their research paper (Military Operation in Malakand Division Pakistan: Causes and Implications. Asian Journal of Social Sciences and Humanities Vol. 3(3) August 2014) noted the army offensive against the local Taliban groups led by Mullah Fazllullah in Malakand Division: "Pakistan's military launched a massive offensive against Taliban groups in Malakand region of KPK in the last week of April 2009. The operation was chosen as a last resort after the failure of two agreements of the provincial government, first with the local Taliban group, led by Mullah Fazlullah, and second with the defunct TNSM headed by Sufi Muhammad. Taliban had refused, in violation of the agreement, to lay down their weapons even after the promulgation of the Nizam-e-Adl Regulation in the restive region. Taliban attacks on security forces including Pakistan Army, Frontier Corps (FC) and police did not stop either. Before the launch of the security operation and while the peace agreement was still intact, militants carried out 18 terrorist attacks in Swat, Dir and Buner districts of Malakand region in the month of April alone. Eight of these attacks targeted security forces, including the army and police.....In 2008 the leader of TNSM Moulana Fazlullah, nicknamed "Mullah Radio" had strong links with TTP which had strong links with jihadi group Asmatullah

Shaheen Bhittani. In February 2009, Baithullah Mehsood joined the Afghan Taliban, mainly Maulvi Nazir, to form Shura Ittihad ul Mujahideen (SIM) and Mullah Omer as their Amir-ul-Mumineen."[3]

The Tehrik-i-Taliban Pakistan (TTP), also known as the Pakistani Taliban, is a militant organization that operates mainly in Pakistan. It shares an ideology similar to the Afghan Taliban but is a distinct group with its own leadership and objectives. The TTP was established in 2007 under the leadership of Baitullah Mehsud. As of recent years, the TTP is led by Noor Wali Mehsud. The group emerged from a loose alliance of various tribal groups in Pakistan's Federally Administered Tribal Areas (FATA), united in their opposition to the Pakistani state and military. The TTP aims to overthrow the Pakistani government and establish a Sharia-based Islamic state. The group opposes Pakistan's alliance with the United States, especially regarding the U.S.-led war in Afghanistan. The TTP uses guerrilla warfare, suicide bombings, and targeted killings to pursue its objectives. While the TTP shares ideological roots with the Afghan Taliban, the two groups have different operational goals. The Afghan Taliban focuses primarily on Afghanistan, while the TTP is focused on Pakistan. The TTP, however, has found refuge in Afghanistan at various times and often aligns itself with broader Taliban networks in the region. The Pakistani military has conducted numerous operations against the TTP, particularly in regions like Swat and South Waziristan. Major operations, such as Operation Zarb-e-Azb (2014), have significantly reduced the group's capacity, forcing many of its members to flee to Afghanistan. After facing military pressure and losses, the TTP has experienced internal divisions, though it remains a potent threat in certain areas of Pakistan. In recent years, some splinter groups have merged back into the TTP, signaling a possible resurgence.[4]

On 26 May 2019, Pakistan army opened fire on innocent Pashtuns in Khar Kamar near Datta Khen in North Waziristan, which resulted in countrywide resentment against the army. The two PTM legislators had arrived with the stated aim of investigating alleged Pakistan Army human rights abuses, subsequently leading protestors to the checkpoint. Recent developments surrounding the Tehrik-i-Taliban Pakistan (TTP) highlight growing concerns for regional security in Pakistan and Afghanistan. The TTP continues to expand its influence, particularly benefiting from its ties to the Afghan Taliban. These connections allow TTP militants to operate from Afghan soil, conducting cross-border attacks into Pakistan with tacit support from the Taliban regime. This complicity between the Afghan Taliban and the TTP has significantly strained relations between Pakistan and Afghanistan. In early 2024, reports showed an increased number of attacks in Pakistan, especially in regions like Khyber Pakhtunkhwa and Baluchistan, areas that have traditionally been hotbeds of insurgent activity. The TTP has also reorganized itself, mirroring the Afghan Taliban's strategy by establishing various "wilayahs" (provinces) and appointing local commanders, thus decentralizing its operations for greater flexibility. Moreover, the TTP's use of sophisticated weapons, some of which are believed to be left over from NATO forces in Afghanistan, poses a growing threat. The organization has been bolstered by military-grade equipment, including night-vision devices, which enhances its operational capabilities.

This resurgence of the TTP, alongside its ties with groups like Al-Qaeda, is a critical security challenge not only for Pakistan but for the wider region. The situation underscores the need for international cooperation to address the growing extremist threat from both the TTP and the broader nexus of insurgent groups in South and Central Asia. Recently, the Tehrik-i-Taliban Pakistan (TTP), along with several affiliated groups in Afghanistan, has issued a threat concerning Khyber Pakhtunkhwa (KPK), Pakistan. These groups, reportedly numbering 30, held a meeting in Shakar Dara, Afghanistan, where they declared their intention to extend control over KPK. The TTP's growing confidence is attributed to its safe havens in Afghanistan, where the Afghan Taliban's reluctance or inability to curtail their activities allows them to operate freely. This close relationship between the TTP and Afghan Taliban has been a concern for Pakistan, especially as the TTP continues to use Afghanistan as a base to launch attacks on Pakistani soil. Pakistan has responded with a multidimensional counterterrorism strategy aimed at curbing the resurgence of the TTP. Despite military efforts and ongoing diplomatic talks with the Afghan Taliban to address the threat posed by the TTP, the group remains a persistent challenge. The TTP's reach has been bolstered by new administrative structures and its growing presence in KPK, as well as in other provinces such as Punjab and Balochistan. Pakistan's leadership continues to engage with Afghanistan to relocate TTP fighters and suppress their cross-border movements, though the effectiveness of these measures remains uncertain given the ideological and tactical ties between the TTP and Afghan Taliban.

The idea that Pakistan's military establishment is divided between the U.S. and China reflects the broader geopolitical balancing act Pakistan has had to navigate in recent years. Historically, Pakistan has maintained a close military and strategic relationship with the United States, especially during the Cold War and in the context of the Afghan War. The U.S. has provided military aid, training, and equipment to Pakistan, making the two countries key allies for decades. However, in recent years, Pakistan has strengthened its ties with China, particularly in terms of defense cooperation, infrastructure projects, and economic investments. The China-Pakistan Economic Corridor (CPEC), part of China's Belt and Road Initiative, has deepened this relationship significantly. China has also become a major supplier of military hardware to Pakistan. During the past five years, the relationship between the two states remained underwhelming due to the army's double face policy that halted the CPEC project under US pressure. The alleged "division" in the military between pro-U.S. and pro-China factions likely stems from these dual relationships. Some officers and officials may see maintaining strong ties with the U.S. as important for military aid, counterterrorism support, and balancing India's influence, particularly as the U.S. strengthens its strategic partnership with India. On the other hand, others may favor China as a more reliable partner in the long term, given China's willingness to invest heavily in Pakistan's infrastructure and its geopolitical alignment with Pakistan against India.[5]

The divide is not necessarily a sharp split but rather reflects different schools of thought within Pakistan's strategic community. In reality, the military establishment likely seeks to balance its relationships with both powers, ensuring Pakistan continues to benefit from U.S. military support while deepening its ties with China for economic and strategic gains. The perception that the Pakistan Army struggled with counterinsurgency operations, particularly in the Swat Valley in 2008, stems from various complexities related to the nature of insurgencies, the geography of the region, and the tactics used at the time. In the Swat operation (Operation Rah-e-Haq), the army initially relied on conventional military strategies such as the use of tanks, jet fighters, and heavy artillery, which are generally effective in traditional warfare but not ideal for guerrilla warfare and insurgencies. Insurgencies are often fought in densely populated civilian areas, where heavy weapons can cause collateral damage, alienating the local population and exacerbating the insurgency problem. This approach in 2008 led to criticism that the military's methods were counterproductive. However, after learning from these early mistakes, the Pakistan Army adapted its strategy. By 2009, in Operation Rah-e-Rast, the military shifted to a more focused counterinsurgency (COIN) approach, using a combination of intelligence-based operations, close cooperation with local militias, and securing local populations through "clear, hold, and build" strategies. The army's later successes in Swat and other tribal regions, such as South Waziristan, are often cited as significant improvements in counterinsurgency tactics.[6]

Counterinsurgency requires a combination of military force, intelligence gathering, political engagement, and efforts to win the hearts and minds of the local population. Early challenges in Swat reflected a learning curve, which over time led to more effective COIN operations in Pakistan. In 2008 Kayani removed DG ISI Nadeem Taj and MG Asif Akhtar based on the "Reforms in ISI" recommended by CIA station chief and CENTCOM. These changes were portrayed in the media as "routine transfers". Pakistan's failure in the world is the failure of ISI. The ISI is a militant organisation not an intelligence agency. Failure to track India's First Armored Division prior to hostilities was then compounded by India's "surprise" attack on 06 September, but the ISI Chief Riaz Hussain justified that ISI was preoccupied with election affairs. The ISI is a failed intelligence organization protecting its corruption, political engineering, joking with the constitution of Pakistan, and imposing barbarism against local citizens. It's a myth that ISI, the self-proclaimed "number one" intelligence agency of the world knows everything. The ISI may in fact be the most incompetent intelligence agency. The intelligence network of ISI has completely collapsed in Afghanistan and a rogue intelligence agency whose officers can't keep their emotions in check cannot be capable of protecting the country against security threats. Pakistan's military and ISI after their failure to convince people in KPK are now increasing the intensity of Bomb Blasts in KPK to convince the public about Military operation in KPK. Pakistan's terrorism challenges and failure of the spy agency-ISI have exponentially grown since the US proxy militia's (Taliban) takeover of Afghanistan with the military and financial support of NATO, Pakistan and the United States. The TTP also boosted its networks in Afghanistan by retrieving sophisticated weapons and modern technology. Pakistan and the US army are complicit with the Taliban for torturing and killing innocent Afghan women and children. The Tehrik-e-Taliban Pakistan (TTP) is operating from Afghanistan-using the US army weapons against Pakistan's security forces. Pakistan is now grappling with a new wave of heightened terrorist activities following the Taliban's takeover of Afghanistan in August 2021. The TTP has emerged as a strong militant group defending the rights of the People of Waziristan. A weak, complicated and controversial infrastructure of the Inter-Services Intelligence (ISI) that couldn't maintain its professional intelligence cadre easily became a militant organisation with numerous militant, extremist and terrorist organizations in South Asia. The ISI is only expert of targeted killing, enforced disappearances and torture.[7]

As a failed agency to authenticate its professional intelligence demonstration against terrorism and extremism, the ISI lost public confidence and access to remote regions of KPK and Balochistan provinces. Internal war between military and civilian officers within the ISI management is not a new story, this story is reverberating in newspapers by the day. Because, its affiliation with extremist and militant organizations confined the agency to a limited space. The ISI (militant group) has trained militants, extremist and terrorist organizations to stabilize neighboring states, change governments and wage jihad against Afghanistan and India. In September 2024, police in Lakki Marwat, KP continued to protest against the targeted killings of police officers and their families.[8] They blame Pakistani military's intelligence agencies, MI and ISI for the killings, and demand that the military vacate their district. The agency never demonstrated a professional approach to national security and domestic governance, pushing Pakistan to the brink dancing to the CIA and MI6 tangos for nothing. In 2024, the government of Shah Baz Sharif authorized the ISI to intercept communication of Pakistani citizens. According to the July 08 2024, directive, "The federal government, in the interest of national security and in the apprehension of any offence, is pleased to authorize [ISI] officers ... to intercept calls and messages or to trace calls through any telecommunication system." Today Pakistan is dancing on the verge of collapse plagued by political instability, lawlessness, and ethnic war in KPK. The state has been embroiled in corruption, nepotism, sectarianism and extremism. Sectarian affiliations in state institutions and political division in law enforcement agencies are turning to the civil war in four provinces.[9]

Journalist Syed Atiq ul Hassan (Friday Times, 12 September 2024) has documented failures of the state and intransigence of Pakistan's military establishment: "Under military rule, democracy in Pakistan was reduced to a façade. The army nurtured a class of politicians who operated under its influence, creating a pseudo-democratic system that was anything but representative of the people's will. Elections were manipulated, political opposition was crushed, and the Constitution was often disregarded or suspended".[10] This is not a new thing, the ISI has been intercepting communications since the 1990s. Alliance making, interfering in neighboring states internal affairs and sabotage is ISI's profitable business. Failed to save dismemberment of Pakistan, failed to counterinsurgency in Balochistan and Waziristan, the agency is expert of enforced disappearance, torture and humiliation, and unable to collect intelligence information from the remote districts of Balochistan, Sindh and Khyber Pakhtunkhwa provinces. Decade's old policy of security state to control Balochistan through Sardars and handpicked MPs has run its course. Social/mass media and tech has produced a cognitive revolution. The Inter-Services Intelligence (ISI) of Pakistan, like many intelligence agencies worldwide, occasionally faces scrutiny regarding its operations and public perception. On 30 January 2023, BBC reported a suicide attack in a Peshawar mosque killing 59 innocent people including children. "The mosque was within the police headquarters area but terrorist were transported safely to carry out suicide attacks. Pakistani Prime Minister, Shahbaz Sharif warned that terrorists wanted to create fear by targeting those who perform the duty of defending Pakistan". The Pakistani Taliban denied involvement after an initial claim by one of its commanders. The Inter-Services Intelligence (ISI) has often been accused of playing double role in major terrorist attacks across India and Afghanistan, the July 2006 Mumbai Train Bombings, the 2001 Indian Parliament attack, the 2006 Varanasi bombings, the August 2007 Hyderabad bombings, the Kabul suicide attacks, and the November 2008 Mumbai attacks.[11]

India Today News Desk, (15 September 2023) noted the ISI military and financial assistance to Kashmiri Mujahedeen in case of Chinese weapons; including pistol, grenades, and night vision devices, which were being transported into the territory through Chinese drones.[12]However, an American journalist and writer, Mansoor Ijaz in his article, (Pakistan's ISI Spy Agency, S-Wing, and Terrorism, Daily Beast, 13 July, 2017) documented evidences related to the murder of journalist Saleem Shahzad by the ISI commandos: "The murder of a prominent Pakistani journalist, Syed Saleem Shahzad, who was kidnapped in Islamabad after repeated threats by Inter-Services Intelligence, Pakistan's premier spy agency, should be a clarion call to the international community about the increasingly strident and lawless behavior of certain elements operating freely inside Pakistan's military and intelligence organizations. Shahzad's abduction occurred a few days after he wrote a forthright article suggesting that the militant attack on Pakistan's main naval base near Karachi on May 22 was in retaliation for an army crackdown on al Qaeda cells infiltrating its inner sanctum. His murder was clearly a warning to other seekers of truth that ISI thuggery knows no limits. The ISI is a danger to civilized societies everywhere, because it nurtures and breeds hatred among Pakistan's Islamist masses, and then uses their thirst for jihad as a foreign policy sledge hammer against Pakistan's neighbors and allies, often for no purpose besides just creating chaos. Its financial, logistics, and intelligence support of myriad jihadist groups in Kashmir thrice brought India and Pakistan to war—once a near-nuclear confrontation. Its S-Wing planning and logistics support for Afghanistan's Taliban from Pakistani soil has so muddied the waters in Afghan-Pakistan relations that President Hamid Karzai turned to India to counterbalance Pakistan's negative influences on his country. War, against both its neighbors, may be big business for Pakistan's army and intelligence organs, but the damage to civil life is nearly catastrophic—and it must now stop".[13]

For years, Pakistan's intelligence agencies have been under deep criticism from the international community, intellectual forums, writers and journalists for their role in terrorism, extremism and the collapse of the Afghan state in 2021. The Dawn newspaper described the intelligence community as "our secret godfathers" in its 25 April, 1994 article. The Civil War in Afghanistan bestowed the ISI with different types of experience and experiments of secret warfare.[14] On 06 October 2016, (Inter-Services Intelligence. Wikipedia, the free encyclopedia) noted a government meeting, in which Foreign Secretary Aizaz Chaudhry exposed international pressure on cracking down against extremist organizations like, Jaish-i-Mohmmad, Lashkar-e-Taiba, and the Haqqani terrorist networks.[15] Wikipedia noted. However, Ghazi Salahuddin noted in his News International article authenticated controversy about the meeting. In that meeting, Chief Minister Shahbaz Sharif noted: "whenever action had been taken against certain extremist groups by civilian authorities, the security agency had worked secretly to free the arrested parties." Moreover, Information Minister Pervaiz Rashid was forced to resign.

Whether the ISI has lost public confidence can be subject to interpretation, often depending on specific incidents, national politics, or international relationships. Calls for reorganization or reform of intelligence agencies, however, are not uncommon, especially when concerns about transparency, effectiveness, or political influence arise. The ISI has often been accused of involvement in domestic politics, supporting or undermining political actors, which can erode public trust. An agency that is perceived to operate beyond its mandate or interfere in democratic processes can lose legitimacy in the eyes of the public. There is an impression in the Pakistani media that ISI has become a state within a state, answerable neither to the military establishment, nor the civilian government. Unfortunately, all these contradictory policies of civilian and military governments left negative effects on Pakistani society. Social, political and religious institutions divided on ethnic and sectarian bases ruined society. The Taliban declared jihad against the Pakistan army in FATA and Waziristan regions and still continue to ruin the lives of innocent civilians. The ISI and MI have so often proved that they are stronger than the country's parliament; they can make parliament, and they can dissolve it. The case of Mr. Nawaz Sharif is not so different from the case of former President Asif Zardari, who received serious threats from the country's secret agencies. This civilian and military intelligence war caused great anger in the police and other law enforcement agencies. In a nine-page statement before the Supreme Court, former Intelligence Bureau Chief Masud Sharif Khattak revealed that former Prime Minister Benazir Bhutto extensively increased the budget of the IB, because the ISI was not willing to report to the Prime Minister.

Introducing stronger parliamentary or civilian oversight of intelligence operations could improve transparency and ensure that the ISI remains within its legal and national security mandate. Reforms aimed at reducing the agency's involvement in domestic politics could help restore public trust and reinforce its focus on national security and intelligence work rather than political maneuvering, establishing clearer mechanisms for accountability in cases of human rights abuses could improve the agency's reputation both domestically and internationally, reorganizing the ISI to better coordinate with other national security and law enforcement agencies could enhance its effectiveness in addressing terrorism, crime, and espionage, modernizing the agency's technological infrastructure and capabilities in cyber defense, intelligence gathering, and surveillance would make it more adaptable to contemporary security challenges. The ISI, being part of the military structure, has historically wielded enormous power in Pakistan's security and political affairs. Its influence has often overshadowed civilian-led intelligence agencies like the Intelligence Bureau (IB). As a result, civilian intelligence agencies are frequently seen as less effective or less influential, further consolidating the military's hold on security-related matters. The ISI has been accused of manipulating domestic politics by supporting certain political parties or undermining others. This involvement weakens the democratic process and sidelines civilian institutions, including civilian intelligence, which should ideally operate independently from political maneuvering.

The Intelligence Bureau, which never received attention from either civilian or military governments during the last 65 years, is now trying to stand on its feet and challenge the militarization of the intelligence mechanism in Pakistan. The Prime Minister allocated huge funds to the Intelligence Bureau to recruit and employ more agents to meet internal and external challenges the country faces. The Intelligence Bureau is the country's main civilian agency that functions under the direct control of the Prime Minister, tackling terrorism, insurgency and extremism. The way military intelligence has operated in the past was not a traditional or cultural way. Inter-Services Intelligence, Military Intelligence and other military intelligence units mostly concentrated on countering political parties. They never gave any importance to internal security threats in the past. Inter-Services Intelligence began as the external intelligence wing of the army, supported militant groups, sent them to India and Afghanistan and served the interests of the military establishment. These self-designed strategies and policies of civilian and military regimes isolated the country in the international community. The list of problems faced by the Pakistani intelligence machine is long. The Intelligence Bureau also played a political role in the past. In 2008, a case was filed in Pakistan's Supreme Court against the alleged involvement of the agency in destabilizing the Shahbaz Sharif government in Punjab. The Intelligence Bureau also spied on journalists and politicians in a non-traditional manner, which badly affected its professional reputation. The Prime Minister realizes that a legislative and structural umbrella is a must under which intelligence agencies must function without military and political interference, while remaining committed to their central mission. On February 25, 2014, Prime Minister Nawaz Sharif approved and published the National Internal Security Policy (2014-2018) and introduced a new mechanism to counter internal and external threats.[16]The involvement of the army and air force in tackling insurgency in the tribal areas and Waziristan caused misunderstanding. Pakistani military and civilian governments relying on US drone attacks did not give any importance to the intelligence reports of the country's agencies.

In the intelligence relationship between police intelligence, the Intelligence Bureau, Inter-Services Intelligence and Military Intelligence, lack of trust has been a longstanding concern in civilian circles. Majority of the members of intelligence agencies of the country belong to different sectarian groups. This illegal affiliation also directed intelligence operations on sectarian bases. Poor data collection with regard to the activities of militant sectarian organizations and their networks across the country is a challenging problem. The failure of Inter-Services Intelligence to intercept consecutive terror attacks on Pakistan's military installations, and its intransigence against maintaining professional intelligence cooperation with civilian intelligence agencies, or even considering Intelligence Bureau as an older civilian brother during the last four decades, forced Prime Minister Nawaz Sharif to restructure the IB and make it more effective to meet internal and external security threats. In Pakistan, unfortunately, different military regimes suppressed political forces and strengthened sectarian mafia groups, subjugated the silent majority through radical mullahs under the cover of Sharia and trained militants to fight inside India and Afghanistan. These policies of dictators destabilized the country. The experience of military regimes has not been a positive one. The army supported sectarian mullahs and weakened democratic forces. As a result the country has been in a state of despondency.

The dominance of the ISI and the broader military establishment in Pakistan has undoubtedly undermined the development of a strong civilian intelligence framework. Without reform, the country risks continuing the cycle of military control over national security and political life. A more balanced intelligence structure, with empowered civilian agencies and greater oversight, would not only restore public confidence but also contribute to a more democratic and accountable governance system. The Prime Minister's decision to restructure the intelligence infrastructure received worldwide appreciation. Mr. Sharif is now in a position to take stern steps and wants to try improving the operational capabilities of his country's intelligence agencies. The creation of an effective intelligence infrastructure to meet internal and external challenges must necessarily be taken as a long-term policy. Civilians may prioritize economic development, diplomacy, and democratic consolidation, while the military focuses more on strategic and security interests, sometimes clashing with civilian-led peace initiatives or political maneuvers. This divergence leads to intelligence agencies, particularly the ISI, operating with relative autonomy, sometimes even in direct opposition to civilian leaders' policies Intelligence agencies in Pakistan, especially the ISI, have been accused of interfering in domestic politics by backing certain political parties, manipulating elections, and undermining civilian politicians who are seen as a threat to the military's interests.

The reported difficulty faced by the Inter-Services Intelligence (ISI) in gathering intelligence from remote districts in Balochistan and Khyber Pakhtunkhwa (KP) highlights several challenges tied to geography, local dynamics, and insurgency activities. Balochistan and KP both have rugged terrains and remote areas, which can hinder the deployment of intelligence assets and complicate communications. These regions also deal with complex socio-political dynamics. Balochistan, for example, has a long-standing insurgency linked to demands for autonomy, ethnic grievances, and resource control. Meanwhile, parts of KP, especially areas bordering Afghanistan, have historically been sanctuaries for militant groups, further complicating intelligence-gathering efforts. The greatest challenge that Prime Minister Nawaz Sharif faces is on the national security front. In most parts of the country, intelligence information collection faces numerous difficulties as the Taliban and other militant groups have become a major threat. This is one of the greatest challenges for the Inter-Services Intelligence (ISI) and civilian intelligence agencies. There are numerous stories of intelligence agency successes and failures in these regions as the ISI faces a modern intelligence war. In fact, the wrongly designed policies of successive governments in Pakistan badly affected the professional abilities of the ISI and civilian agencies as they were used against each other for political purposes. From the 1980s, the real journey of the ISI, Intelligence Bureau (IB),

Chapter 5

Military Courts, Fair Trials Violations, and Rough-Handling of Pashtun and Baloch Prisoners

The 1973 constitution of Pakistan authenticates fair trial. No doubt every citizen's right is protected by the constitution, but no one has full access to justice in the country. The military harass and torture civilians and political workers, their houses are raided and their family member are humiliated, raped and imprisoned. There is no law to intercept the rogue and terrorist army from enforced disappearances, rape, torture and killing of innocent Pashtun and Bloch. The BBC reporter, M Ilyas Khan reported from Dera Ismail Khan the killings of thousands of people by the Pakistan army. M. Ilyas Khan also reported cases highlighted by the PTM, in which the army killed women and children with impunity.[1] The Constitution of Pakistan remains on paper, no military ruler and democratic government exhibited respect to it. "In May 2016, for example, an attack on a military post in the Teti Madakhel area of North Waziristan triggered a manhunt by troops who rounded up the entire population of a village. An eyewitness who watched the operation from a wheat field nearby and whose brother was among those detained told the BBC that the soldiers beat everyone with batons and threw mud in children's mouths when they cried. A pregnant woman was one of two people who died during torture, her son said in video testimony. At least one man remains missing. M. Ilyas Khan (Uncovering Pakistan's secret human rights abuses 02 June 2019) reported.[2] The brutality of the Pakistan Army (Pak Army torture kills Pashtun man forcibly disappeared three years ago, News Intervention Bureau -May 6, 2024) 'once again come to the forefront in the Pashtun region. The family of Wali Salam, a Pashtun man of North Waziristan, received his lifeless body on May 4, 2024, sparking outrage and condemnation. According to reports, Wali Salam had been subjected to undeserved torture by the Pakistan Army after being forcibly disappeared three years ago'.[3]

However, the News Intervention Bureau reported Pakistan's backlash in Quetta for brutal torture on Baloch Long Marchers on 23 December 2023. "The long march against Baloch genocide has shaken the Pakistan Army to its core. The protest that started from Turbat after the extra-judicial killings of four innocent Baloch youth soon culminated into a mass movement which attracted participants from across the communities. Be it Sindhis or the Pashtuns, every community extended unconditional support to the movement and long march was organized at the behest of Baloch Yakjehti (Solidarity) Committee (BYC). After brutal torture of marchers in Islamabad, Baloch have organized a Quetta protest that got support from PTM. The Pashtun Tahafuz Movement (PTM) again participated in the Quetta sit-in protest outside the High court and expressed unconditional support to the cause of BYC. The Provincial President of PTM, Noor Bacha in his address to the sit-in, warned Pakistan against continuing the oppression of Baloch and Pashtuns". The News Intervention Bureau noted.[4] Pashtun leaders have often accused the Pakistan army of human rights violations. Amnesty International condemned the Pakistani government for harassing women in the 'Baloch Long March journeyed about a thousand miles from Turbat in the southwestern province of Balochistan to the capital city, Islamabad to protest the alleged extrajudicial killing of young Baloch men late last year. The peaceful protesters, Amnesty International noted were 'consisting largely of families of victims of enforced disappearances including people as old as 80 and children as young as two years old, had been sleeping in near-freezing temperatures at the sit-in at the National Press Club, Islamabad since 22 December 2023.[5]

Asian Legal Resource Centre (Pakistan: Alternative Report to the Human Rights Committee under the International Covenant on Civil and Political Rights. Asian Legal Resource Centre, July 2016) in its report to the human rights committee, has highlighted some aspects of violations of law and human rights by the government. The report to the human rights committee noted the absence of an efficient and proper criminal justice system has mired the rule of law.[6] Amnesty International in its January 24, 2024 report (Pakistan: Amnesty International condemns harassment faced by Baloch protestors in Islamabad) warned that "The Pakistani authorities should be ashamed of the harassment meted out to the Baloch Long March protestors. This is not the end the Baloch women would have hoped for when undertaking the perilous journey with their children to demand justice for their families. The authorities have been heartlessly indifferent to the plight and demands of the peaceful protestors camped out in the severe cold for the past month," said Carolyn Horn, Programme

Director, Law and Policy at Amnesty International. The denial of the rights to freedom of expression and peaceful assembly have compounded the tremendous social, financial and psychological costs borne by the families of the disappeared. The voices of the people must not be ignored in the run-up to the national elections in Pakistan. Human rights must be upheld before, during and after the elections." Amnesty report noted.[7]

Civil rights existed on paper only. The army, police and government don't respect the constitution-joking the taunting with their illegal acts. Extrajudicial killing, torture, rape and enforced disappearances have become a new culture in the country. Prisoners are not presented in court within 24 hours of arrest as provided by the constitution. The illegal detention may last for months while the loved ones of the detainee run from pillar to post to try to locate their whereabouts. In the army units and field intelligence unit's underground cells political workers and human rights activists are being raped and tortured. The Killing of innocent children in Peshawar army schools (December 16, 2016) by Pakistan army commandos raised many questions about the intentions of the rogue army.[8] War criminal General Raheel Sharif later on visited the ruined school. The 20 points National Action Plan (NAP) was used to protect the killers. To undermine insurgency and terrorism Parliament of Pakistan amended the constitution and empowered the military courts to try the suspect civilian terrorists. This sparked criticism against the judiciary. The Supreme Court ruled that it had no jurisdiction to examine the constitutional amendment and strike it down. As the Supreme Court of Pakistan never raised the question of 85 innocent civilians in military custody. Over 100 innocent Pakistanis have suffered illegal, unconstitutional military trials; 09 May 2023, which was used as an excuse by the fascist army to teach a lesson to politicians and political activists.

Trying civilians in military courts is against international law. Article 14 of the International Covenant on Civil and Political Rights (ICCPR), which Pakistan has ratified, guarantees the right to a trial before a competent, independent, and impartial tribunal established by law. Experts and writers, Masoom Sanyal and Mahika Suri in their well-written analysis (In Defence of Democracy: The Pakistani Supreme Court's Decision against Military Trials of Civilians-Nov 30, 2023) have highlighted civilians trial in military courts: "International Law on the matter of military trials of civilians is not entirely crystallized but is sufficiently clear to indicate that such trials ought to be conducted only in case of extremely serious offences such as espionage. In the case of Castillo Petruzzi v Peru, the Inter-American Court of Human Rights observed that "when a military court takes jurisdiction over a matter that regular courts should hear, the individual's right to a hearing by a competent, independent and impartial tribunal previously established by law and, a fortiori, his right to due process are violated" (para. 29). The Article 14 of the International Covenant on Civil and Political Rights (ICCPR) also guarantees a right to "fair and public hearing" by a "competent, independent and impartial tribunal." Pakistan is a signatory to the ICCPR and has ratified it. According to the International Commission of Jurists, the Human Rights Committee has been of the consistent opinion that Article 14 of the ICCPR should be interpreted as prohibiting the trial of civilians in military courts. Additionally, the Constitution of Pakistan also provides for an explicit fundamental right to a fair trial, by virtue of Article 10A. Thus, military trials of civilians are not only prohibited under international law but also violate the fundamental right to fair trial guaranteed in the Constitution of Pakistan".[9]

On 28 May 2024, Daily Dawn reported families of those facing military courts called for their fair trial. 'The families of PTI activists faced military court proceedings in cases regarding the May 09 2023 violence demanded a fair trial for their dear ones. Over a dozen family members of PTI activists who were facing trial before military courts, and their lawyers Rabbiya Bajwa and Abuzar Salman Niazi, addressed a press conference at the Lahore Press Club. Ms Bajwa said that there was a criminal silence over the violation of the basic human rights in Pakistan, adding that they would launch a campaign to wake the people to stand against the violation of human rights and the Constitution of Pakistan.'[10] International Commission of Jurists in its analysis (Military "justice" system: a glaring surrender of human rights. Issue: Independence of Judges and Lawyers, Analysis Brief, 2019) revealed figure of prisoners prosecuted by the army: "According to the military, in the four years since military courts were empowered to try terrorism-related offences, they have convicted at least 641 people. Some 345 people have been sentenced to death and 296 people have been given prison sentences. Only five people have been acquitted. At least 56 people have been hanged. An earlier law giving military courts authority to try civilians will lapse on 30 March 2019. Last week, the Cabinet approved a proposal to extend the tenure of military courts for another two years. The Government is currently in consultation with opposition parties to get consensus on the extension".[11]

On 24 November 2015, the President of Pakistan amended the Army Act, and allowed intelligence agencies to detain civilians even before the passing of the 21st Amendment. The army was authorized to detain, kill, and torture suspects and try them in military courts where no human rights organization or journalist forum were allowed to cover the court proceeding. Dr. Muhammad Zubair, (28 January 2019) in his article highlighted the changing shape of the Army Act: "It also authorized military courts to hold in-camera proceedings and keep identities of individuals associated with the cases secret. Moreover, it gave protection and indemnity to court officers for any act done in 'good faith' in pursuance of the military trials. Contents of the presidential ordinance came to public knowledge only nine months later when it was placed before Parliament for approval, which was granted on 11 November 2015 through the Pakistan Army (Amendment) Act, 2015. The constitutional amendment included a sunset clause of two years, with the possibility of extension. The first two-year term of the military courts ended on 7 January 2017. In March 2017, under the watchful eyes of the military leadership, and after three months of negotiations, the government and opposition parties agreed to a two-year extension. It was claimed that the 'extraordinary situation and circumstances' continued to exist and that the extraordinary measures 'have yielded positive results in combating terrorism'. Thus, Parliament passed the Constitution (Twenty-Third Amendment) Act, 2017 and the Pakistan Army (Amendment) Act, 2017. However, this time Parliament provided four basic rights to accused persons facing military trials: informing them of charges at the time of arrest, their production before courts within 24 hours, allowing them to engage private defence counsel and application of the regular law of evidence in the court proceedings"[12]

Pakistan's human rights commission was in hot water when the army tightened the rope around the neck of the civilian government. The HRCP only expressed concerns over the planned extension of military courts. However, the International Commission of Jurists (ICJ) also criticized the military trial of civilians as a 'disaster for human rights' in Pakistan. An Indian analyst and research scholar, D. Suba Chandran (NIAS, 11, December 2017) in his research paper on Pakistan's Military courts highlighted procedure of courts, and the involvement of military establishment in judicial matter:

The military courts were established through the 21st constitutional amendment (Pakistan Army (Amendment) Bill, 2015) passed with huge support following the tragic terrorist attack on an Army Public School in December 2014 in Peshawar. The TTP led massacre witnessed the killing of nearly 140 persons in a School in Peshawar, most of them children. In

January 2015, both houses of the Parliament passed the bill unanimously thereby establishing military courts for speedy trials of terrorists. The bill had a clause providing for the closure of military courts by 7 January 2017. The military courts also became a part of Pakistan's National Action Plan (NAP); along with the Zarb-e-Azb, these three were seen as Pakistan's primary counter terrorism strategy. While the Army is still continuing with the Zarb-e-Azb, the achievements and failure of the NAP have become a political issue during the recent months, whereas the military courts technically came to an end on 7 January 2017. According to media reports, close to 270 cases were tried by the military courts; of which the majority of them (around 160) were sentenced to death (though a small number were actually executed) and the rest to prison. Despite a 90 percent conviction, civil society does complain about lack of transparency in the above trials. Though there were discussions in the media during the late 2016 itself on the impending deadline, there were no political debates within the Parliament on providing an extension to the military courts. With no action, the tenure of the military courts automatically came to an end in early January.[13]

Some political circles supported the idea of military courts that high courts couldn't prosecute militants. The matter was not that simple. On a number of instances, civilian courts' judges were openly threatened by Islamic militant groups such as the Taliban and the Lashkar-e-Taiba. A number of lawyers were killed for prosecuting extremists. Many judges fled the country after receiving death threats. Military courts in Pakistan never convicted a single corrupt military official. These courts received tenacious criticism from civil society and international human rights organizations. Protection of Pakistan Act 2014 can easily deal with judicial matters, and can settle terror-related cases. Ayaz Gul (January 16, 2019) in his analytical article has reviewed the operational mechanism of these courts and criticism of the International commission of jurists:

The military tribunals have been in operation since January 2015. At that time, the Pakistani parliament authorized them for two years to conduct trials of suspected terrorists in a bid to deter growing terrorism in the country. The ICJ denunciation comes as Prime Minister Imran Khan's government consults with opposition parties on legislation to extend the tenure of the courts. The ICJ cited "serious fair trials violations in the operation of military courts, including: denial of the right to counsel of choice; failure to disclose the charges against the accused; denial of a public hearing; a very high number of convictions – more than 97 percent–

based on "confessions" without adequate safeguards against torture and ill treatment."...The Pakistani army and civilian officials reject the charges and maintain the legislation allowing the trials binds the special tribunals to conduct "fair and transparent" hearings. Political parties have backed the military courts, noting Pakistan's regular judicial system does not offer protection to witnesses. Moreover, judges and attorneys prosecuting suspected hardcore militants have complained of receiving death threats, or have come under attack. In January 2015, Prime Minister Nawaz Sharif's government promised to reform the civilian criminal justice system and presented the military courts as a temporary solution. Since then, the government has not taken any significant measures to reform the judiciary. From January 7, 2015 to January 6, 2017, military courts convicted 274 individuals and handed down 161 death sentences. At least 17 people have been executed after being convicted by a military court.[14]

Lawyer Kamaran Murtaza expressed deep concern over the apex court judgment and said: "Article 10 of the Pakistani constitution gives every citizen the right to an open trial, and this is not possible in the military courts. Forget about the fair trial, nobody even knows the names of the convicts the military courts have thus far sentenced, and he would appeal against the Supreme Court's decision as it violates fundamental constitutional rights of the people." The HRCP chairperson hammered political parties for not taking advantage of the consensus against Islamist militancy and surrendering their powers to the army. "It is unfortunate that the nationwide resolve against the Taliban and other extremist groups did not translate into political action. It remained a military affair. International human rights forums have deeply criticized the confession by torture in military dark cells and demanded the removal of this cruel justice system". On 16 January 2019, the International commission of jurists deeply criticized the illegal function of military courts in Pakistan. In its briefing paper, the ICJ documented serious fair trials violations in the operation of military courts, and warned that high number of convictions–more than 97 percent–based on "confessions without adequate safeguards against torture and ill-treatment:

"The trial of civilians by military courts is a glaring surrender of human rights and fundamental freedoms, found the ICJ in its Briefing Paper Military Injustice in Pakistan released today. The Pakistani Government must not extend the tenure of military courts to try civilians for terrorism-related offences, the ICJ said. "Military trials of civilians have been a disaster for human rights in Pakistan," said Frederick Rawski, ICJ's Asia

Director. "As a recent judgment of the Peshawar High Court has confirmed, proceedings in these tribunals are secret, opaque, and violate the right to a fair trial before an independent and impartial tribunal," he added. In the briefing paper, the ICJ has documented serious fair trials violations in the operation of military courts, including: denial of the right to counsel of choice; failure to disclose the charges against the accused; denial of a public hearing; failure to give convicts copies of a judgment with evidence and reasons for the verdict; and a very high number of convictions – more than 97 percent – based on "confessions" without adequate safeguards against torture and ill treatment. The ICJ has also demonstrated how military courts are being used to give legal cover to the practice of enforced disappearances. The use of military courts to try civilians is inconsistent with international standards, the ICJ recalled. According to the military, in the four years since military courts were empowered to try terrorism-related offences, they have convicted at least 641 people. Some 345 people have been sentenced to death and 296 people have been given prison sentences. Only five people have been acquitted. At least 56 people have been hanged"[15]

On 12 January 2019, Dr. Mehdi Hasan, Chairperson of the Human Rights Commission of Pakistan (HRCP) expressed grave concern at the government's decision to table a bill in favour of extending the tenure of military courts, which were otherwise due to end their term. In a statement issued the HRCP categorically stated that 'the institution of military courts was an anomaly in any democratic order that claims to uphold the fundamental rights and freedoms of its citizens: "It is the state's duty to uphold the rule of law in a manner that ensures that every citizen is entitled to due process and a fair trial. Equally, it is the state's duty to uphold the rule of law to ensure the security of its citizens. These are not mutually exclusive obligations. Moreover, there is little evidence to show that military courts have succeeded in increasing respect for the rule of law. The perception of 'speedy justice' is no substitute for rooting out the militant extremism that led to the institution of these courts in the first instance or indeed for taking the time to train and equip domestic judicial and police mechanisms that are, and ought to remain, responsible for maintaining civilian law and order under a civilian mandate".[16]

In the aftermath of the December 16 school attack, Pakistan also lifted a seven-year-long moratorium on death penalties. The military, responding to public anger over the Peshawar killings, was moving fast. The military promised that it will not abuse its new powers by prosecuting politicians,

journalists or rights activists, as happened in the 1980s. The mandate of
the new courts was set to expire after two years, and the trials were subject
to civilian oversight. Journalist Imad Zafar once argued that the political
system has been the target of milablishment propaganda machine. The
hatred between the two political camps, Imad Zafar viewed it reaching
boiling point and no one liked to be contradicted or criticized for his
political affiliations or ideologies. The military establishment's power
and control over state resources and institutions is immense. This means
creating a counter-narrative has always been the toughest of jobs for the
many political parties that have tried. Daily Dawn in its 06 March 2017
analysis of military courts highlighted consecutive conviction of military
courts:

"Since February 2015, a total of 274 individuals have been convicted in
military courts. So far, the army has sentenced 161 individuals to death, 12
of whom have been executed and 113 have been given jail terms (mostly
life sentences). There are roughly 11 military courts that have been set
up across Pakistan; three in KP, three in Punjab, two in Sindh and one in
Balochistan. With the sun today having set on Pakistan's military courts,
Dawn.com recaps this paper's position against military courts with excerpts
of past articles. In April 2015, Sabir Shah disappeared from Lahore's central
jail. His family and lawyers did not know where he had gone. Five months
later, the family was informed via an ISPR press release that Sabir had been
awarded a death sentence by the military courts. Sabir's lawyer claims he is
unaware of the evidence that may have been used to convict his client. Sabir
was originally indicted on murder charges. The trial was underway at the
civilian courts when he was mysteriously moved to a military internment
Centre. In August 2016, families of 16 civilians found guilty by the military
courts filed a review petition at the Supreme Court of Pakistan in what
turned out to be an iconic hearing. "These trials before the military courts
need to proceed again after sharing complete evidence and the case record
with the accused and also ensuring complete freedom to the accused to
engage a counsel of his choice," argued Asma Jahangir before a five-judge
Supreme Court bench, headed by Chief Justice Anwar Zaheer Jamali. At
first, the 21st Amendment, as it is popularly known, was met with much
debate, but over time, military courts weaved themselves into the fabric
of Pakistan's criminal justice system". Pakistan's military courts-here's why
it should never rise again: Murky procedures, no transparency or right to
appeal in civilian courts-a snapshot of Pakistan's military courts.[17]

However, ISPR in 2016 issued a press statement in which its chairman indicated that 135 out of 144 people convicted in military courts had "confessed" to their crimes. That the confession rate was higher than 90 percent points towards a disturbing possibility; that confessions might be elicited using questionable interrogation methods. This statement was rejected by the International Commission of Jurists and noted: "suspects tried by military courts remain in military custody at all times, even after the magistrate records their "confessions". However, Amnesty international in its report (27 March 2019) noted some statements of victim families and the illegal disappearances of Pakistani intelligence agencies:

"We are repeatedly given advice that if we stop protesting, end our activism against enforced disappearances and sit at home, our Baba will come back." Sasui Lohar, daughter of Hidayatullah Lohar, forcibly disappeared on April 17, 2017 from Nasirabad, Sindh, Pakistan. In April 2017, Hidayatullah Lohar, school teacher (headmaster), blacksmith and political Sindhi activist was forcibly disappeared from the school where he taught. He was taken away in a "double-cabin grey coloured" vehicle by men in police uniform and civilian clothes. Since then the authorities have refused to disclose his whereabouts. Despite the presence of eye-witnesses, his family had to petition the Larkana High Court to order the area police station to register the First Information Report. Hidayatullah Lohar is one of Sindh's "missing persons". His family has been patiently seeking truth and justice through the courts and on the streets of Pakistan since his disappearance. His daughters, Sasui and Sorath Lohar are at the forefront of the campaign against enforced disappearance in the southern province of Sindh. Lohar's case was also registered in the Commission for Inquiry of Enforced Disappearances of Pakistan (COIED) and a number of Joint Investigation Team (JIT) (appointed by the COIED) hearings have taken place in the province on the commission's order but to no effect. The JITs comprise of government stakeholders, including the interior ministry, police officials, federal investigation agency officials and intelligence agencies.[18]Amnesty international on 27 March 2019, in its reports warned:

The issue of disappearances has been occasionally raised in public and parliament by political parties, including PPP, PML (N), MQM, BNP (M), and NP (when on Opposition benches). Initially, the media and courts were vocal on the issue. When Iftikhar Muhammad Chaudhry was Chief Justice of the Supreme Court of Pakistan, the apex court entertained a petition of the Balochistan Bar Council. Although, in Pakistan's power structure, law courts are not empowered to punish the Army personnel guilty of enforced disappearance of Baloch people, the Chaudhry-headed bench exerted pressure on the Pakistan Army, FC and intelligence agencies to release missing persons and stop inhuman practice of enforced disappearances. The said petition led to a tussle between the apex court and the Pakistan Army, which resulted in the dismissal and arrest of judges by General Pervez Musharraf. The Pakistan Army and intelligence agencies have been using enforced disappearances as a covert policy to bear down on the Baloch freedom movement and have been vociferously disputing the reports of enforced disappearances of people".[19]

However General Ghafoor admitted in a Press conference on 29 April, 2019: "We know you have a great attachment to missing persons (issue). We too have. We don't want any person to go missing but when there is a war, you have to do a number of (undesirable) tasks. It's said that everything is fair in love and war. War occurs to be ruthless."[20] The DG ISPR justified the enforced disappearances with his comments "everything is fair in love and war".[21] Moreover, Sayed Irfan Raza in his Dawn (30 January 2019) analysis noted the standpoint of military courts about the missing persons. In 2019, Pakistani human rights defender Idris Khattak was forcibly disappeared, activist Muhammad Ismail was arbitrarily detained on trumped up charges, while his daughter and women rights activist Gulalai Ismail fled the country. The authorities also denied entry to a representative from the Committee to Protect Journalists' (CPJ), warned news anchors not to express their opinions, while journalists from the Dawn newspaper faced threats for their reporting. Student protesters including Alamgir Wazir were arrested and charged for their activism.[22] In his Asia Times, (17 September 2019) article, Imad Zafar argued:

"Pakistani establishment is not simply powerful in its own right, with the controlled media and hegemony over state resources, but the current engineered discourse has been backed by Riyadh and Washington. Not a single analyst could have predicted that a regime backed by these superpowers could be defeated. However, all that changed when the establishment proved incapable of pre-empting India's annexation of Kashmir. That proved to be the last nail in the coffin of the current political discourse. According to whistleblowers in the power corridors who do not wish to be named, there is a rift within the security establishment, with many high-ranking officials wanting not only an end to military involvement in political matters but for certain heads to roll. The announcement by Fazal-ur-Rehman, president of the Jamiat Ulema-e-Islam (F) party, of a planned "long march" to Islamabad in October and to hold a sit-in there is not a coincidence by any means. It is believed by many whistleblowers that Fazal has the backing of certain quarters within the establishment who do not want the current dispensation to continue. These people are angry over the Kashmir fiasco and the political engineering that resulted in the current political and economic turmoil in Pakistan".[23]In January 2018, Human Right Watch in its report warned that notwithstanding the establishment of military courts, and an elected government of Prime Minister Imran Khan, cases of human right violation, rape, enforced disappearance, torture in darker prisons exacerbated:

"In March, parliament reinstated secret military courts empowered to try civilians after the term for military courts ended in January 2017. Pakistan human rights groups said that many defendants facing military courts were secretly detained and tortured to coerce confessions. Several remain forcibly disappeared. Authorities do not allow independent monitoring of military court trials. The Pakistan government failed to sufficiently investigate and prosecute allegations of human rights violations by security forces. Security forces remained unaccountable for human rights violations and exercised disproportionate political influence over civilian authorities, especially in matters of national security and counterterrorism. In March, parliament passed a constitutional amendment reinstating secret military courts to try terrorism suspects for another two years. Security forces were implicated in enforced disappearances and extrajudicial killings throughout the country. The government muzzled dissenting voices in nongovernmental organizations (NGOs) and media on the pretext of national security. Militants and interest groups also threatened freedom of expression. Women, religious minorities, and transgender people faced violent attacks, discrimination, and government persecution, with authorities failing to provide adequate protection or hold perpetrators accountable. The inclusion of the transgender population in the 2017 census and the first-ever proposed transgender law were positive developments. The human rights crisis in Balochistan continued with reports of enforced disappearances and extrajudicial killings of suspected Baloch militants. Baloch nationalists and other militant groups continued attacking non-Baloch civilians".[24]

On 22 May, 2020, OpIndia reported cases of abduction, torture, humiliation and organ trade by Pakistan's rogue military units in Baluchistan. Organizer paper reported alleged involvement of Pakistan field units in abduction, forced disappearances, torture and forced organ harvesting of people living in ethnic areas of Balochistan, Organizer reported. The report also claimed that corpses of such ethnic minorities were wrapped by the army in white cloth and family members were intercepted to see faces of their sons and brothers. Such dead bodies have been buried with missing organs. OpIndia reported that the army are burying the dead in desert. The report of the Organizer claimed that the army covers the bodies such that the stitch marks are not visible to the family. Interestingly, the army also does not allow post-mortem to be conducted on such dead bodies. Organizers also reported that 'illegal organ harvesting has become a flourishing trade in the Islamic Republic of Pakistan. The country had, however, banned the commercial sale of human organs in 2010. As per the law, anyone found involved in organ harvesting and trade of organs can face up to a jail term of 10 years and a maximum fine of PKR 1 million'. Organizer reported.

Chapter 6

How do Militant Organizations Respond to Counterterrorism? Introducing the LIVE Typology, with Examples from Proscription in Pakistan

Muhammad Feyyaz and Brian J. Phillips

Abstract

How do militant organizations respond to counterterrorism? A vast literature seeks to understand the effects of counterterrorism, examining outcomes such as levels of violence. However, violence is only one way that militant groups can respond to pressure. We focus on terrorist designation or proscription, the sanctions many states and international organizations impose on militants as an attempt to weaken them. We introduce a new typology of armed group responses to counterterrorism: (L)egal tactics like lawsuits or petitions, (I)dentity shifts like name changes or fragmentation, (V)iolence increases or decreases, and (E)conomic or financial tactics such as changing funding sources. These four approaches can be summarized by the acronym LIVE. Empirically, we illustrate the model with examples from the case of militant organizations in Pakistan, an important and under-studied case. Overall, the LIVE typology can be helpful for anticipating the repertoire of responses to counterterrorism, and for explaining armed group behavior generally.

Keywords: Counterterrorism proscription terrorist designation typology Pakistan

Introduction

On January 14, 2002, the Pakistani Ministry of the Interior officially proscribed the militant organization Jaish-e-Mohammad (JeM)—banning the group, confiscating its propaganda, seizing its assets, and imposing financial restrictions on the group and its members.[1] The counterterrorism method of proscription, also called terrorist designation[2] in some countries, is increasingly used globally, with hundreds of organizations now proscribed.[3] JeM, like other groups, responded to proscription in multiple ways. First, anticipating proscription, the group opened bank accounts under other names and transferred money to the new accounts and front businesses.[4] After proscription, JeM changed its name to Khuddam-ul-Islam (KuL) and fragmented somewhat, with a smaller faction naming itself Jamaat-ul-Furqan (JuF). (Both entities were soon proscribed.) Individuals associated with the former JeM attempted twice to assassinate the then-president of Pakistan, General Pervez Musharraf, shortly after the JeM successors were proscribed in 2003.[5] JeM then kept a relatively low profile for almost a decade. It resurfaced publicly in 2011, beginning a multiyear campaign of hundreds of attacks.[6]

How do militant organizations respond to counterterrorism? There are many studies of counterterrorism effects, with scholars examining how groups respond to leadership decapitation, terrorist designation, and general repression, among other tactics.[7] Much of this research studies how policies affect violence by the targeted groups. However, changes to attacks are only one consequence of counterterrorism. Militant groups file lawsuits, change their names, merge with others, and diversify their funding sources. This range of possible tactics, which can seriously hinder counterterrorism, speaks to research on militant group adaptation.[8] Studying additional consequences is essential for understanding counterterrorism more holistically, and for a more accurate picture of organizational dynamics of terrorism. Yet the literature lacks a general typology for the range of ways militant groups might respond to counterterrorism pressure.

We introduce a new framework for understanding how militant organizations respond to government counterterrorism. The framework refers to four general categories of militant group behaviours—Legal, Identity change, Violence, and Economic (LIVE)—that could follow counterterrorism actions. We describe how government actions can lead to these behaviours. The typology offers contributions to scholars seeking to explain responses to counterterrorism, scholars trying to understand militant group behaviour generally, and governments trying to anticipate consequences of their counterterrorism tactics. In the next section, we briefly review some relevant literature, situating our study among several valuable lines of research including terrorist innovation and adaptation. Then, we outline the LIVE typology, explaining the types of groups most likely to use each type of response, and the implications for counterterrorism. We then illustrate the typology using examples from proscribed militant groups in Pakistan—an important and under-studied case. The organizations respond in diverse and interesting ways, suggesting challenges for law enforcement and emphasizing heterogeneity in counterterrorism effects. The manuscript concludes with ways that the typology can be used for research, including highlighting some of the limitations that could be addressed.

Research on counterterrorism, militant organization responses, and tactical adaptation

One of the most prominent streams of terrorism research is the scholarship studying counterterrorism effectiveness.[9] Lafree and Freilich group counterterrorism tactics into five categories: military responses, criminal justice responses, de-radicalization and disengagement programs, community-level and primary prevention programs, and political settlements and conciliatory actions.[10] Scholars have extensively studied the effectiveness of these types of counterterrorism approaches. For example, researchers have examined leadership decapitation, with some studies finding that it tends to reduce the violence of targeted groups or reduce their longevity.[11] Other studies find mixed effects of leadership targeting.[12] While it is important to understand violence, as counterterrorism generally seeks to reduce violence, it is unclear how leadership targeting affects groups in other ways. For example, does it lead to group fragmentation, internal group changes, or the adoption of new types of violence? Beyond leadership decapitation, other work studies topics such as repression and concessions, but it also mostly looks at violence as the outcome.[13]

A more recent line of counterterrorism research looks at sanctions against militant organizations, such as the U.S. Foreign Terrorist Organization list. The goal of terrorist designation seems to be to reduce terrorism, with related goals such as weakening groups that use terrorism and reducing anti-state violence generally.[14] To bring about these goals, the formal listing of entities as terrorists places emphasis on certain organizations so that security agencies and countries can coordinate, and it provides a legal framework to punish individuals who might support named terrorists.[15] Some work suggests that terrorist designation or proscription sometimes reduces violence.[16] A few scholars have analyzed other consequences of terrorist designation, like how it affects civil war peace negotiations.[17] When groups are designated as terrorists, their responses seem to depend on how adaptable they are.[18] Scholars have also argued that the process of proscription is a "ritualistic performance" manifested by debates in parliaments that ultimately extends power at the expense of curtailing rights, freedoms and political participation.[19] However, most research on the effects of terrorist proscription examines levels of violence as the primary outcome. It is less clear how groups might otherwise respond to proscription.

Beyond research directly examining counterterrorism, inquires have focused on how militant organizations adopt new tactics or adapt generally. Vasseur et al. define adaptation as "organizational changes a violent non-state actor consciously makes in response to changes occurring in its operational environment (or the pressures resulting from these changes)." They specify that adaptation and learning are related but distinct processes.[20] Furthermore, they identify 46 types of adaptation, including changes in motivation, changes in structure, change in geographic location, or changes in tactics. This list is a valuable starting point, but a more parsimonious grouping of tactics could be helpful as well. Much of the research on adaptation concentrates on violence as the key output, such as suicide bombing. For example, Bloom argues that inter-group competition leads to groups adapting suicide terrorism.[21] O'Rourke argues that groups increasingly use female suicide terrorists for functional reasons—these types of attackers are simply more effective.[22] Radtke and Jo study how groups that are more adaptable can better weather United Nations sanctions.[23] Tschantret examines how Chinese repression encouraged local militants to evolve.[24] Kenney's important work shows how governments and terrorists co-evolve in response to each other, looking at the examples of both drug-trafficking organizations and al Qaeda.[25] More broadly, scholars have looked at the transformation of rebel groups into political parties.[26]

Overall, militant organizations frequently change, in a variety of ways. This is often a direct result of counterterrorism. Much of the research on counterterrorism consequences and organizational evolution studies violence as the key output. This is perhaps because violence is indeed important. Additionally, with the existence of large databases on terrorist attacks, it is straightforward to study how violence levels change after government interventions. Studying other outcomes is more difficult, at least when done quantitatively. However, other outcomes like group identity change or economic effects are still critical to understand. They can be mediating factors that lead to changes in violence, or they can indicate other changes, such as group weakening. Knowing more about the varied effects of counterterrorism can help governments anticipate the consequences of their actions, and to best prepare for the next steps in counterterrorism campaigns. Instead of listing all of the ways groups might adapt, or focusing in-depth on one, we try to group together the various ways into several parsimonious categories, a typology.

The LIVE typology

We suggest that terrorist organisations responses to government sanctions can be grouped into four categories: legal, identity of the organization, violence, and economic. Violence is an outcome often studied, but the other responses are also important because they can permit groups to survive and continue to use violence and otherwise confront the state. All four types of responses create costs for counterterrorism. Legal challenges can congest the judicial system, and if the groups win their lawsuits, this could impose costs on counterterrorism agencies and force them to change practices. Identity-based responses to counterterrorism are additional complications for counterterrorism actors monitoring and seeking to deter terrorists, and such changes can allow the groups to thrive in ways not previously possible. Economic responses present similar problems. They mean that governments need to monitor and try to interrupt additional funding sources. If a group shifts to a fundraising source like kidnapping or drug production, this adds to crime in the region—a costly spillover effect. We generated these categories and the set of tactics or examples within each category, from analyzing the literature described above, along with the broader counterterrorism and counterinsurgency literature.[27] We then inductively finalized the typology as we gathered data from the Pakistan case. In the following section, we discuss each of these categories, although counterterrorism implications are discussed more in the conclusion.

Legal

As for legal responses, this category of actions includes activities like suing the government, filing a formal legal petition, or appealing government decisions like proscription. These kinds of responses seem to be more common in democratic countries, because in authoritarian countries, such processes might not be legal or taken seriously. Not all terrorist organizations are likely to use this approach. Organizations with political wings, above-ground entities that attempt to participate in non-violent politics, are probably the most likely to respond legally to counterterrorism. Groups that legally petition a government are probably also domestically oriented, with a substantial presence in one country, as opposed to transnational, stateless, or completely underground groups. While it might seem surprising to think of terrorist organizations filing lawsuits instead of throwing bombs, these tactics are rather common. This is generally consistent with the idea of social service provision by militant organizations—these groups do not only fight, but often seek to replace the government (either for the whole country or in a secessionist region), and, therefore often carry out actions mirroring government bureaucracy. Many militant groups, before they took up arms, were legal political parties. And many such groups shift (back) into legal political parties once a civil war ends. Furthermore, research by Jo and co-authors shows that insurgent organizations frequently comply with international law, for example in their treatment of prisoners or the use of child soldiers.[28] As a result, terrorist organizations filing lawsuits or using similar approaches is not so unusual.

Identity

Groups also respond to counterterrorism by changing the fundamental identity of their organization. One example of this is the group changing its name (as a number of groups do in the Pakistan case discussed below), but there are many other ways an identity can change. When an organization fragments, its identity is often changed, as perhaps a hardline group breaks off, making the rump organization more politically moderate. Alternately, when two organizations merge, this can lead to one distinct, new type of organization, and thus a new identity. There are other, more subtle ways that terrorist group identities can shift. Organizations can, for example, start emphasizing or de-emphasize a particular ethnic or ideological identity. Unlike legal responses, which seem more likely in countries with stronger norms of rule of law, identity responses could happen in any type of state. What might be more pertinent are organizational factors. Groups that change the identity of their organization in response to counterterrorism might be weaker than groups that can maintain the same identity over time. The strongest groups probably do not need to alter their identity in the face of counterterrorism pressure. At the same time, identity-based responses could indicate a degree of flexibility or innovation that the weakest groups might not be capable of. Another organizational factor that might affect the likelihood of a group's name change is whether the group is clandestine or trying to operate in the open. A truly clandestine group might never need to change its name or otherwise alter its identity. However, when groups operate more "above ground," for example by providing social services or having a political wing, they might feel the need to change their name to continue to operate legally.

Violence

Violence is the third aspect of the LIVE typology. Counterterrorism has the goal of reducing violence, so practitioners watch to see if subsequently violence decreases, stays the same, or increases. Militant groups use violence for a variety of reasons, for example to demonstrate their resilience, to punish an opponent, to terrify a public so that it puts pressure on the government, or to directly coerce a government into changing a policy.[29] After some counterterrorism action, militants might be too weak to use violence as they had before. Or they might use less violence to deter the government from attacking, or to keep receiving concessions conditioned on less violence.[30] Alternately, militants might respond to counterterrorism by using more violence to demonstrate their (true or purported) strength. Armed groups might also respond to counterterrorism by changing their violence qualitatively, such as adopting new tactics.

Under what conditions might we be more likely to observe changes in violence as a response to counterterrorism? On the one hand, democratic countries might see violent increases less often, since groups in these kinds of countries have non-violent alternatives to affect political change. On the other hand, some research suggests that democracies, or at least partial democracies, are more susceptible to terrorism because such governments need to respond to violence against civilians to try to win over voters.[31] Democracies are also targeted because democratic governments use concessions since they are restricted against using authoritarian approaches.[32] As for organizational attributes, religiously-motived groups seem especially inclined to increase their violence when they are able to.[33] Such groups generally have less concern about the costs of human life, since they are often less concerned about popular support. Religiously oriented terrorist groups are more focused on impressing a higher power that they think accepts or encourages the loss of life, especially when the victims are not of the same religion as the perpetrators.[34] By contrast, it seems likely that groups with other motivations, such as leftism or ethnonationalism, should be relatively likely to respond to counterterrorism—especially concessions—by reducing violence.

Regarding changing types of violence, armed groups seem to learn tactics from other such organizations. For example, groups learn complex tactics like suicide bombing from each other.[35] Some of this learning might be via simple observation, including through the news media. But there is also evidence to suggest that groups learn tactics from groups that they are already cooperating or aligned with.[36] Other work suggests that groups in competition with each other are especially likely to adopt new types of violence.[37] If these groups are already likely to adopt, then counterterrorism pressure could interact with interorganizational factors to make tactical adoption more likely.

Economic

The fourth aspect of the LIVE typology is economic. When militant groups face counterterrorism pressure, they sometimes need to dramatically change their financial methods. Economic responses include starting a fundraising drive, budget cuts (e.g., ceasing to publish a magazine or provide social services), diversifying funding sources, or engaging in a new tactic like kidnapping or drug trafficking to raise money. Terrorist organizations depend on funding to train, carry out attacks, and simply pay their workers. Many such organizations also provide social services. These activities all require a substantial amount of funding. Counterterrorism could put pressure on funding sources, or otherwise require a group to acquire resources quickly, suggesting a change in economic activity.

Certain types of terrorist organizations seem likely to respond economically to counterterrorism. Groups that depend on diaspora support can be hit hard by sanctions such as international terrorist designation. At the same time, a group's broader economic environment can condition economic responses. Some groups operate in countries ripe for black market operations—coca in the Andes Mountains, opium in Central Asia or Southeast Asia, or precious gems in Sub-Saharan Africa, for example. These groups might be likely to start to engage in the drug trade or related industries when economically pressured. Other groups, due to geography, do not have the option to increase or decrease their involvement in such markets.

Finally, it is possible that some groups may respond to counterterrorism either by embracing a combination of LIVE strategies at the same time or by sequentially adopting them.

Examples from Pakistan

In this section, we present examples of each of the four types of responses to counterterrorism. We present evidence from Pakistan since 2001, an important front in the so-called war on terrorism (WOT), but also seriously under-studied compared to countries like Iraq or Afghanistan, or even historical cases like Northern Ireland.[38] Studying Pakistan on its own is valuable to better understand this crucial case. It is also methodologically helpful to study one case to study it with the appropriate depth required, and to hold background factors constant.[39] Furthermore, this case offers exemplification of all four facets of the LIVE typology in a single context. The evidence we find is likely to be relevant elsewhere. The patterns in Pakistan are at least applicable to the many ethnically diverse democratizing or partial democracies around the world. We also focus on militant group responses to terrorist proscription in particular to focus on one type of counterterrorism. Responses should be generally similar for other types of counterterrorism, although the conclusion to the paper discusses other possibilities.

Brief Case background

Academic research on terrorism in Pakistan abounds. However, no systematic study can be reckoned to have correctly located the temporal origin of the terroristic phenomenon in this country. A thorough examination of the country's conflict history since its inception in 1947 due to the partition of British India generally situates the origin of terrorism during the early 1970s, stemming from the Baloch insurgency. It was against this backdrop that the parliament passed the Suppression of Terrorist Activities (Special Courts) Ordinance in late 1974, which became an Act in February 1975.[40] The Act also pioneered the inclusion of the word terrorism in any legislation in Pakistan since the country's establishment.[41]

Comparatively, the second phase of terrorism, which can be characterized in terms of strategy, a subversive war, was carried out by the local mercenaries in the 1980s at the behest of hostile intelligence agencies (Afghan, Soviet Union, India) to deter Pakistan from supporting the Afghan Jihad against the Soviet forces in Afghanistan.[42] The mid-1980s witnessed the growth of sectarianism precipitated by the Iranian revolution and the ongoing Islamization governance by the military regime of General Zia ul Haq.[43] The formation of first Shia sectarian organization, Tehreek-e-Nifaz-Fiqh-Jafaria (TNFJ) in 1979 in tribal areas in the wake of emboldening by Iran's eagerness to organize Shias in Pakistan and in its reaction, the

91

emergence of first Sunni sectarian militant group Sipah-e-Sahaba Pakistan (SSP—Soldiers of the Companions of the Prophet) in Punjab during 1986 laid the foundation what would later become an internecine sectarian war in Pakistan.[44] SSP's Pashtun cognate was Tehreek Nifaz-e-Shariat-e-Muhammadi (TNSM) formed during the late 1980s.[45] These organizations are more broadly known as politico-sectarian movements. Indeed, they have committed violence against Shia clergy and common Shias; some scholars are reluctant to categorize them as classic terrorist entities.[46]

The first archetypal Pakistani underground terrorist organization, Lashkar-e-Jhangvi (LeJ), a Deobandi supremacist, a rebel group within SSP, emerged in the mid-1990s.[47] Over time, it became one of the deadliest terrorist groups, especially after the 9/11 attacks, through collaboration with Al Qaeda, to wage a destructive anti-state and sectarian war inside and beyond Pakistan.[48] The US invasion of Afghanistan brought a radical transformation in the militancy landscape of Pakistan, from previously predominantly sectarian to contemporaneously non-sectarian religious, anti-state, and inter-field [inter faith] conflict.[49] Most notable was the influx of foreign terrorist elements in the tribal territory of Pakistan, adjoining Afghanistan, and now merged into Khyber Pakhtunkhwa province. The US-led drone warfare, which started in 2004, starkly exacerbated the spate and character of violence.[50] Pakistan's deadliest terrorist organization, Tehreek-e-Taliban Pakistan (TTP), came into being in late 2007.[51] In the coming years, the former tribal territory was inundated by an infinite number and types of militant groups. These included several outfits that were loosely affiliated with TTP or the splinter groups operating from diverse locations, mostly Punjabi. They were mainly the renegades of mainstream Kashmiri fighters Lashkar-e-Taiba (LeT), JeM, Harkat-ul-Mujahideen al-Alami, Harkat-ul-Ansar (HuA) and some sectarians such as LeJ.[52] The factionalisation and defections initially occurred when Pakistan decided to join WOT, and later when a military assault was launched in a mosque, the Red Mosque, in Islamabad in July 2007 to flush out terrorists belonging to Al Qaeda, TTP, and other militant organisations.[53]

Bloody confrontations between the Pakistan military, supported by the US drone operations, created mayhem in Pakistan. From 2006–07 onward, the country went through an unabated series of brutal terrorist campaigns— the non-sectarian religious and sectarian (now with an altered anti-state agenda), least of all the Baloch insurgency, triggered around 2006— claiming tens of thousands of civilians' lives besides causing tremendous loss to the national economy.[54] Apart from the locally proscribed

Balochistan Liberation Front (BLF), the Baloch Liberation Army (BLA) is another major terrorist group, designated by the US as a foreign terrorist organization, leading the Baloch armed struggle. Other than the defectors, Kashmir-bound Pakistani groups, LeT and JeM, generally did not partake in the terrorist campaign inside Pakistan.[55] Similarly, Jamaat-ud-Dawa (JuD, organization for the propagation of faith) established in 1985, which is the parent preaching organization of LeT and the Falah-e-Insaniat Foundation (FIF), a sprawling public-service charity, both established in 1990, have mainly directed their efforts outward.[56]

The military-led counterterrorism operations by Pakistan in 2014 set a severe blow to the Pakistani Taliban and affiliated terrorist groupings' human, organizational, and infrastructural potential. It significantly reduced the terrorist threat to the country, ironically reemerging with more profound assertions with the ascent of the Afghan Taliban rule in Afghanistan.[57] Apart from the military operations, successive Pakistani governments have been promulgating other measures to address terrorism, extremism, and the militancy problem, including the proscription of terrorist groups and organizations and charities supporting them.[58] The subsequent discussion empirically contextualizes and analyses LIVE typology by juxtaposing it with varied responses by different armed groups to the proscription by the Pakistani government.

Legal examples

The earlier discussion has indicated the type of organizations potentially amenable to legal routes during counterterrorism, and increasingly so in developed democracies. Present-day Pakistan neither exemplifies a liberal democracy nor an authoritarian country; it can be described as a political dispensation with militarized overtones, in other words, a struggling democracy. Its checkered political history due to militarization of politics owing to frequent military interventions and infighting among the political actors has meant elusiveness of the rule of law almost throughout its existence.[59] The observation should preempt an expectation that the pursuit of a legal path by the militants, specifically the terrorist organizations, occurs like a norm in this country. Nonetheless, we can locate five examples, three organizational and two concerning individuals, relevant to the current analysis. The legal provision empowering the federal government to ban militant outfits and freeze their assets was made part of the Anti-Terrorism Act 1997 through an amendment issued by the Musharraf government on August 15, 2001.[60] It explains why proscription of the violent organizations commenced during this period, and not earlier.

Tehrik-e-Jafria Pakistan, (TJP, the Movement of Followers of Jafria Shia Sect), founded in 1979, was banned by Musharraf's regime in January 2002 for anti-Sunni attacks.[61] TJP is a political extension of its original formation, TJFJ, and has been part of Muttahida Majlis-e-Amal (MMA, United assembly for action), a pro- [Afghan] Taliban Mullah led political coalition of several religious parties, which established the provincial government of Khyber Pakhtunkhwa and Balochistan provinces after the October 2002 Pakistan's national election. TJP leadership protested the ban as unjustified. Its leader, Sajid Naqvi, declared, "We will go [to] court against this decision …. and prove that his action is utter injustice … and an insult to tens of millions of Shiite people."[62] Legal battles continued for years, and the TJP (also known as the Shia Ulema Council) filed a petition in 2016 asking to be de-proscribed.[63] However, it was not successful.

SSP was banned twice, in 2002 by the military regime of General Musharraf and in February 2012 by a civil government, when it was functioning under a changed name, Ahle Sunnah Wal Jamaat (ASWJ).[64] Upon the second proscription, Maulana Mohammad Ahmed Ludhianvi, the head of ASWJ, publicly declared he would challenge the order in court.[65] At the time, he said, "It's taken us so long [to] rein in our activists—it will become very difficult to control their emotions if the ban is enforced."[66] He apparently never filed a legal petition; the public declaration arguably ameliorated the possible loss of support or membership that might follow proscription, or also reduced the likelihood of extreme acts that his comments alluded to. At the very least, the ASWJ leader's announcement signaled that the group was concerned about proscription (against arguments that proscription is meaningless), and that it was considering fighting it in court.

Another type of legal appeal, beyond going directly to the courts, is when a militant group attempts to address proscription through a bureaucratic process. In some instances, proscription review committees composed of government officers have been sought to plead revocation of listing. Tehreek-e-Labbaik Pakistan, a militant sectarian political party that the government banned in April 2021, exercised this option to no avail.[67] However, it was finally de-proscribed later that year after reaching a peace deal with the government.[68]

Beyond organizations responding to counterterrorism sanctions with legal appeals, some proscribed individuals take this approach as well. Hafiz Muhammad Saeed, the head of JuD, who the UN also implicates as chief of LeT, and whom the US and India blame for the 2008 Mumbai attacks, which killed nearly 170, including scores of foreigners. Saeed was listed as a terrorist by the UN Security Council (UNSC) in December 2008, a month after the Mumbai attacks, "pursuant to paragraphs 1 and 2 of resolution 1822 (2008) as being associated with Lashkar-e-Tayyiba (QDe.118) and Al Qaida (QDe.004) for "participating in the financing, planning, facilitating, preparing or perpetrating of acts of activities by, in conjunction with, under the name of, on behalf or in support of' both entities."[69] JuD and FIF are designated by the US as "terrorist fronts" of LeT. Saeed filed a petition in 2017 to the UN for delisting, which was later rejected.[70]

In early 2018, Pakistan announced plans to take over the entire infrastructure of JuD and its charities, e.g., FIF, present in over 100 cities of Pakistan.[71] JuD termed the government move illegal and resolved, "We will not keep silent. We will fight a legal battle."[72] The government subsequently proscribed it and all affiliated organizations in 2019. One unique variation in legal responses involves another individual, JeM leader Mohammad Masood Azhar. His name was proposed several times by the Western powers and India for UNSC sanction since 2009 but was persistently vetoed by China at the behest of Pakistan, citing a lack of "solid evidence."[73] He was finally listed on May 1, 2019 following appeal for his alleged role in the Pulwama attack on Indian security forces in Kashmir.[74] In this case, proscription efforts were challenged through vetoes by a UNSC member in collaboration with an ally, and the listing itself led Azhar going underground ever since. Indian authorities have termed People's anti-fascist Force (PAFF) as another manifestation of JeM, but the latter has not been publicly heard since the banning of its leader.

Does the recourse to legal action by the militant organizations empirically correlate with the period when Pakistan was more democratic (since 2008), as we had suggested? There is some evidence of this, as we find more examples of groups responding with legal charges in the more democratic years. There are exceptions, like the TJP in 2002 declaring it would fight its proscription in court. However, consistent with the typology, legal responses seem to have occurred more in democratic years.

Identity examples

A common variant within the identity adaptation is the name change, which is a more popular strategy employed by Jihadi and sectarian organizations. The proscription data by the Pakistani government reveal that the group's name change is not an occasional activity; instead, almost every Jihadi and sectarian group undertakes it as a regular feature to survive. Some groups repeatedly undertake this exercise. In the jihadi category, for instance, soon after proscription by the Musharraf regime, JeM changed its name to KuL, HuA, a Kashmiri-based militant group labeled itself Jamiatul-Ansar (Jam-A), and LeT became Pasban-e-Ahl-e-Hadith. The UNSC listed JuD in May 2008 as a front of LeT in UN Resolution 1267. The following year, in January 2009, it changed its name to Tehreek-e-Tahafuz Qibla Awal.[75] Identically, SSP has availed this practice several times. It renamed itself as Millat-e-Islamia Party (MIP) in 2002 and ASWJ when MIP was banned again in 2003. The government de-proscribed the ASWJ chief, but the movement continues to remain on the government's proscription list.[76] The charities, the so-called front of jihadi organizations such as the Al-Rehmat Trust and Al-Rashid Trust, have also used renaming. After the US designated Al-Rehmat Trust in 2010 "for providing support to and for acting for or on behalf of JEM," it reassigned itself the title Maymar Trust.[77] The Aid Organization of the Ulema became the successor organization of Al Rashid Trust after its listing by the UN in October 2001.[78]

Intriguingly, sometimes, militant groups combine multiple actions to maintain freedom of movement. For example, in 1997, the US classified HuA as a terrorist organization. It then splintered into two groupings and changed the names to Harkat-ul-Mujahideen (HuM) and Harkat ul Jihad e Islami.[79] HuM was recognized as the reincarnated HuA, which later re-designated itself Jam-A during the Musharraf regime. Similarly, after the January 2002 curb, TJP not only decided to challenge its ban in the court in 2001, it announced that it was renaming itself Millat e Jafria Pakistan.[80] The movement survives to the present day by having changed its name several times. Nevertheless, it remains proscribed. The case that militant groups shift ideology solely to address implications stemming from proscription is challenging to trace within the militancy landscape of Pakistan. However, the alleged surrogates of LeT and JeM operating in Indian Kashmir reportedly reactivated themselves in August 2019 as The Resistance Front (TRF) and PAFF to secularize their original religious identity after India revoked the special status of Jammu and Kashmir in 2019.[81] Unlike in the cases mentioned above, where the groups' identity remodeling occurred in reaction to proscription, in Kashmir, it ensued to localize the resistance to evade attention and prospective proscription after a blanket lockdown and a "crippling curfew" was imposed by the Indian government across Kashmir.[82]

Perhaps, within the identity examples, a more interesting sample is of an ethnic makeover. After LeT was banned in January 2002, some of its cadres, along with some dozen from other Kashmir-directed groups, not only relocated themselves into Pakistani Kashmir in anticipation of proscription and crackdown, the group designated many commanders after the names of various towns from Indian Kashmir to feign as Kashmiris. The underlying purpose of masquerading activity was to lead the public, the state, and the international community to believe in their non-Pakistani and more Kashmiri identity.[83]

Violence examples

Pakistani groups and organizations have exhibited a variety of responses to their proscription, including indifference to such restrictions by showing complete disregard for enforcement. TTP, BLF, BLA, and LeJ are prime examples of dissident behaviour. Within the increasing attacks examples, three Sindhi separatist groups emerge as more suitable illustrations— the Jeay Sindh Qaumi Mahaz- Aresar Group (JSQM-A), Sindhudesh Revolutionary Army (SDRA), and Sindhudesh Liberation (SDLA). JSQM-A is a politically nationalist party that allegedly supports separatists. The Interior Ministry proscribed them in May 2020. In June 2020, two groups, SDRA and SDLA, committed 10 terrorist attacks in the Sindh province at three locations: seven in Karachi, three in Southern Sindh, two in Larkana, and one in Ghotki city. The key targets, among others, were the law enforcement agencies (Rangers) and a government charitable program office.[84] Importantly, in sharp contrast to historically known for their moderate violent behaviour, the June orchestrations by the Sindhi insurgents created an impact due to the sheer number and the intensity, and more notably, synchronization.[85]

Other groups also carried out new or spectacular attacks shortly after being proscribed such as KuL and JuF. The Musharraf government banned both again on November 15, 2003. The next month, President Musharraf suffered two assassination attempts involving militants from the two groups.[86] There are far fewer examples of groups decreasing attacks or giving up violence, which partially explains why terrorism has not diminished in Pakistan since late 2001. This trend is more associated with the jihadi groups for a reason. LeT curtailed its operations after being banned by the government in January 2002.[87] In another case, JuD decided to suspend activities, i.e. temporarily, "remain dormant" in response to proscription while allegedly preparing to stage come back later.[88] It must be mentioned that the decision to decrease their operations may not have been autonomous, as underscored by some scholars, because they worked under the watchful eye of Inter-Services Intelligence (ISI, Pakistan's leading spy agency).[89] A more phenomenal response, possibly following a similar direction, was by

JeM, which—after reported assassination attempts on the president—went underground for a decade after its prohibition and resurfaced in 2011.[90]

Some militant groups have disappeared from the scene during the last decade, obviously reducing their violence. Curiously, proscription did not induce similar reactions among the more deadly terrorist groups, e.g., TTP, LeJ and Baloch groups. They are proscribed by the host and several other countries, including the US, but proscription has yet to be able to tame them conceivably due to countervailing incentives. Their past successes in blunting counterterrorism are presumably a critical reason for this behaviour. In the typology section, we speculated that religiously-motivated groups might be the most likely to increase their violence after proscription. We did not find this to be the situation in Pakistan. However, this seems to be due to the relative uniqueness of the Pakistan case, where jihadi groups often have connections to the ISI, as mentioned. In other cases, and consistent with the literature, increases in violence are probably more likely among religious groups.

Economic examples

The legal and institutional deficiencies in strategic counterterrorism-related financing by Pakistan have been a significant impediment until recently to realize dividends accruing from proscription of militant groups.[91] Not only have terrorist, jihadi, and sectarian organizations and charities escaped desired effects for a long time but in the past, mainstream political parties have been directly involved in fundraising to "liberate" Kashmir.[92] This mindset still pervades some public sections, deriving from the history of partition. JeM is an apt example of cleverly repositioning its funding channels before its banning in 2002 and after its resurfacing in 2011. In anticipation of forfeiture of assets during the former case, apart from opening accounts under pseudonyms, JeM withdrew savings from the banks and invested in legal business, i.e., real estate, production of goods, and commodity trading.[93] When the group resurfaced in 2011, within no time, it revived its charity, Al-Rehmat Trust, founded in 2001 for humanitarian assistance and education.[94] A few reports suggest that the trust had commenced financial operations in 2007, much before JeM became public, to collect donations for militants' families and support the Afghan Taliban.[95] JeM's fundraising campaign disguised under Al-Rehmat Trust, supposedly also to recruit and train the youth and build mosques, remained intact from within Pakistan and Gulf states until the charity was brought under "Watch" by the Interior Ministry. Al-Rashid Trust, mentioned above, is another charity that had links with militant organizations. It was often touted as one of Osama Bin Laden's many sources of income.[96] When the banks froze accounts of the charity under the Musharraf regime, it comfortably decentralized its finances by opening new accounts in individual names, leaving an extensive reservoir of untapped sources and assets in the Middle East, Great Britain and South Africa.[97]

Some smaller groups have reportedly switched to clandestine fundraising to avoid proscription's financial effects. This is consistent with the expectations outlined in the typology. The tactics entail using an underground network of experienced supporters rather than publically collecting funds.[98] Another common means is anonymous donations from the community, traders, and businessmen, mainly to sectarian militants that the groups continue to rely upon in Pakistan, which are difficult to track.[99] Finally, insofar as the financial sustenance of the mainstream terrorist groups is concerned, particularly following their proscription, they survive by turning to organized crime and acting as alleged proxies of hostile states to further the latter's geopolitical interests. TTP and BLA have been connected to India by some Western observers and Indian sources for receiving "coveted funding."[100]

Conclusion

Militant organizations respond to counterterrorism in a variety of ways. To provide a theoretical framework for the set of responses, this manuscript introduced the LIVE typology, emphasizing legal, identity-based, violence, and economic responses. This grouping is diverse enough to acknowledge differences between these types of responses, yet also parsimonious to allow researchers and practitioners to use the typology as a heuristic or shortcut when describing potential militant reactions. Looking at the case of how militant organizations respond to counterterrorism sanctions in Pakistan, we find interesting examples. Groups took advantage of legal options, filing petitions with courts or government agencies to be de-proscribed. Some were successful, while others were not. Many groups underwent identity adaptations as a result of counterterrorism pressure, such as name changes and shifting ideologies. Regarding violence, multiple groups increased their violence as a direct reaction to proscription. This is consistent with literature on the backlash of counterterrorism.[101] Fewer groups seemed to reduce their violence. Finally, regarding economic adaptations, the organizations in Pakistan have been quite adept at shifting financial sources under counterterrorism pressure. This seems problematic for policymakers trying to clamp down on terrorist financing.

Has proscription been successful as a counterterrorism response in Pakistan? It appears that the measure has produced mixed results. It has been able to reduce or regulate militants' public presence in some cases, with some effects on political, moral and financial support. However, it has been far less successful in ultimately dismantling or suppressing the most violent organizations. The ability of groups to adapt through the four mechanisms we identified has meant that most groups continue to survive. The study also finds that certain conditions and the character of militant organizations (e.g., a state-sponsored proxy or not) affect how they adapt to counterterrorism. However, this aspect warrants further exploration by studying other contexts. Beyond contributing to studies about Pakistan, our findings advance research on terrorist proscription. This policy is increasingly used around the world, but we find that it leads to unintended consequences, and does not seem to often achieve the desired consequence of reducing violence. However, policymakers and practitioners could use the LIVE model when thinking about policies to enact, and when building expectations about likely responses to policies.

The LIVE typology has limitations. The categories and implications are likely to be conditional on context-specific factors, such as international relations, for instance, entailing the banning of terrorist groups that are other governments' proxies. In such cases, the proscription might function domestically without however resolving the international roots of the violence. More broadly, different countries often have very different ideas of which groups are "terrorists."[102] Perhaps an explicitly international dimension will have to be integrated into the typology, or there can be more specific domestic and international versions. Future research can build on our work in several other ways. First, we looked at the case of Pakistan, but do militants respond to counterterrorism sanctions similarly in different contexts? In other countries, do some parts of the LIVE typology matter more than others? We found that many groups changed their names, and several filed lawsuits against the government, but this seems to not occur in some other countries. What explains differences in responses to counterterrorism across different countries or regions? Future analyses could be conducted using quantitative data, such as relatively new databases on armed groups,[103] or more specifically the Tominaga, Lee, and Lyu database on designated terrorist organisations.[104]

The model suggests a number of implications regarding which types of groups might react certain ways, along with suggestions for related counterterrorism. These can be seen as hypotheses that can be tested. Do our propositions hold in other contexts? In what way can the typology be improved, or what better typology might exist? Second, beyond how do groups respond do counterterrorism, how do other actors respond to counterterrorism? The present research could be built upon to better understand how civil society, allied governments, rival governments, international organizations, and other actors respond. For example, sometimes there is a public backlash against proscription,[105] but this has not been studied enough from a social science perspective. Finally, we mostly discussed terrorist designation or proscription, but to what extent can the LIVE framework help understand reactions to militarized crackdowns, or other approaches like concessions? How can governments tailor their responses accordingly to achieve desired results? There is some research on these important topics, but much more can be done.

Disclosure statement: o potential conflict of interest was reported by the author(s). Additional information. Notes on contributors. Muhammad Feyyaz Muhammad Feyyaz holds a PhD in politics from Queen's University, UK. He has taught at various universities in Pakistan including the country's apex civil and military institutions, namely NDU, Islamabad and the National School of Public Policy, Lahore. His research interests lie at the intersection of metaphysical and critical approaches to research and pedagogy and the theory and practice of persistent political violence, especially terrorism, counterterrorism, civil war, and insurgency. Brian J. Phillips: Brian J. Phillips is a Reader in the Department of Government at the University of Essex and an affiliated professor at CIDE in Mexico. His research and teaching interests include terrorism, civil conflict, and crime.

How do Militant Organizations Respond to Counterterrorism? Introducing the LIVE Typology, with Examples from Proscription in Pakistan. Muhammad Feyyaz &Brian J. PhillipsORCID Icon. Published online: 26 Aug 2024. To cite this article: Muhammad Feyyaz & Brian J. Phillips (26 Aug 2024): How do Militant Organizations Respond to Counterterrorism? Introducing the LIVE Typology,with Examples from Proscription in Pakistan, Terrorism and Political Violence, DOI:10.1080/09546553 .2024.2385015. © 2024 The Author(s). Published with license by Taylor & Francis Group, LLC. CONTACT Brian J. Phillips brian.phillips@essex.ac.uk Department of Government, University of Essex, Wivenhoe Park CO4 3SQ, UK TERRORISM AND POLITICAL VIOLENCE .https://doi.org/10.1080/09546553.2024.2385015. © 2024 The Author(s). Published with license by Taylor & Francis Group, LLC. This is an Open Access article distributed under the terms of the Creative Commons Attribution License (http://creativecommons.org/licenses/by/4.0/),which permits unrestricted use, distribution, and reproduction in any medium, provided the original work is properly cited. The terms on which this article has been published allow the posting of the Accepted Manuscript in a repository by the author(s) or with their consent. Aims and scope Terrorism and Political Violence advances scholarship on a broad range of issues associated with terrorism and political violence, including subjects *such as: the political meaning of terrorist activity, violence by rebels and by states, the links between political violence and organized crime, protest, rebellion, revolution, the influence of social networks, and the impact on human rights. The journal draws upon many disciplines and theoretical perspectives as well as comparative approaches to provide some of the most groundbreaking work in a field that has hitherto lacked rigour. Terrorism and Political Violence features symposia and edited volumes to cover an important topic in depth. Terrorism and Political Violence. Taylor & Francis make every effort to ensure the accuracy of all the information (the "Content") contained in our publications. However, Taylor & Francis, our agents (including the editor, any member of the editorial team or editorial board, and any guest editors), and our licensors, make no representations or warranties whatsoever as to the accuracy, completeness, or suitability for any purpose of the Content. Any opinions and views expressed in this publication are the opinions and views of the authors, and are not the views of or endorsed by Taylor & Francis. The accuracy of the Content should not be relied upon and should be independently verified with primary sources of information. Taylor & Francis shall not be liable for any losses, actions, claims, proceedings, demands, costs, expenses, damages, and other liabilities whatsoever or howsoever caused arising directly or indirectly in connection with, in relation to, or arising out of the use of the Content. Terrorism and Political Violence is a hybrid open access journal that is part of our Open Select publishing program, giving you the option to publish open access. Publishing open access means that your article will be free to access online immediately on publication, increasing the visibility, readership, and impact of your research. The journal draws upon many disciplines and theoretical perspectives as well as comparative approaches to provide some of the most groundbreaking work in a field that has hitherto lacked rigour. Terrorism and Political Violence features symposia and edited volumes to cover an important topic in depth. Subjects have included: terrorism and public policy; religion and violence; political parties and terrorism; technology and terrorism; and right-wing terrorism. The journal is essential reading for all academics, decision-makers, and security specialists concerned with understanding political violence.*

Chapter 7

The Emergence of a Nonviolent Nationalist Movement among the Tribes of Waziristan in Pakistan

Muhammad Irfan Mahsud

Abstract

In the second decade of the 21st century, the emergence of Pashtun Tahafuz (protection) Movement (PTM), among the tribes of Waziristan, rose to talk about the rights of Pashtuns after major military operations against the militants in doing so challenging government policies in the erstwhile tribal areas. The research has thoroughly investigated reasons of the emergence and popularity of PTM, its achievements and political ecosystem. The study has employed new social movement and asymmetric federalism theories. The study has argued that the protracted conflict coupled with government policies of securitization in erstwhile Federally Administered Tribal Areas (FATA) of Pakistan and feeling of discrimination among the Pashtun youth has led to the creation of a pro-Pashtun movement in 2018. The movement has been kept nonviolent, promotes progressive values and provides an alternate platform for the youth to address grievances thus halting their enrollment within militant groups. The paper utilizes ethnographic-based data collection tools, such as semi-structured interviews, informal discussions and personal observations to reach its findings.

Impact Statement

This study considers the emergence of the PTM in the erstwhile FATA since 2018 with special attention for (North and South) Waziristan which forms half of the territory of the erstwhile FATA and wherein the movement took its origin. Based on qualitative data and field research conducted in Waziristan (both North and South) between December 2019 and January 2020, the study explores the dynamics that turned the movement into a leading actor in the social and political life in Waziristan and beyond. The finding suggests that the emergence of PTM as a leftist, secular and peaceful movement progressively adds a new dimension to what was traditionally considered as the 'Pashtun identity', and that is defined by aggressivity, a strict adherence to Islam and the reference to an immutable cultural code known as Pashtunwali.

Keywords: Pashtun ethno-nationalism nonviolent movement Waziristan Pashtun Tahafuz Movement

Background and Introduction

This region comprising Waziristan and tribal areas has been poorly understood in the West as well as in Islamabad (Hopkins & Marsden, Citation2012). This misunderstanding has led many renowned (local and foreign) scholars, historians and journalists to believe this region is famous only for revolts, agitation and militancy. Elisabeth Leake has noted that the area comprised of Waziristan and its surroundings have been generally remained out of state control from the colonial period into the 21st century. Leake believes that the British and the Pakistani state has struggled to integrate this region into the mainstream (Leake, Citation 2017). Hopkins argues that the tribal areas and Waziristan in particular has hosted many religious based revolts against the colonial intrusion in the 19th century (Hopkins, Citation2009). Since 1947 and the inception of Pakistan as an independent state, the former *Federally Administered Tribal Areas* (FATA)[1] remained a troubled area that have been iron-fisted by Islamabad. The Soviet invasion of Afghanistan in 1979 and the subsequent participation of tribesmen from Waziristan radicalized the youth therewith experience violent approaches firsthand. Since 2004, both the rise of militancy and the subsequent military operations have nurtured a conducive context for the tribal youth to become politically more active. This conflictual situation carries substantial economic[2] and social deteriorations for the local population as well as its displacement (Chughtai, Citation2013). Amid the chaos the tribal youth participation in violent activities was considered to be the main reason for the emergence of most violent militant organizations in the world.

Keeping in view the enormous youth budge, the federal government in 2017 tried to cope with this unstable situation by creating a *FATA Youth*

Jirga [council][3] whose aim was to enroll a share of young tribesmen in the institutionalized political field and to therefore prevent them from indulging into politically more active. But this move had limited effects because the initiative was poorly implemented by the government (lack of funds and staff) and the tribal youth was not very interested in it. A year later the killing of a young man, Naqeebullah Mehsud, by Karachi police forces in what was later identified as a fake encounter (Shah, Citation 2020) was the ultimate event that led to the formation of the *Mahsud Tahaffuz Movement* ('Mahsud Protection Movement', MTM).[4] The MTM was subsequently renamed *Pashtun Tahaffuz Movement* ('Pashtun Protection Movement', PTM) to be more inclusive of all the Pashtuns tribes.

This study considers the emergence of the PTM in the former FATA since 2018 with a special attention for (North and South) Waziristan[5] which forms half of the territory of the tribal belt and wherein the movement took its origin. Based on qualitative data and field research conducted in Waziristan (both North and South) between December 2019 and January 2020, the study explores the dynamics that turned the movement into a leading actor in the social and political life in Waziristan. Primary data were collected through informal discussions and through 27 semi-structured interviews with members of the PTM and non-PTM tribal people as well as government officers. Interviews took place in South and North Waziristan and in the cities of Bannu, Tank, Dera Ismail Khan and Peshawar. Due to the sensitivity of the study, pseudonyms are used instead of real names, but professional occupation is indicated. In the first part, I introduce the historical context that led to the creation of the PTM. In the second part, I further present the movement in itself and introduce the reader to its political ecosystem in the third and last part. Ultimately the paper assumes that the emergence of PTM as a leftist, secular and peaceful movement progressively adds a new dimension to what was traditionally considered as the 'Pashtun identity', and that is defined by aggressivity, a strict adherence to Islam and the reference to an immutable cultural code known as Pashtunwali (Jan, Citation2010).

Methodology

The study is qualitative in nature, and I have collected primary data through semi-structured interviews, informal discussions and personal observations in the given area of research. To answer the main question of the study: What is the nature and dynamics of ethnicity based nonviolent movement that has emerged among the tribes of Waziristan? The respondents included members of tribal civil society in settled districts, leaders and activists of the PTM, tribal youth, tribal elders, professionals, businesspersons and government officers. Qualitative research is needed because the study needed in-depth analysis and understanding. Along with individual interviews and informal discussions, I also conducted focus group discussions of the students belonging to North and South Waziristan. To improve the study, secondary sources are also consulted such as articles on PTM in different newspapers, journals and reports.

Sample size

The purposive sampling strategy was selected in North and South Waziristan. Hence, twenty-seven identified people from tribal districts of South Waziristan, North Waziristan, settled districts of Bannu, Tank, Dera Ismail Khan and Peshawar were interviewed between 01 December, 2019 to 10 January ,2020. Moreover, the general rule of saturation (same response/information for a question asked) is also used in a survey type of query whether PTM is right or wrong in their demands and stance. Due to expected degree of homogeneity of the views, the sample saturated quickly.

Ethical considerations

Due to the sensitivity of topic, security of the participants was my primary concern. Since there is still a security situation and working on PTM is a sensitive subject, I have skipped certain parts/techniques such as details and method of approaching the interview respondents including recording. For example, after a formal consent a video record session, respondents said that they have lied in the interview. The respondents were having problem with written consent and video recording. After through thinking and taking help from scholarly work written on conflict methodology in the same area (Waziristan) (Dawar, Citation2021), I decided to take an informal consent and not to record (particularly video recording) interview sessions. Therefore, the interviews are conducted with the consent of the interviewees and pseudonyms are used instead of real names of locals. I did not follow the formal method of recording the discussion, as it would put them in an uneasy situation. Therefore, an informal chat in the local dialect was carried out in areas of research with the local respondents. This approach also helped me in gaining their trust and confidence, which resulted in developing a rapport with interviewees, which is an important component for any research.

Limitation of the study

Holding discussion on PTM is tantamount to anti-state and many were and still would be reluctant to discuss it with anyone outside their community or close circle; hence, I used purposive sampling in the North, South Waziristan and Tank due to security and other concerns. The interviewees, particularly tribal elders, businessmen, professionals, in these areas were reluctant to answer the questions regarding the movement. Due to heavy security presence, people were usually tense and activities were limited. However, with the assistance of my local connections and gatekeepers, I was being able to conduct interviews and informal discussions with local people. Prior experience of research in the area, ability to speak local language and understanding of local culture and traditions helped me overcome limitations to a much greater extent.

Theoretical Framework

Social movements are not a new phenomenon. Western states (US and Western Europe) witnessed a number of protests/agitations against government policies and prevalent social practices since 1950s be that civil rights, feminist, environmental or anti-colonial social movement. Many authors including Phongpaichit (Phongpaichit & Baker, Citation1999) tried to develop theories regarding evolution, growth and future of social movements. The New/social-movement Theory (NSMT) operates when collective action takes place in the wake of discrimination to collective identity like ethnicity/gender (Buechler, Citation1995; Sen and Avci, Citation2016). NSMT is relevant in societies where there is a tussle between individual rights and state's rights (McAdam et al., Citation1988) (middle or lower middle class in case of Pashtun nationalist uprising). NSMT asserts that in the effort against status-quo, leaders/members of social movements are usually skilled, educated and aware of their rights and duties. Traditional Social Movement Theory (SMT) functions on the basis of class exploitation by another (Marxist approach) (Welton, Citation1993), therefore, SMT is not suited for the study. NSMT better explains the contemporary social movements (Buechler, Citation1995; Sen & Avci, Citation2016) such as Pashtun nationalist movement because it focuses the rights of the individual citizens and its relationship with state excessive authority. In the region of Waziristan, excessive securitization and the security check points every few kilometers affected freedom of movement of the inhabitants whereby creating the environment of insecurity. Moreover, the personnel of military trained to maintain order in the area with no priority to give due regard to local culture and tradition were considered a threat to local tribal identity.

The dispensation of federalism and its asymmetrical trajectory can be taken into account while understanding the rise of Pashtun nationalism in Pakistan (Ahmed & Khan, Citation 2022). The concept of symmetry and asymmetry were discussed by Tarlton for the first time. Asymmetry can be understood where unit/province share more or less common concerns in the federal system, however, in the case of 'symmetry' unit/province do not share common concerns/features (Tarlton, Citation1965). According to Smith asymmetry exists where some federating units are more powerful than the others (Smith, Citation2005). In Pakistan, federating units such as Punjab province has more share in the power structure. The federal government is usually formed when a political party has secured majority in Punjab. Almost half of the percentage of the officers/personnel in judiciary, military and other important state intuitions are from Punjab. Therefore, Punjabi elite is usually held responsible for the backwardness of area such as the ex-FATA where right to vote to the inhabitants was given in 1997. Constitutionally, politicians/legislators from tribal areas were not allowed to make/amend law for their constituency. Since 1947, inhabitants of ex-FATA have been denied fundamental human rights. Ultimately in 2018, the region was merged into mainstream Pakistan, however, law implementation, execution and implementation are still a challenge.

Historical perspective: brief contextualization of the PTM's creation

Although the legal regime was enforced by the then government after the approval of local community representatives (tribal elders) in the tribal belt since 1947 created frustration and a sense of deprivation among the local people in the long run. This already-tense situation was further aggravated by militant activities that developed in the area in the since 1980s and ultimately chaos started openly in 2000s.

Legal rule

In 1947, despite ruling now an independent country, the first government of Pakistan decided to apply to the erstwhile FATA a set of laws that was inherited from the British Empire: the *Frontier Crime Regulation* (FCR) (Hopkins, Citation2015). The FCR consisted of a special constitutional status that allowed arbitrary violence by government institutions including physical state apparatus and their subsequent impunity.[6] Under the aegis of President Zulfiqar Ali Bhutto, the new Constitution that was enforced 1973 replicated the FCR (that was also kept enforced) in the form of Article 247. In addition, Art. 247 delineated the administration of the ex- FATA by placing it under a presidential regime: (Nichols, Citation2013) firstly, the region was governed by the President of Pakistan through his local representant, the Governor of the area; secondly federal civil servants were the administrative operative personnel for the area (Hopkins, Citation2020). Since its very origin this un-representative system mainly led by non-local civil servants had triggered frustration of local people against the Central State (Fozia & Khan, Citation2017; Mahsud et al., Citation2023). Throughout the decades after the creation of Pakistan, the situation kept worsening by the actual enforcement of FCR and Art. 247, because of the corrupted behavior of the administration. The deprivations caused due to legal framework in erstwhile FATA has validated and given rise to asymmetrical trajectory of federalism in Pakistan.

Hideouts for (foreign) militants

The 2001 'War on Terror' added other dimensions to the historically volatile situation that was prevailing in the tribal belt. Because of its porous border with Afghanistan and its unprotected inner boundary with the neighboring Baluchistan province (Beattie, Citation 2019), the territory of Waziristan was used by the outlaws/militants more frequently (Schetter, Citation2013). The area became a safe enclave in post 2001 period for the Arab, Uzbek, Chechen and Afghan militants who were thus able to easily enter or exit the Afghan war zone (Johnston & Sarbahi, Citation2016; Qazi, Citation2011). But after the fall of the Taliban regime, Waziristan-based militants melted with local ones and turned against the local administration/government (Abbas, Citation2010). It is because, under the immense pressure of US government Pakistan army penetrated into Waziristan early in 2003–2004 and initiated chain of military operations first in South Waziristan against the foreign militants. These foreign militants were under the protection of tribesmen as guests in their houses, in local culture known as *Hamsaya*, taking them by force and invading privacy of houses was considered a sheer disregard of local culture and traditions which gave rise to doubts and resentment among the inhabitants and local militants for the government forces (Mahsud, Citation2019). Eventually in December 2007, foreigner and local militants therefore re-organized locally within small groups that later amalgamated within the *Tehreek-e-Taliban Pakistan* (*Taliban Movement in Pakistan*, TTP) (Abbas, Citation2008; Markey, Citation2013). TTP was created by Beitullah Mahsud (Abbas, Citation2009), a local tribesman. On the one hand, militants started being violently active against Islamabad (that is to say people or infrastructures that embodied the Pakistan State). On the other hand, they progressively superseded the (arbitrary) FCR rule of law by their (arbitrary) legal system. Militants enjoyed the support of the local clergy and were later joined by a small share of local unemployed and illiterate young men (Arshad, Citation2010).

But militants were not exclusively warmly welcomed by the tribal people. Local political chiefs thus voiced their concerns to the represent of the central State regarding the development of armed militancy in Waziristan. Nonetheless, in the post 2002 period the population get stuck between the violent attacks of militant organizations and the violent military operations directed by Islamabad. The central State responded to militancy by sending the Army in Waziristan, first to South Waziristan for it was the militancy's hotbed (Mahsud, Citation2019). Consequently, despite the FCR being still enforced, on the ground it lost its *raison d'etr* because the military commandment's orders overtook the civil agents' power. Their authority was therefore curtailed. After years of military operations, in 2020 militancy is considered to be tamed in the former FATA. But the insurgency has had deep and long-term effects on the local society. However, with the resurrection of Taliban in Afghanistan in 2021, sharp surge of militant activities has been noted in Waziristan which can attract yet again military actions. Along with the murder of numerous tribal chiefs, around one million tribesmen and women were compelled to migrate from their homeland (Hameed, Citation2015). In the localities they settled, and especially in urban areas, these new *Internally Displaced Persons* (IDPs) faced discrimination and harassment from the residents as well as overall insecurity. People from Waziristan consequently experienced great distress and anxiety particularly the Mahsuds for they are the largest tribal group in South Waziristan [*see footnote n°3*]. Besides, a large chunk of the traditional leaders being murdered which created leadership vacuum.

Three crucial events

Before getting into the details of the events it is important to identify that there Waziristan host many tribes the three major and influential tribes are Mahsud, Wazir and Dawar, each of these tribes has provided leadership support to the PTM. Through personal communication with journalists, tribal elders, military officers and FGDs with PTM activists I have deduced that three events then led to the creation of the PTM. As a first step, in 2014, a video showing security personnel dancing in a 'ganr khat', a traditional female garment from the Mahsud tribe, provoked severe protests among the Mahsud tribesmen in Dera Ismail Khan. According to Ishtiaq Mahsud, a local journalist covering the tribal protests, dissents were followed by a massive social media campaign that forced the authorities to apologize for showing disrespect to the local culture.[7] In personal communication with Ahmed Dar it was revealed that the military high command in district Peshawar was displeased with the way matter was handled by the officers on station. In the course of this event, analyzed through focused group discussions with PTM activists and local journalists, coupled with the long-lasting feeling of humiliation resented by the Mahsuds, Sailab Mahsud, a journalist, created the 'Khat Tehreek' [Shirt Movement] in order to preserve the Pashtun values. Slogans such as 'Da Sanga Azaadi Da' [What Kind of Freedom is This] and 'Pakhtun Ta Zwandon Ghawaro' [We Want Life for Pashtun] became popular and slowly awakened a new Pashtun nationalism. Local tribal elder including Muhammad Qayyum and Muhammad Hashim hailed Salib Mahsud as the Pashtun nationalist leader and a force behind the emergence of PTM. FGDs with PTM revealed that whenever the authorities detained PTM activists, it was Saliab Mahsud who came to the forefront to rescue. Naeem Tarar, a Lt Colonel posted in Dera Ismail Khan and Tank District in 2014–2015, highlighted the Manzoor Pashteen himself was released a couple of times from their custody due to the intervention of Salib Mahsud through campaigning and protest in front of press clubs in district Tank and Dera Ismail Khan. As a second step, in 2017, a landmine explosion in Shamkai, a village of South Waziristan, again triggered massive protests against the authorities because mines were buried in Waziristan's soil by the Army to fight back militants. Muhammad Zeb, a bureaucrat serving in South Waziristan in 2016–2017 and Ishtiaq Mahsud, a local journalist, noted that for the first time, the protests were coordinated. Under the leadership of Manzoor Pashteen, a young Mahsud tribesman, *Khat Tehreek* evolved into the *Mahsud Tahaffuz Movement* (MTM) whose claims were broader than those of the Khat Tehreek in order to encompass all the historical issues faced by the Mahsuds.

As a third step, in January 2018 the death of Naqeebullah Mahsud at the hands of the Karachi police (Ali, Citation2018) this time prompted protests from Pashtuns all over the country. Torchbearers were the Mahsuds. All protestors gathered under the umbrella of the MTM.[8] They launched a national campaign on social networks as well as on electronic and print media to demand justice for Naqeebullah Mahsud. But their claims went far beyond this death. Protestors asked for the release of 32000 tribesmen (Baloch & Bugti, Citation2018) that were arbitrary arrested by the security forces[9] and they informed the rest of the country about the abuses that the tribal people had been subjected to for decades (Arsalan, Citation2018). Journalists A and B in district Tank and Dera Ismail Khan, Tribal elders including A and B in Dera Ismail Khan and Naeem Khan lawyer in district Tank have agreed on the fact that it was at the occasion of these demonstrations that the MTM changed its name for the PTM so that it better stands for the entire tribal population and not only for the Mahsuds. Nevertheless, a Mahsud retained the leadership because the PTM was placed under the direction of Manzoor Pashteen and benefitted from the support of Sailab Mahsud. FGDs with PTM activists highlighted that the PTM is actually an ethnic based Movement of Pashtuns in general and Mahsuds in particular. To answer the question on the roots of PTM and its torchbearers, personal communication with local administration and military officers revealed that without participation of the Mahsud tribesmen the movement will collapse like a house of cards. Ahmed Dar and Naeem Tarar, military officer in the area from 2015 and 2018–2019, were of the opinion that it is actually the participation of Mahsud tribe in PTM and TTP which led to success if participation of this tribe is rolled back both the movement/organization will collapse in a matter of days. After the historical overview of the PTM's foundation, we will now go deeper into the movement's ideology and its membership.

Inside the PTM

This second part will now explore the political manifesto of the movement. It will also give indications as to the members' sociological profile. Those elements are crucial to weigh up the PTM's success.

PTM's ideology and strategy

Contrary to a political party, the PTM has no formal structure. A formal organized structure can be continently controlled by the government, it can lead to a bone of contention and discord among the PTM leadership. In addition, its members come from 'ordinary' background on the grassroot level, they do not come from political or landlord dynasties. Regarding its goals as well as its method, PTM's inspiration is to be found in the pro-Pashtun nationalist and leftist *Khudai Khidmatgar Movement* ('the Servants of God Movement', KKM) that was created in 1929 by Khan Abdul Ghaffar Khan *aka* Bacha Khan (Banerjee, Citation2000). The KKM was operative in the settled areas, notably Peshawar, Mardan and Charssadda (Gandhi, Citation2008; Shah, Citation1999). At the time of British colonialism, the KKM aimed at social reform through non-violent actions. By using peaceful protests, the KKM was thus the first of its kind. According to Bacha Khan, non-violence was supposed to be diffused through education of both males and females (A. Khan, Citation2018). That is the reason why he established several schools in the settled Pashtun areas.[10] Ultimately Bacha Khan tried to unite all the Pashtuns be they located on the Afghan or on the Pakistan side of the borders but Bacha Khan failed to attract the Afghans in his movement. There was a misconception among the Pashtun youth and power elite in Pakistan that KKM's motto was 'Lar Aw Bar Yao Afghan/Pashtun' [roughly: 'Pashtuns on both sides of the Durand line are the same']. In reality, there is no evidence to support the fact that slogan was ever used during the struggle of KKM. In any case, almost a century later, the PTM navigates in the same stream as the KKM (Akhtar, Citation2021).

Since 2018, the movement presents itself as a peaceful and secular one that puts the respect of Human Rights for the Pashtun as its core goal.[11] Its 6-point manifesto mingled immediate demands with long-term requests:

1. Police officer and people involved in Naqeeb's killing should be punished;

2. A committee must be set up in order to evaluate extrajudicially killings and fake encounters committed by the authorities in the area;

3. The missing persons' cases must be taken to the Court of Pakistan, while forced disappearances must immediately end;

4. Waziristan ground should be cleared of landmines;

5. Local people should not be systematically suspected of being associated to or supporters of the militancy;

6. Inhumanity in the tribal belt must be stopped (Saddique & Xiumei, Citation2019).

All these points contribute to defend the Pashtun identity and rights in connection with NSMT, that is to say to achieve tribesmen' full equality with their fellow citizen within the state of Pakistan. Religious issues are never raised by the PTM. The movement considers that the state itself has ill-played with local people's religious sentiments since 1979. According to the PTM's narrative, 'with the help of religious political parties in the 1980s, President Zia relied on tribesmen's religious feelings to launch a 'Holy War' in Afghanistan against the USSR' (Abbas, Citation2014). For the PTM, 'this state of affairs crucially damaged the socio-political fabric of Waziristan' (Ahmed, Citation2004). The movement considers the post-9/11 situation in Waziristan to be the outcome of this policy. Therefore, the main target of the movement's claims is the State and government. The unprecedent blatant criticism on state institution is one reason for the popularity of PTM in public but it has led to the restriction of their coverage on electronic and print media. Claims are nevertheless limited to Pashtuns from both sides of the Durand Line ('Lar Aw Bar Yao Afghan/Pashtun'), whereas at the domestic level, the PTM does not favour an inclusive approach of the tribal areas that would encompass different minorities. To reach its goal, the PTM choses a non-violent strategy and uses two types of actions: peaceful sit-ins, and demonstrations and electoral participation.

Albeit a loosely structured movement, the PTM enjoys strong supports outside Waziristan. An important share of the Pashtuns who lives in Pakistan outside the tribal areas participates to the multiples protests that took place across the country. The movement is hence successful in triggering people's attention in Waziristan as well as in exporting itself outside the area. In Europe and in the United States, the Pashtun diaspora has also responded positively to the PTM's project (Caron & Khan, Citation2022) and organize the same kind of non-violent protests (PTM Europe Holds Protests against Pakistan, Citation2018). Electoral competition is another tool within the PTM strategy that proved to be fruitful. A few months after the PTM's inception, Mohsin Dawar and Ali Wazir, two founders of the movement, decided to run for the general elections of summer 2018. They contested seats in their homeland of North and South Waziristan and were elected to the National Assembly (NA) (Two PTM leaders make it to the NA, Citation2018). We will now meet the PTM's leadership and explore its membership.

Sociological overview and prominent members

The sociology of PTM members differs from traditional political or religious parties. Most of the members are young, students for many, and comes from low or average economic background. As already stated, activists originate from the Pashtun group that is based in Khyber Pakhtunkhwa and in Baluchistan. Waziristan was the first bastion and continues to be the hotbed of the movement, specifically the city of Dera Ismail Khan District which is the stronghold for the Mahsuds (M. Pashteen and A. Wazir are settled there since 2009–2010 when they escaped the conflict that was ragging in (South) Waziristan. From Waziristan, the PTM's audience then expanded throughout Khyber Pakhtunkhwa and in Baluchistan because of the movement's ability to raise issues such as unlawful imprisonment, extra judicial killings and harassment at the security check-posts, topics that have been abandoned for a long time by the existing political parties. In Waziristan, young Pashtuns think[12] that many of its supporters turned to the PTM because they do not consider the existing Pashtun leadership able to empower the Pashtun minority and/or enhance their rights within the Pakistan federal system.[13] On the contrary, the PTM embodies a refreshing and promising opportunity in order for the locals to be more integrated politically and economically wise.

The three main leaders of the PTM are Manzoor Ahmed, *aka* Pashteen, from South Waziristan; Ali Wazir, from South Waziristan; and Mohsin Dawar, from North Waziristan – the two last ones being elected at the NA. Pashteen is the main orator of the movement and his speeches have helped the movement to gain attention in two main directions: on the one hand, he refers to a Pashtun (non-violent) nationalism and appeal to the Pashtuns' pride; on the other hand, he directly addresses the Pakistan state. Pashteen also cleverly plays with his image by emulating Bacha Khan's modest attire for instance. Moreover, the traditional cap that he always wears has now become the symbol of the Pashtuns' peaceful protests.[14] In addition, he is popular among the Pashtuns for refusing a reserved seat at the NA that was offered to him by Imran Khan's government.[15] Before joining the PTM Ali Wazir and Mohsin Dawar were active members of another pro-Pashtun and leftist party, the *Awami National Party* (ANP) [cf. infra]. Both of them took their distance with the ANP because the party failed to deliver any substantive improvements, directly and indirectly, for the cause of the people living in tribal areas (including IDPs living in the province) despite ruling the Khyber Pakhtunkhwa province from 2008 until 2013.[16,17] Although, ANP did not govern former tribal areas directly but their silence on the atrocities and brutalities committed by the physical state apparatus against the Pashtuns both in tribal areas and KP province continued in the post 2006 period which pushed many important Pashtun nationalist members to revisit their affiliation. Regarding the movement, the former link of two of its leading members with the institutionalized political parties (here, the ANP) is telling because in Waziristan, most of the political men and their proponents now declare their support to the PTM. Examination of the leadership is also of a great importance in terms of ethnicity. For the first time indeed, a Pashtun-led movement is ruled by leaders of different tribes (a Mahsud, a Wazir and a Dawar) and from different place of origin (South and North Waziristan). Despite this diversity, there is no ethnic-wise cleavage within the PTM, and all the three leaders are respected without any interference of their ethnic background. Notwithstanding, Mohsin Dawar has left the movement because of political differences/reasons but the predicament for the rights of the tribesmen is continued. We will now end this second part by examining the movement's successes as well as its limitations.

Achievements and limit

As already stated, the objectives of the PTM were twofold. On the one hand, they were related to concrete demands in the Naqeebullah case, and on the other hand, they encompassed those to address the general situation of the tribal areas. On the first aspect, 2018 demonstrations were successful: the Supreme Court took notice of Naqeebullah's murder as well as of the missing persons. Hundreds of arrested men were subsequently released (Arsalan, Citation2018). Tribesmen also considered that this demonstration successfully cultivated a sense of responsibility among the security personnel who operated in the erstwhile FATA, especially in Waziristan. For instance, police operating in cities is deemed to be now more respectful while dealing with tribal people[18] and Islamabad abolished the permit cards for the locals.[19] On the second aspect, the movement played an important role to speed up mainstreaming process of erstwhile FATA initiated by the political/civil forces i.e., political parties, intelligentsia, civil society and the NGOs coupled with fast changing strategic importance triggered by the proposed US withdrawal from Afghanistan and the subsequent resurrection of Taliban thereby jolting the power-elite. This move was done as early as in May 2018. The central government passed the 25th Amendment of the Pakistan constitution that revoked the Special Status of the FATA and merged the area within the Khyber Pakhtunkhwa. The Amendment was easily passed by the NA (Waseem, Citation2018) as well as the Khyber Pakhtunkhwa Assembly with two-third majority (with 99-7 in favor). Furthermore, peaceful protests in Pakistan and in the Western world have helped the PTM to gain international attention (Aslam & Neads, Citation2021) from advocacy NGOs such as Amnesty International or Transparency International. Every so often, they publish reports of the Human Rights situation in tribal areas that are hoped to put pressure on Islamabad.

Despite this important attainment, some members are doubtful as to the long-run efficiency of the PTM's exclusive pro-Pashtun attitude. The PTM restricting its claims to the sole Pashtun group while ignoring the plight of other ethnic minorities in Pakistan might therefore be detrimental for the movement's image and struggle.[20] For instance, murders of Shia followers in Karachi, Quetta or Dera Ismail Khan are not condemned by the PTM. Ethnic minorities such as the Baluch-, the Sindhi- or the Urdu-speaking that also suffer from what they consider to be unfair state policies toward them, doubt the PTM's aptitude to fruitfully questions the Pakistan power's structure. They consider the PTM to be a strictly pro-Pashtun movement that does not carry the plight of other communities which suffers more or less the same fate/treatment.[21] In that respect, the PTM leaders are confronted to a tricky situation. While they try to keep their non-violent position, virulent anti-Punjabi slogans were shout during the movement's protests (Mallick, Citation2020), notably by the Pashtun youth. Punjabi elite can be held responsible for the Pakistan other minorities' backwardness because 'there is a debate about the backward areas in Southern Punjab' (Mughal, Citation2020). Ultimately, the combination of strictly Pashtun nationalism and rejection of Punjabis could fuel the already existing communal strife in Waziristan. We will now end this discussion/analysis by exploring the PTM's local and transnational ecosystem.

Political ecosystem of the PTM

Since its inception in 2018, the PTM has changed the political ecosystem it is embedded in – 'political' refers to non-violent institutionalized political parties and violent groups alike.

The local political landscape

Beyond its political ecosystem, the emergence and subsequent appeal among Pashtuns of the PTM can be explained by two main sets of reasons. The first one refers to the concrete situation of Pashtuns on the ground as stated in Part 1 of the study. The second set of reasons is the failure of the three pro-Pashtun organizations, the ANP, the *Pashtunkhwa Milli Awami Party* (PMAP) and the *Qaumi Watan Party*, in successfully opposing the government to obtain improvements of tribesmen's socio-economic situation. These political parties prefer their own electoral interest rather than the development of the area (Qaiser, Citation2016). But more importantly, the field research shows that the Jamiat Ulema-e-Islam (JUI) and the Jamaat-e-Islami (JI), two religious political parties, endure the same decrease of popularity especially among the young Pashtuns. Religious elite in Pashtun tribal region has been instrumental in various uprising against the colonial rule and enjoyed enormous public support since centuries (Haroon, Citation2007). Whereas since 1947 they have been very popular among the population of Waziristan (Borchgrevink, Citation2010) due to its high degree of religiosity (Haroon, Citation2008, Citation2012), the emergence of the PTM not only damaged the vote bank of religious political parties but also challenged their silence on the atrocities that have been brought by the conflict in the last two decades on the people of Waziristan.[22] It is the first time in their history that these religious parties are that neglected by voters. This finding might seem paradoxical because until then, the armed militancy operating locally in the name of jihad had positive side-effects only on the religious parties.[23] But during the general elections in 2018, the *Jamiat-e-Ulema Islam* lost seats to the PTM.

The rise of the PTM also has side-effects on the militancy for the movement seems to provide a way of exit for young militants and/or an alternative way to raise their voice and struggle against what they consider to be the oppressive state apparatus.[24] Consequently, enrollment in militancy decreases: in 2014 TTP counted around 35,000 fighters while they were only around 2,000 in 2020.[25] In addition, the PTM impacts the militant groups themselves. Many local militant factions indeed declare being sympathetic towards the PTM. Solidarity might be ethnic-based for the PTM as well as the militant groups are run by Pashtuns. Militants also condemned Naqeebullah Mahsud's murder and announced their will to avenge this death.[26] The most striking case is Mufti Noor Wali Mehsud, one of the TTP's *amir* [chief], who publicly displays his support to the PTM by wearing the 'Pashteen hat'. The militancy's support to the PTM sometimes creates tensions within the militancy *milieu* for on an individual basis, not all the militants are of the same inclination towards the PTM. However, a clash is imminent between militant groups and PTM. In September/October 2022, PTM has registered protest in various areas in the tribal belt and Pashtun areas in Pakistan against the increasing militant activities. The most significant one was noted in October 2022 in Swat Valley where thousands of people came together staged demonstration and urged government to take concrete steps to end militancy in the region (Khaliq, Citation2022). This protest is significant because it is the first time PTM members have openly condemned militant groups/activities.

The (noxious) Afghan support

Despite calls from the PTM, Islamabad's continuous lack of interest in improving the situation in Waziristan created a space for the Afghans to join in the movement. Kabul (under Ashraf Ghani) hence publicly declared its strong support to the PTM (Oxford Analytica, Citation2018; Threlkeld & Easterly, Citation2021). Kabul might be strategic in doing so since the Afghan authorities intend to use the Pashtuns to pressurize Islamabad. Same for the Western-based diaspora who displays its support to PTM by using the social networks (Khan & Shah, Citation2021) with the aim of damaging Pakistan's image abroad. Along with the Pashtun group (which forms 42 to 45% of the Afghan population) (Barfield, Citation2022), the other ethnic minorities of Afghanistan also support the PTM (Jafri, Citation2021) for two main reasons. On the one hand, Kabul has territorial claims over some parts of the Pakistan tribal belt and beyond (Omrani, Citation2009; Rubin & Armstrong, Citation2003; Spain, Citation1961) that are shared by the population. On the other hand, a large bulk of Afghans blames Islamabad for the troubles that the successive governments have created in their country for decades (Hussain, Citation2008; Rashid, Citation2010). However, on the Waziristan ground people are of the opinion that the Afghan support might be detrimental to the PTM because the litigation between Islamabad and Kabul over the Durand Line combined with the deteriorated relationships between the two countries have exacerbated the crackdown on the PTM (extra judicial killings, harassment and imprisonment) (European Asylum Report Office, Citation2019). The Afghan support also nurtures rumours like the PTM taking support from India and other countries hostile to Pakistan (Shah, Citation2020). In addition, the Afghan backing creates a distress among the urban leftist supporters of the PTM that is the reason why they disapprove the slogan 'Lar Aoo Bar Yoo Afghan/Pashtun'. Pretty well-integrated within the Pakistan power structure themselves, they feel that Pashtuns enjoy the same situation and are well integrated in various parts of Pakistan.[27] Pro-Afghan motto also somehow legitimates Kabul's claims over tribal areas located in Pakistan, something that they strongly oppose. In addition, they fear that the Afghan public support will further cultivate hatred against Pashtuns living in other parts of the state.[28]

The resurrection of Taliban in Afghanistan in 2021 (Muraviev, Citation2022) has decreased the support and popularity of PTM in Kabul. The Taliban (TTP and Afghan Taliban) are radical Islamists and therefore detest Pashtun nationalism based on their progressive/secular approach. This development has also put NSMT to test the prediction of what future has in store for the social movements in this context. The completion of Pak-Afghan border fencing (Jones, Citation2009; Oztig, Citation2020) might have an impact in relation to cross-border militant activities. There is a good chance that TTP may start attacks on PTM demonstrations which might prove fatal for the security of state, unity and rights of the Pashtuns within Pakistan.

The study has not touched upon many important topics related to PTM particularly the developments in 2021–2022 the region and its impact on the movement and beyond. For example, in 2022 and onward period there is a sudden surge in militant activities in Waziristan and the tribal belt of Pakistan which can undermine and boost the influence of PTM. Another important area of research can be the awareness and community resilience build by the movement vis-à-vis militant resurrection. There is some interesting scholarly work done in the area of community resilience in Waziristan (Makki & Akash, Citation2022) but relevant questions can be raised in a larger context, for example, the tribal belt, Khyber Pakhtunkhwa and Balochistan province where youth is supportive to PTM. There is potential in nonviolent agitation (in nascent stages) in Baluchistan province against the power-elite (Ahmed & Khan, Citation2022) which can be important to study in relation to PTM.

Conclusion

We saw why, how and on which ground the PTM emerged as a staple actor in the political life in Waziristan and beyond, in the Khyber Pakhtunkhwa and Baluchistan provinces. In addition, by promoting non-violence, the PTM also transforms the traditional perception of the 'Pashtun identity'. PTM is not emphasizing on religious issues which highlights the progressive nature of the movement. But the movement has many hurdles to face. The PTM is confronted to a boycott by the mainstream (electronic and print) media because of its blatant criticism on government institutions. Without their support, it will be increasingly difficult for the PTM to thrive and to successfully pursue its activities. This situation can be detrimental for the movement because it can affect its actual efficiency on the ground. The decrease of militant activities can be both positive and negative at the same time. Negative, because it can give Islamabad free hands to get rid of the PTM. Positive, because it can provide the PTM with opportunities to further organize the Pashtun people and therefore be more active in pressuring the authorities. Fourthly, the PTM must expand and strengthen its basis by attracting young urban Pashtuns. By doing so, the movement could take advantage of their networks and connections with state officials. The PTM has already lost the Afghan support due to the resurrection of Taliban in Afghanistan in 2021 which can have negative impacts for the movement. In any case, social movements generally cannot sustain in the long-term take for example 'Arab Spring'. Therefore, this movement has the potential to engage in active politics. PTM has the potential to transform into a progressive political party. Along with severing the inhabitants of Waziristan and the Pashtun belt PTM, as a progressive group, can play an active role in the much-needed counter violent extremism in the region.

Disclosure statement: No potential conflict of interest was reported by the author(s). Additional information. Notes on contributors. Muhammad Irfan Mahsud: Muhammad Irfan Mahsud is an Assistant Professor at the Department of Peace and Conflict Studies, National Defence University (NDU) Islamabad, Pakistan. Holding a PhD in Political Science from the University of Peshawar, his expertise encompasses research on violent and non-violent movements, ethnonationalism, religious militancy, radicalization, CVE, socio-political transformation triggered by forced migration, climate change and armed mobilization in Pakistan. In 2016–2017, Dr. Mahsud was honoured with a PhD fellowship at the University of California, Los Angeles (UCLA), USA. Proficient in qualitative research methodology, he has presented at international conferences, published in prestigious journals, and contributed to book chapters. Serving on peer review boards, Dr. Mahsud is a sought-after panelist on national television talk shows, providing insights on various issues. Engaged in research projects with UNDP, USAID, and the Higher Education Commission of Pakistan, his dedication lies in advancing understanding and resolving complex peace and conflict matters in Pakistan and the broader region. Cogent Social Sciences is a multidisciplinary open access journal with a mission to make research and knowledge accessible to everyone without discrimination. Our vision is based on inclusivity, dissemination and the power of collective wisdom. The journal's broad scope facilitates the discovery of connections between disciplines and communities. We strive to help researchers communicate with a global audience and interact with experts from across the social science community and beyond. Each submission is evaluated on its own scholarly merit and research integrity, and our expert academic editors take an objective and constructive approach to peer review. Article-level metrics let the research speak for itself. Cogent Social Sciences considers original research and review articles in the following sections and broad topical areas: Area Studies - African Studies Publishing submissions that are theoretically and empirically grounded. The Interventions must address multiple and intersecting crises confronting the world. With a particular focus on the climate crises; resources-based conflicts; tenure security; political actions of the subalterns as they confront authoritarian and hegemonic system(s). In addition, we also welcome submissions on food security and famines; the development question; land question; labor question; national question, gender, and social reproduction. As well as the perennial dynamics of migration. Area Studies - Asian Studies Provides a forum for research about Asia with multi- and interdisciplinary approaches. Topics covered include sustainability, management, society, environment, economy, and education of Asian countries or regions. Area Studies - Middle Eastern Studies The Middle Eastern Studies section of Cogent Social Sciences seeks to advance the understanding of complex social, political, and cultural dynamics within the Middle East through an interdisciplinary approach. This section welcomes submissions that integrate various disciplines, including but not limited to gender studies, conflict resolution, political science, sociology, and cultural studies. By fostering a platform for innovative and inclusive research, we aim to contribute to the production of alternative and subjugated knowledge while promoting global engagement and inclusivity. This section looks to promote interdisciplinary research. We encourage research that *synthesizes multiple academic disciplines to provide a holistic understanding of Middle Eastern issues. This includes facilitating cross-disciplinary collaborations that enrich the scholarly discourse and address multifaceted challenges from multiple perspectives. The Middle Eastern Studies section of Cogent Social Sciences aspires to become a leading platform for interdisciplinary research, supporting alternative and subjugated knowledge while fostering global engagement and inclusivity. By implementing these strategies, we aim to contribute to a more diverse, inclusive, and comprehensive understanding of the social sciences. Criminology & Criminal Justice. Promotes critical reflection and international scholarship through exploring trends in crime control and the comparative organization and operation of criminal justice systems. We encourage work that looks at how key sociological constructs such as age, class, gender and race and ethnicity interact with definitions of criminality and the contemporary management of crime. Open access. Cogent Social Sciences is an open access journal and only publishes open access articles. Publishing open access means that your article will be free to access online immediately on publication, increasing the visibility, readership, and impact of your research. The emergence of nonviolent nationalist movement among the tribes of Waziristan in Pakistan. Muhammad Irfan Mahsud, To cite this article: Muhammad Irfan Mahsud (2024) The emergence of nonviolent nationalist movement among the tribes of Waziristan in Pakistan, Cogent Social Sciences, 10:1, 2333084,DOI: 10.1080/23311886.2024.2333084. © 2024 The Author(s). Published by Informa UK Limited, trading as Taylor & Francis Group. Published online: 02 Apr 2024. CONTACT Muhammad Irfan Mahsud irfanmahsud@ndu.edu.pk. His areas of interest include climate change and security, violent and nonviolent movements, conflict, transformation and peace building in the tribal belt of Pakistan and religious militancy in Pakistan. This is an Open Access article distributed under the terms of the Creative Commons Attribution License (http://creativecommons.org/licenses/by/4.0/), which permits unrestricted use, distribution, and reproduction in any medium, provided the original work is properly cited. The terms on which this article has been published allow the posting of the Accepted Manuscript in a repository by the author(s) or with their consent. Rewriting Editor: Read Robert, Economics, University of Lancaster, Lancaster, UK. SUBJECTS: Asian StudiesAnthropologyAsian PoliticsGovernmentSecurity Studies - Pol & Intl RelnsAnthropology - Soc Sci.*

Chapter 8

Still Under Sanctions, Still Unrecognized: A Dossier of Reports on Afghanistan, International Relations and Aid Ahead of Doha III

The AAN Team 09 Jun 2024

The United Nations is due to host a third meeting of Special Envoys on Afghanistan in Doha, on 30 June-01 July 2024, to discuss Afghanistan. It is aimed, according to a UN spokesperson, at increasing "international engagement with Afghanistan in a more coherent, coordinated and structured manner." The Islamic Emirate of Afghanistan (IEA) has said it will attend if its conditions are met. It was not invited to the first meeting and declined to go to the second. While the Islamic Emirate is still not recognized and Afghanistan remains under UN sanctions, there are differing views on the way forward. Regional countries, keener to get better relations with the IEA are seemingly emerging as a block. Meanwhile, donor countries range from those still wanting to isolate the Emirate as long as it curbs the rights of women and girls and refrains from broadening the currently 'exclusive' government, to those capitals warming to the idea of better relations. In the run-up to Doha III, we wanted to bring together the reports we have written on the earlier meetings, as well as papers exploring aid and international relations in this new dossier.

Almost three years since the IEA took power, there have only been small shifts in Afghanistan's relationship with the outside world, but nothing fundamental has changed. UN and United States sanctions, which, at the takeover, suddenly applied not to an armed group but to a ruling party and therefore, the country, are still in place, albeit with waivers. No country has recognized the Emirate as Afghanistan's government, but some have gone a lot further than others in terms of sending and receiving diplomats, not a small number at the ambassadorial level. The coveted Afghan seat at the UN General Assembly is still not held by an IEA appointee. International aid, a mainstay of the Islamic Republic's public finances and economy, fell sharply when the Taliban took over, but after some months, was restored, at least in part. However, it has been largely humanitarian and almost completely off-budget. More recently, the amount of aid has declined and is set to fall further. International players may continue to insist that the Emirate respects the rights of Afghan women and girls, and minorities and form an inclusive government, but the IEA continues to assert its sovereignty over domestic matters and to decry attempts to meddle in Afghanistan's internal affairs. Its demand to be respected and recognized as Afghanistan's legitimate government has been consistent, along with pushing for sanctions to be lifted. Trade, rather than aid, is its preferred route to a more flourishing economy. The UN initiative to convene meetings in Doha emerged in recognition that this impasse was harming Afghan citizens.

The meetings were intended to be a forum for special envoys of countries with an interest in Afghanistan, mostly its neighbors, or regional players or donors, to try to establish a consensus on how to deal with the Emirate. That consensus has yet to emerge. Indeed, at the last Doha meeting, splits seemed to be emerging. AAN reported extensively on the first two Doha meetings, including the discussions beforehand and reactions afterwards, from the Emirate, Afghan women's rights activists, civil society actors and others. We also delved into the associated debates and votes at the UN Security Council, including over UNAMA's mandate renewals. We have also covered civilian aid, which is an important aspect of international relations, looking at: how the continuing skewing of aid towards the humanitarian has affected the Afghan economy; how the IEA perceives the aid industry; and whether, as the United States Special Inspector General for Afghanistan Reconstruction (SIGAR), John Sopko, has alleged that the Islamic Emirate or its officials are diverting humanitarian aid. In these reports, AAN has uncovered a much more complex, nuanced and interesting situation than media headlines had suggested. In the run-up to Doha III, we have put together reports on the Doha meetings, aid and international relations published since our last dossier.[1] They are presented in chronological order, with the most recent first. It also seemed useful to provide a brief timeline of events to do with the Doha meetings.

Timeline of Doha-related events

25 April 2023 – The Doha meetings were initiated when Secretary-General António Guterres appointed senior Turkish diplomat Feridun Sinirlioğlu as a Special Coordinator to conduct an "independent assessment" which would provide recommendations for "an integrated and coherent approach among different actors in the international community in order to address the current challenges facing Afghanistan." 1-2 May 2023 – Shortly after the Sinirlioğlu appointment, Guterres hosted the first meeting of Special Envoys (Doha I), to which the Emirate was not invited. Its aim was "to reinvigorate international engagement around key issues, such as human rights, in particular women's and girls' rights, inclusive governance, countering terrorism and drug trafficking." The special envoys also discussed their expectations from the independent assessment report. 10 November 2023 – Sinirlioğlu presented his report to the Security Council. It identified five key issues (including human rights, counterterrorism, counternarcotics, economic issues and inclusive governance), presented a "performance-based roadmap" to get to an "end state of Afghanistan's full reintegration into the international system" and proposed three mechanisms to do that, the large group of interested countries and bodies that already exists, a smaller and more active International Contact Group and, most controversially a UN Special Envoy, complementary to UNAMA, who would focus on "diplomacy between Afghanistan and international stakeholders as well as on advancing intra-Afghan dialogue." The IEA has proven implacably opposed to the last mechanism, arguing, among other things, that such envoys are appointed to countries embroiled in civil war, which Afghanistan is not.

31 December 2023 – The UN Security Council voted on the Sinirlioğlu report, but failed to reach a consensus after much discussion. In the end, it was neither fully endorsed nor rejected.

18-19 February 2024 – At Doha II, Special Envoys discussed Afghanistan in the absence of IEA representation – it had declined to attend. Differences of opinion emerged, especially between regional players, keener to strengthen ties with the IEA, and Western countries who tend to be the major donors, who range between pro-isolating France and Germany to pro-greater engagement Norway and Japan.

18-21 May 2024 – UN Under-Secretary-General for Political and Peacebuilding Affairs, Rosemary DiCarlo, visited Afghanistan to discuss the meeting with the government, diplomats and civil society. She extended an invitation to Doha III to acting Foreign Minister, Amir Khan Muttaqi, (UN press briefing here). The Emirate has yet to confirm whether or not it will attend

30 June-1 July – The Doha III meeting is due to be held with the aim, said the UN Secretary-General's spokesperson, of increasing "international engagement with Afghanistan in a more coherent, coordinated and structured manner."

Afghanistan is back on the world's agenda. The UN Security Council has met behind closed doors to hear about the recently held United Nations-convened meeting of Special Envoys on Afghanistan in Doha. The current rulers of Afghanistan, the Islamic Emirate, decided not to attend the Doha gathering and are adamantly against the planned appointment of a UN Special Envoy to coordinate and facilitate the world's engagement with the country, as foreseen by the UN Security Council's latest resolution on Afghanistan. Ahead of the Security Council's meeting to renew the mandate of the UN Assistance Mission in Afghanistan (UNAMA), which is due to expire on 17 March, AAN's Roxanna Shapour looks at what is known about the 'Doha II' gathering, at the debate among the emerging political blocks about the shape of future engagement with Kabul and how Afghans themselves view a seemingly hamstrung political process that is happening in faraway meeting rooms behind closed doors.

United Nations Secretary-General António Guterres will host a second meeting of Special Envoys on Afghanistan in the capital of Qatar, Doha, on 18-19 February 2024. Unlike the last gathering in May 2023, the Emirate has also been invited, although it has not yet confirmed that it will send a delegation. The two-day meeting is expected to focus on the UN Security Council-mandated Independent Assessment Report, particularly its recommendation for appointing a UN Special Envoy for Afghanistan, something the Emirate has emphatically opposed. Meanwhile, a January meeting of the regional countries in Kabul appears to have signalled a shift in Emirate thinking, that engagement closer to home might yield better outcomes and strengthen its position vis-à-vis its Western interlocutors. AAN's Roxanna Shapour looks at the debate around the assessment report, especially as it has solidified into the merits of appointing a UN Special Envoy, and what an Emirate tilt to the region might mean for discussions in Doha on international engagement. The United Nations Security Council has passed a resolution on the Independent Assessment on Afghanistan, which former Turkish Minister of Foreign Affairs Feridun Sinirlioğlu had put together. UNSC Resolution 2721 only passed after a month and a half of Security Council meetings, mainly held behind closed doors and two weeks of intensive negotiations on its language. The result is a resolution which failed to fully endorse the Sinirlioğlu report. AAN's team here summarises the developments around the Independent Assessment, from how it came to be proposed to its contents and the resolution passed on 29 December, the last working day of the Council in 2023.

While the Islamic Emirate of Afghanistan (IEA) maintains that it deserves full-scale recognition, it has not been given the country's seat at the United Nations. In early December 2023, the UN General Assembly will again consider whether or not to allow the Islamic Emirate to take Afghanistan's seat at the world body. The argument plays out in the context of a worldwide discussion about whether and how governments should deal with a regime that critics say denies women and girls almost every individual right, has a dire general human rights record and is narrowly based. AAN's Thomas Ruttig has been analyzing the impasse, noting the intra-Republic rivalry to also represent Afghanistan at the UN, and scrutinizing UN procedures and considerations to try to make sense of it all. This paper is an attempt to give an overview of the Afghan economy in light of two new World Bank reports, one on the economy, two years on from the re-establishment of the Islamic Emirate of Afghanistan (IEA), and a second on the welfare of households. The Emirate has not published budgets for this year or last, which makes the wealth of detail and analysis provided by these reports, both at the macro level and for families and businesses, important. This paper also draws on presentations by ministers and senior officials at televised 'accountability sessions' held over the summer in which the economy was a strong theme. The presentations were generally upbeat, portraying a picture of progress, but the larger general picture appears much bleaker, finds AAN's Kate Clark.

Diversion of aid in Afghanistan is in the news again, this time with allegations by the United States Special Inspector General for Afghanistan Reconstruction (SIGAR), John Sopko, that the Islamic Emirate or its officials are diverting humanitarian aid. Language in a draft US appropriations bill would prohibit any US assistance going "directly or indirectly" to the Taliban, something which Sopko has warned could have "serious" consequences for aid organizations. The Emirate has denied the allegations. Guest author Ashley Jackson* has been looking into the Taliban's actual influence over aid, hearing from aid workers on the ground about their experiences and delving into the role of both donors and the Emirate in its delivery. She asks if aid diversion is any worse – or better –

than the historical 'norm' in Afghanistan and suggests that, whatever its level, there is a need for a candid dialogue that would lead to practical and ethical steps to ensure aid reaches those most in need.

Despite publicly claiming to welcome international aid, the Taliban government has exercised a growing influence over humanitarian operations within Afghanistan at both national and local levels. This includes bans on women working for NGOs and the United Nations and, more recently, an order to hand over all internationally funded education projects to the Ministry of Education. These more high-profile national orders have been issued alongside hurdles and increasing suspicion at the local level, from demands for beneficiary lists to the detention of aid workers. In this report, Sabawoon Samim and Ashley Jackson look at the factors driving these restrictions on aid delivery and the dynamics that shape Taleban attitudes toward aid and aid workers. The 1-2 May 2023 gathering in Doha, hosted by United Nations Secretary-General António Guterres, brought together the representatives of 21 countries – the five permanent members of the Security Council, major donors and regional players, plus the European Union and the Organisation of Islamic Cooperation. They spent two days talking about how to engage with the Taliban, who have now been in power for 20 months, but are still unrecognized as Afghanistan's government. The gathering took place in the shadow of the extension of an Islamic Emirate ban on women working from NGOs to the UN and a chaotic few weeks for the UN. AAN's Roxanna Shapour and Kate Clark have been sifting through Guterres' press statement and the various reactions to the gathering. They ask some questions about the gathering in Doha – and try to answer them.

United Nations Secretary-General António Guterres is due to host a two-day meeting on Afghanistan with foreign envoys, beginning tomorrow, 1 May 2023, in the capital of Qatar, Doha. The Taliban have not been invited. AAN understands from sources from invited countries that the idea for the meeting emerged from visits to Kabul in January by senior UN officials trying to negotiate with the Islamic Emirate on its ban on NGOs employing Afghan women. UN Deputy Secretary-General Amina Mohammed, in particular, came away with the sense that there needed to be a political plan for dealing with the Emirate. In recent days, however, the Doha meeting has become mired in controversy over her reported suggestion that the representatives would be looking into the question of recognizing the Taliban's government. This suggestion was swiftly and categorically denied by the UN Secretary-General's spokesperson. The Taliban's extension of their ban on employing Afghan women to the UN, made almost a month ago, has only complicated everything further, as AAN's Kate Clark reports (with input from Roxanna Shapour), including appearing to throw the UN into disarray.

Anyone who lived in Afghanistan during the first Islamic Emirate will find the current stand-off between the Taleban and NGOs – and now the United Nations – over the issue of women working familiar. There is the same clashing of principles: the Emirate's position that women must largely be kept inside the home to avoid the risk of social disorder and sin, and the humanitarians' that the equitable and effective delivery of aid is impossible without female workers. The choices on the humanitarian side also feel familiar, and all unattractive: comply, boycott or fudge. AAN's Kate Clark has spoken to people who were working in the humanitarian sector in Afghanistan in the 1990s, and who continue to follow Afghanistan, to get their insights into the similarities and differences – and what, possibly, might help. Recent complex negotiations surrounding UNAMA's mandate in Taliban-run Afghanistan have shone a light on longstanding divisions among UN Security Council members concerning key issues, such as human rights, women's rights, peace and security and governance. This year, on 16 March 2023, member states agreed to resolve their differences by passing two Afghanistan-related resolutions; one that extended the UNAMA mandate until 17 March 2024 and another that requested an independent assessment of in-country efforts, with a report to be presented to the council before 17 November 2023. Meanwhile, the new Humanitarian Response Plan, which requests USD 4.6 billion to support 23.7 million Afghans in need, was launched in early March after a two-month delay. Defining the coming months as an "operational trial" period, the HRP plans for enhanced monitoring to ensure minimal conditions are met. AAN's Jelena Bjelica and Roxanna Shapour take a look at the latest developments related to the UN and humanitarian aid to Afghanistan and wonder what the efforts to increase scrutiny might bring.

Edited by Kate Clark

About The Afghanistan Analysts Network (AAN): AAN is an independent non-profit policy research organization. It aims to bring together the knowledge, experience and drive of a researchers, analysts and experts to better inform policy and to increase the understanding of Afghan realities. It is driven by engagement and curiosity and is committed to producing analysis on Afghanistan and its region, which is independent, of high quality and research-based. We are committed to be bi-taraf but not bi-tafawut – impartial, but not indifferent. Since its establishment in 2009, AAN's publications have informed and influenced the work of Afghan and international policymakers, journalists, development workers and academics and others interested in Afghanistan and its region. AAN's analysts are regularly asked to speak at conferences and briefings around the world, and frequently appear as commentators in the media. AAN has a light institutional structure that includes an Executive Board with overall responsibility for AAN and its work, and a small team of analysts and researchers working from the AAN's office in Kabul. The Afghanistan Analysts Network is registered in Germany as an association (eingetragener Verein, e.V.) with registration number VR28652B, and as a non-profit research organization at the Ministry of Economy in Kabul under registration number 341, dated 17.6.1388. AAN's work is supported by an international advisory board and members. AIM AND PRIORITY AREAS. AAN's focus is on research and on producing high-quality, impartial analysis about Afghanistan and its region. AAN's aim is to provide solid ground for informed policy-making nationally and internationally, to ensure that Afghanistan stays on the international agenda and that lessons are learnt for future policy-making. We wish to contribute to fact-based, thoughtful and nuanced reporting and debate about Afghanistan among analysts, academics and the general public – in Afghanistan and internationally. AAN's research approach is conflict-sensitive, rights-based and with a focus on gender and marginalized groups. It focuses on eight priority areas crucial for sound policy-making on Afghanistan: War and Peace.

AAN's Executive Board is responsible for the overall research agenda, management and fund-raising. The Executive Board members also serve as senior analysts. The AAN Executive Board. Kate Clark, Co-Director and Senior Analyst @KateClark66. Kate Clark has worked at AAN since 2010. She was Country Director (2014-16) and has been a co-director since 2017. Kate's interest in Afghanistan began in 1991 when she went to Peshawar in Pakistan on holiday and spent time with Afghan refugees there. In 1999, she was posted to Kabul as the BBC correspondent – at the time the only western journalist based in the country. She reported on drought and war, but also on football and tourism, travelling widely on both sides of the frontline. Kate was expelled by the Taleban in early 2001, but returned to cover the 2001 war, contributing to award-winning coverage. After 2002, Kate was based in London, but returned to make radio and television documentaries about the insurgency, weapons smuggling, opium and war crimes. At AAN, Kate focuses on the war, including civilian casualties, the Afghan Local Police and 'campaign forces' and detention and torture. She has also written on Afghanistan's plants, birds and the environment. Kate has an MA in Middle Eastern Politics from Exeter University in Britain and previously worked in the BBC Arabic Service. She has also lived, studied and worked in the Middle East. Jelena Bjelica, Co-Director and Senior Analyst @jb_aan. Jelena joined the Afghanistan Analysts Network as an analyst in October 2015 and she was elected by the AAN General Assembly as a co-director in November 2019. Between 2010 and 2014, she worked with the United Nations Office on Drugs and Crime (UNODC) in Afghanistan and later with the Afghanistan Center at Kabul University (ACKU). Before joining the UN, Jelena worked as journalist. She spent ten years covering Kosovo, Macedonia and South Serbia regions, for a number of publications from southeastern and central Europe, including establishing a Serbian language fortnightly newspaper in Prishtina, Kosovo. She has published two books on human trafficking and organised criminal networks in the Balkans and Central Europe. In 2003 she received the Reporters Without Borders' Press Freedom Award for her reporting on human trafficking in the Balkans. Her academic publications have also looked at organised crime and the subversion of international aid. Jelena holds an MA in journalism from Cardiff University. She has published in Serbian, French, Albanian and English. Former AAN Executive Board members . Martine van Bijlert @mvbijlert, Martine is a co-founder of the Afghanistan Analysts Network. She also served as AAN co-director from 2009 to 2017. Martine grew up in pre-revolutionary Iran and studied the Sociology of Non-Western Societies at Leiden University in the Netherlands. Her interest in the region was rekindled when she visited Quetta, first as a volunteer at a dental clinic for Afghan refugees in 1990 and later to study the return and new arrival of refugees in 1992-93. Since graduating, she has worked as a community development officer for MEDAIR in Grozny, Chechnya (1995) and Kabul (1997-98), with stints as an asylum officer for the Immigration and Nationalisation Service in the Netherlands in between; as political secretary at the Netherlands Embassy in Tehran (2000-04); political adviser to the European Union Special Representative for Afghanistan in Kabul (2004-07); and, after that, as an independent analyst on Afghanistan. Over the years, Martine has focused on Afghanistan's local politics, in particular in Uruzgan and surrounding provinces, the political economy, including the Kabul Bank scandal, elections and the possibilities for peace and reconciliation. Martine has published widely, travelled extensively throughout Afghanistan and is fluent in Dari. She is also a photographer and a novelist. Sari Kouvo. Sari is a co-founder of the Afghanistan Analysts Network and served as AAN co-director from 2009 to 2019. Since 2004, Sari has shared her time between work in Afghanistan, international civil society organisations, the European Union and academia. Sari holds a permanent position as Associate Professor of International Law and Senior Lecturer in Legal Theory in the Department of Law at Gothenburg University in Sweden. She has held visiting fellowships and lectured at various universities, including the Australian National University, Kent University, NATO Defense College, Vrije Universiteit Brussels, Åbo Academy University and Birkbeck University of London. Sari has published widely on issues relating to international law, human rights, transitional justice, gender and Afghanistan. Thomas Ruttig, Co-Director and Senior Analyst @thruttig. Thomas Ruttig is a co-founder and was co-director of the Afghanistan Analysts Network until 2021. He has worked on and in Afghanistan since he graduated in Afghan Studies from Humboldt University, Berlin (Germany) in 1985: as a GDR diplomat, including at the GDR Embassy in Kabul (1985-89), as political affairs officer for two United Nations missions in Afghanistan (2000-2003, including as UNSMA head of office Kabul, adviser to the Afghan Independent Emergency Loya Jirga Commission and UNAMA head of office Islamabad and Gardez), deputy to the EU Special Representative for Afghanistan (2003-2004); political adviser to the German Embassy in Kabul (2004-06), visiting fellow at the Berlin think-tank Stiftung Wissenschaft and Politik (SWP; 2006-2008) and independent political analyst, author and consultant, including as advisor to the Netherlands' PRT in Uruzgan province (2008-2009). He has altogether spent more than 13 years in Afghanistan and speaks Pashto and Dari. Thomas also has extensive experience as a foreign news editor and freelance journalist, mainly on Afghanistan, Central Asia, foreign affairs and development issues (1989-2001). He has published on a wide range of subjects, with a focus on Afghanistan's political forces, democratic development and peace. He regularly writes for German and other newspapers, mainly Berlin daily taz (die tageszeitung), and also blogs about Afghanistan in German, under Afghanistan Zhaghdablai. At AAN, Thomas focuses on war&peace issues, elections, democratic rights and political parties and Afghanistan's modern political history. He has also written on poverty, migration, the environment, Afghanistan's mineral resources and its postal system, Loya Jirgas, Afghans in World War I, Afghan-Bukharan, Afghan-Central Asian and German-Afghan relations. Advisory Board: AAN's Advisory Board consists of figures who have been and remain closely involved in Afghanistan. Members of AAN's Advisory Board are: Ambassador Ann Wilkens. Chairperson of the Swedish Committee for Afghanistan's Advisory Board; former Swedish Ambassador to Afghanistan and Pakistan. Doris Buddenberg. Former Resident Representative of UNODC Afghanistan. In November 2021, the Chair of the Advisory Board since our establishment, Ambassador Francesc Vendrell, died. He was the former Personal Representative of the UN Secretary-General (2000-01) and EU Special Representative for Afghanistan (2002-08). Dr Bernt Glatzer (†2009) German ethnologist, was a member of AAN's original advisory board.

Chapter 9

The Taliban War against Women and Children in Afghanistan

Viciousness and brutalism against women has become an unwritten law in Afghanistan where women are being targeted at home, workplace and by in-laws within the infrastructure of their cultural ports. Afghan religious clerics have been promoting the narrative that women must be at home, or in graveyards since decades. Every day, hundreds of women are being killed, harassed and abused in cities and villages of the country. Afghan women have no right to attend colleges, and universities, or adopt a private job without the consent of their husbands. The exponentially growing violence against women in four provinces of Pakistan calls for practical attention of government and international human rights forums to provide a reasonable protection to women at home and work place. This expert opinion report highlights violence against women in Afghanistan. This author has spoken to legal experts, barristers, Police officers, and some nongovernmental organizations protecting the rights of women. This chapter has made every effort to authenticate fear of persecution of Afghan women. We live in an era of fear market where only ignorance drives our thoughts and responses every day. We observe many incidents of auctions in terror markets across the globe, in which innocent women are being sold for suicide terrorism. These are spreading successfully because we do not do our homework. Islam has often been used by Afghan religious clerics for their own ambitions and motivations.

Every so often, Hadeiths of Prophet Muhammad (PBUH) were misquoted and misused by Taliban to declare jihad against women. That being the case, war on women in Afghanistan has also now entered a crucial phase. Pakistani Mullah, Imam Abdul Aziz of Red Mosque Islamabad, in his recent interview with a local journal (Quran orders to become terrorists, SAMVADA-25 August 2021) communicated that the Holy Quran had ordained Muslims to become terrorists against enemies of Allah.[1] How can Pakistani lawyers and human rights organizations change the power dynamics of extremist Taliban clerics that keep out women from their social and political movements? This is an important question but it might be a troublesome attempt to shake the power corridor of Afghanistan's religious establishment. "No nation can rise to the height of glory unless to seek the support of women in building a nation." Mohammed Ali Jinnah of Pakistan warned while speaking to the Muslim Union of Aligarh University on10 March 1944.[2]

In 2020, the World Economic Forum in its report placed Afghanistan as the least trouper in addressing gender-based violence. The country remained corrupt in the gender index of 2020. Domestic abuse and violence is not just a physical violence in Taliban misgovernment, it is a threatening behavior of Mullahs and their government officials.[3]Damaging and dangerous customary practices of terrorist Taliban and social elements against women and girls in are the pillars of patriarchal architecture based on male dominated society.[4]Implanted in tribal culture; it sometimes assumes violent form in a crime of heinous nature. Legal and judicial response to this kind of violent culture has been underwhelming. In Afghanistan, women's status revolves around various regions and classes and is very much based on different cultural traditions and values. Traditionally, women are thought to be subordinate to men and always retrieve their rights far less than their legal entitlement. A woman who is killed, beheaded or persecuted in tribal society is not considered a crime but judged as it as part of tribal honour traditions.[5] Abandonment and renunciation of a woman's access to justice is a complicated issue, where women are considered as a curse. Countless Bills, Ordinances and Laws were passed in yesteryears to exhibit their false resolve of protecting women from violence and honour killings.

In every political and social forum, women are considered a commodity by the terrorist Taliban. This led to the development of the culture of illiteracy, culture of violence and abuse. The US State Department in its recent report highlighted some aspects of women treatment by different government departments, and law enforcement agencies. The girl's virginity test has also been a contradictory issue in law courts that they need to live through a DNA test. The law does not explicitly criminalize spousal rape and defines rape as a crime committed by a man against a woman." Rape is a criminal offence in Afghan law, but in the case of a poor woman, it is interpreted differently. Influential and political entities pressuring practice of law and inculcating the police to act according to their instructions. Pakistan present the same picture. In the country report of Pakistan, the US State

Department (Country Reports on Human Rights Practices for 2021 United States Department of State. Bureau of Democracy, Human Rights and Labour-04 January, 2021) reported the Lahore High Court declaration of virginity tests, including the so-called "two-finger test" for examination of sexual assault survivors, "illegal and against the Constitution," and without forensic value in cases of sexual violence[6]

Moreover, women have been targeted by their families and husbands in case of honour killings, forced marriages and conversions, imposed isolation, and used as chattel to settle tribal disputes. Honour killing is traditionally named a form of brevity that the killer fulfils his religious and traditional duty. If a woman talks to a strange man on the phone, she is also punished for that by her husband. The police are normally hesitant to take the cases of domestic violence and consider that kind of case as family matters." On 15 July 2022; a woman in Pakistan named Koratul Aeen Baloch was tortured to death by her husband in front of her four children in Sindh province (MM News)".[7] As mentioned earlier, women in Afghanistan have limited rights in a male dominated society and face different kinds of violence such as sexual violence perpetrated by their family members, domestic abuse including spousal murder, beating, threatening of stoning to death, honor killings, torture, acid attacks and child custody problems.

There is a consensus in Afghanistan society that growing rate of violence against women is a nationwide pandemic with alarming low conviction rate due to the political and administrative influence on exercising legal powers by courts. In September 2021, Asian development Bank in its report suggested that there must be an open access to law courts for victim of sexual abuses.[8] The report mentioned Islamabad High Court case that repudiated cultural norms that supports violence against women: "In defiance of the explicit commands of Islam, child marriage, rape and honor killings are not uncommon in our society today. Women are forced into marriage against their will. Heinous traditions of honor' killing or girls given in marriage as a form of compensation and other forms of exploitation are being practiced in a State where 97% of the population professes to be Muslim. The tribal and other societal norms seem to have taken precedence over the Islamic injunctions. Female children are not safe. "The alarming aspect is that there is no outrage against the practices and mind-sets which are a blatant violation of the unambiguous injunctions of Islam. The practices and attitudes highlighted above are prevalent in our society and are public knowledge. (Abrar-ul-haq, and Ashraf, 2017) of these practices is the female victims whose heartrending stories are heard by the Courts across the country on a daily basis. These norms are not only offensive but blasphemous".[9]

On 20 July 2021, a Pakistani woman, Noor Moqadam, was killed by her living-partner in a house in Islamabad. The murder caused nationwide revulsion and prompted demands for more to be done to ensure women's safety. Moqadam's death drawn attention to the plight of women and girls in Pakistan where violence against women is not considered a serious problem. CNN noted. It brought calls for an overhauling Pakistan's criminal justice system, which has very low conviction rates, particularly for crimes against women.[10]Moreover, on Lahore-Gujranwala Motorway (M-11), three vandals raped a woman in front of her children. On 09 September 2021, Dawn reported the woman running out of fuel on a motorway of Lahore.[11]Daily Times reported (News Desk, February 03, 2021) the woman called her relatives in Gujranwala who advised her to call the motorway emergency numbers and also set off to help her. According to the complaint registered with the police by one of the woman's relatives, the car was broken into by two men who stole money and jewelry. They raped her in front of her two children in a nearby field, and then escaped. Police said she was traumatized, but later on, she did provide them with some basic descriptions of her attackers. The newspaper reported.[12] Journalist Sofhia Saifi in her CNN report (The beheading of a diplomat's daughter shows how badly Pakistani authorities are failing to protect women.[13]

The Ministry of Human Rights in Pakistan told CNN that more than 28% of women between the ages of 15 and 49 have experienced physical violence. Lawyer and women's rights campaigner, Sahar Bandial told CNN that 'Pakistan's criminal justice system saw domestic violence offenses as a "private matter" between couples and families'. People are much more comfortable with the concept of stranger violence because it externalizes the threat, a Pakistani lawyer and founder of Digital Rights Foundation, Nighat Dad told CNN.[14]" Girls, Gay, Women, transgender and religious minorities in Pakistan continue to face violence, discrimination, and persecution, with authorities failing to provide adequate protection or hold perpetrators to account, a US based Human Rights Groups noted. Human Rights Watch (HRW) in its 2022 report painted a bleak picture of civil liberties in Pakistan.[15]

In several cases in 2021, agencies blocked cable operators and television channels that had aired critical programs. "The Human Rights Watch report noted.[16]However, daily the Nation in its 23 November 2022 news report noted that Pakistani newspapers have come across many such cases where children are raped, men are tortured, and women are forced to marry or murdered for the sake of masculine honour. The Nation reported.[17] The issue of honour killing and rape under the Taliban administration in Afghanistan is deeply complicated when it comes to cultural principles of Pashtuns, Tajik, Hazara, Uzbek and Balochis tribes where they fulfil their duty of honour killings if a girl or woman enters into friendship with a stranger. Police and courts are not taking direct action against the honour killer unless cases are reported. Honour killing is an act in which a male member of a family kills a female relative for tarnishing the family's image. However, a Pakistani woman asylum seeker, Islamic Sharia Law and the Hudood Ordinance have fixed 100 lashes for her crime. The Holy Quran has strictly prohibited sex without marriage. In this report, I have already quoted verse from the Holy Quran that warn (Chapter-17: Verse-32): "And do not approach unlawful sexual intercourse". Indeed, it is ever an immorality and is evil as a way."[18] Cohabiting by an unmarried couple is illegal in Islam. Pakistani cultures do not permit cohabitation, largely owing to strongly held beliefs against pre-marital sex. Her son may possibly be killed as an illegal child born without marriage.

In fact, killing a woman in Afghan society has cultural and social backgrounds. Women are accused by family members that they bring shame and dishonor to their families, and they are rarely provided with any opportunity to prove their innocence in law courts. Pakistan is also a male dominated society where women have no right to interfere in the decision making process of tribal elders, and they can be killed in a variety of behaviors that include talking with a strange male. According to the report of the women's rights organization, Aurat Foundation-Pakistan, "a man killed his wife on the basis of just a dream he had about her committing adultery. In Afghanistan, women can also be killed for ostensibly disrespecting their husbands".[19] Pakistan is an Islamic country; its laws are made up according to Islamic teachings. In all four provinces access to justice for women has broken as the majority of women don't like to appear before a male judge, or they may possibly fear the wrath of their husbands and family members.

Barrister in the Supreme Court of Pakistan and Legal Consultant of the Ministry of Interior in Pakistan, and a former Deputy Attorney General, Muhammad Arif Choudhry told me: (27 November 2022) "Although the laws are in place but they hardly come to rescue this vulnerable segment of society from number of reasons. Mainly the social value system is an impediment on the way of implementation of these laws. The Victims in many cases are not aware of their rights guaranteed by the law due to illiteracy. In cases when someone dares to approach the law enforcement agencies, police etc. which is under direct control of the influential of the relevant areas, FIRs are not registered to ignite the machinery of law. Judicial system is also controlled by corruption, social segregation of women does not allow them to approach the police or appear before court of law for redressed of their grievances. Mainly the religious fanatics hold control of the society through their obscurantist views and unfortunately the have following in the society. In each community, Mosque is the epicenter of such myopic individuals. Society is ridden by male chauvinism which is the main cause of keeping the masses ignorant and particularly the women folk are the worst target of such conduct". Barrister Choudhry Arif said.[20]

However, to further elucidate the issue of Cohabitation, I contacted a competent lawyer, Mr. Miftahuddin Haroon of Wentworth Solicitors in Paddington London, and asked a question about the issue of cohabitation in Afghanistan. Mr. Miftahudding said: "Pashtun Culture doesn't allow cohabitation without marriage. If man and woman are found in cohabitation they are publicly stoned to death. Afghanistan is an Islamic country that doesn't allow cohabitation without marriage". Haroon said.[21] Mr. Akhtar Jaffery said that in Sindh and Khyber Pakhtunkhwa provinces, women have no access to justice.[22] A woman has to testify in front of all irrelevant people in the courtroom about the cases of rape and sexual abuse. As mentioned earlier, violence against women is a social and cultural problem. The United Nations Declaration on Elimination of violence against women has argued that domestic violence against women is not only limited to her physical, sexual or psychological violence, rather its included intimate partner violence, partner sexual abuse, dowry related violence, marital rape, sexual harassment at domestic work place.[23] Recent police reports from Pakistan authenticated that in 2020 and 2021, more than 5,279 women were raped in Punjab province, and incidents of 500 honor killings were reported by Human Rights Commission of Pakistan.

Appendix 1

The Propagation of Virtue and Prevention of Vice Law

The Islamic Emirate of Afghanistan. Ministry of Justice

In the name of Allah, the Beneficent, the Merciful

Praise be to Allah, the Lord of the Worlds. Blessings and peace upon the foremost of the messengers, and on all his family and companions.

The Law on the Promotion of Virtue and Prevention of Vice.

Article 1

This law is based on decree number 9 issued by the esteemed Amir al-Mu'minin, may

Allah preserve him, on 28/3/1444AH, corresponding to 2/8/1402 in the Hijri solar calendar [25 August 2023].

Aims

Article 2

1. The aim of this law is to organize matters related to the promotion of virtue and prevention of vice, and

2. To lay out the duties and capacities of those who are charged with enforcing this law.

Terminology

Article 3

These are the meanings of certain terms referred to in the course of this legal document:

1. *Ihtisab* [enforcement]: Conducted by the enforcer to promote Islamic law –*sharia* – and all virtuous acts that are in accordance with Islamic law and to prevent any deviation from Islamic law.

2. *Muhtasib* [enforcer]: The person who has been delegated by the Amir al-Mu'minin, or by a person authorised by the Commander of the Faithful, to carry out the task of enforcement.

3. *Muhtasib fihi* [that which is being enforced]: Actions that are subject to an enforcer's enforcement.

4. *Ma'ruf* [virtue]: Every word or deed that is approved of by Islamic law.

5. *Amr bi'l-ma'ruf* [promotion of virtue]: To require obedience to the Messenger of Allah صلى الله عليه وسلم, along with action in accordance with Islamic law.

6. *Munkar* [vice]: Every word and deed that is disapproved of by Islamic law.

7. *Nahi an il-munkar* [prevention of vice]: To prevent any such word or deed that does not accord with Islamic law.

8. *Muhtasib alaihi* [the one upon whom enforcement is being conducted]: The person from whom an enforcer requires virtuous conduct and avoidance of that which sharia disapproves.

9. *Ta'zir* [punishment]: Action taken that is in accordance with Islamic law, and this particular law, by the enforcer when some manifest act that contradicts sharia takes place.

10. *Sharia hijab*: Clothes which cover a woman's whole body from everyone [ie men] who is not her mahram [everyone who is not her close male relative] so long as those clothes are not thin, short or tight.

Area of enforcement

Article 4

This law will be implemented in all departments, in public places and for everyone who lives in the country of Afghanistan.

Responsibility for implementation

Article 5

The Ministry of Promotion of Virtue, Prohibition of Vice and Hearing of Complaints is responsible for implementing the orders contained in this law.

Establishment of virtue and prohibition of vice

Article 6

1. The Ministry of Promotion of Virtue, Prohibition of Vice and Hearing of Complaints is responsible for exhorting people to virtue and prohibiting vice, in accordance with Islamic law and Hanafi jurisprudence.

2. The Ministry of Promotion of Virtue, Prohibition of Vice and Hearing of Complaints is responsible for promoting peace and brotherhood among the population and to deter them from ethnic, linguistic and regional prejudice.

Limitation of responsibility for establishing virtue and extirpwating vice

Article 7

Everyone is able to stand up for virtue and against wrongdoing, but the responsibility for doing so has been limited to enforcers.

Abbreviation

Article 8

The Ministry of Promotion of Virtue, Prohibition of Vice and Hearing of Complaints will, hereafter, be referred to as the Ministry in this legal document.

Chapter 1

Rules for the enforcer, the enforcer and that which is being enforced, conditions, Manner and principles of enforcement.

Qualifications and attributes of a Muhtasib (enforcer)

Article 9

A person is fit to be appointed as an enforcer if he fulfils the following conditions:

1. Islam.

2. Is bound by Islamic tenets (has reached puberty and is of sound mind).

3. Has knowledge of the Islamic injunctions which he is promoting, along with the things which he is prohibiting.

4. Has a good idea of the benefits of removing vice and asserting virtue, when to be engaged in the prohibition of one, and promotion of the other.

5. A sense of justice.

6. Has the capacity to promote and prohibit.

A person is able to work as an enforcer if he fulfils the following conditions:

1. Is himself a manifestation of virtue and avoids all forms of iniquity and vice.

2. Is sincere, not ostentatious, nor seeking any worldly reward or respect of men.

3. Is kind.

4. Practices forbearance and patience.

Conditions and principles relating to enforcement and the enforcer

Article 10

Conditions and principles relating to enforcement and the enforcer are as follows:

1. Respect for everyone's [social] standing and human dignity, ensuring good treatment for everyone when promoting virtue or prohibiting vice.

2. Prohibition of any wrong behavior they see with their eyes.

3. Prohibition of any wrong behaviour they hear with their ears.

4. When promoting virtue or prohibiting vice, not prying into people's private sins; avoiding entering their homes, except in cases when it is allowed, according to Islamic law.

5. Prohibition of any wrong behaviour that is testified to by two persons whose testimony is acceptable.

6. Prohibition of wrong behaviour in such a manner that it does not lead to another wrongful act of similar or greater seriousness.

10 The Law on the Promotion of Virtue and Prevention of Vice, working translation

7. In establishing virtuous behaviour and eliminating iniquity, adhering to justice and not being discriminatory in any way.

8. When promoting virtue or prohibiting vice, dealing with more important matters before attending to other less important matters.

9. Explaining the harm in his actions to a perpetrator of vice. 10. Exhorting and admonishing in a soft manner.

11. Only using force when there is no fear of any untoward incident taking place as a result of it.

Conditions relating to the enforcee

Article 11

1) Conditions relating to the enforcee are as follows:

1. To be engaged in some wrongdoing, from which one is, from an Islamic point of view, obliged to refrain.

2. To be avoiding some good deed, which one is Islamically obliged to carry out.

2) The enforcer is obliged to promote virtue and prohibit wrongdoing when the conditions mentioned are present, in the case of the enforcee.

Conditions relating to that which is being enforced

Article 12

Conditions relating to that which is being enforced are as follows:

1. The word or action that is subject to enforcement, or that which leads up to it, is present.

2. Without having to conduct any investigation, the matter to be enforced should manifest itself in such a manner that the enforcer can either see it or hear it, or credible information about it reaches him in a manner consistent with this law.

3. The wrongdoing should be evident without it having to be ascertained through investigation.

Injunctions related to women covering themselves

Article 13

1. A woman is required to cover her entire body.

2. A woman should cover her face in order to prevent some *fitna* [social disorder or chaos, which can itself facilitate sin] taking place.

3. Women's voices (in a song, a hymn, or a recital out loud in a gathering) are also something that should be concealed.

4. A woman's clothes should not be thin, short or tight.

5. It is the responsibility of women to hide their body and their face from men who are not their *mahram* – close relatives.

6. It is obligatory for Muslim and righteous women to cover themselves in front of non-believing or loose women, so that no fitna may ensue.

11 The Law on the Promotion of Virtue and Prevention of Vice, working translation

7. It is forbidden for unrelated men to look at a woman's body or face. Likewise, women are not allowed to look at strange men.

8. If an adult woman leaves home because of some urgent need, she is duty-bound to hide her voice, face and body.

Laws for the covering of the male body

Article 14

1. The part of a man's body that should be covered is from his waist down to his knees. Knees are also required to be covered.

2. Men are required to adhere to the order contained in the first clause of this article, along with other injunctions related to segregation.

3. While pursuing pastimes and exercise, men are obliged to wear clothes that conceal the required parts of the body. Their clothes should not be very tight, nor should certain parts of the body be apparent.

Duties of the enforcer related to people covering themselves

Article 15

Enforcers are obliged to promote virtue and prevent vice with regard to both men and women, in accordance with the orders contained in this law.

12 The Law on the Promotion of Virtue and Prevention of Vice, working translation

Chapter two

Duties and responsibilities of enforcers

Actions that are required of the enforcer with regard to the veneration of Islamic holy places, the prophets on whom be blessings and peace, the gracious companions, may Allah be pleased with them, and pious predecessors, May Allah have mercy on them.

Article 16

1. An enforcer is duty-bound, in accordance with Islamic law, to ensure that Emirate functionaries and the general population accord due veneration to Islamic holy places, the prophets on whom be blessings and peace, the gracious companions, may Allah be pleased with them, and pious predecessors, May Allah have mercy on them.

2. An enforcer is duty-bound to punish any person who contravenes the order contained in clause number one, in accordance with the orders contained in this law.

The enforcer's duties with regard to the press and news organisations

Article 17

An enforcer is duty-bound to ensure that those working for the press and news organisations observe the following virtuous rules when publishing reports:

1. To publish reports that do not contradict Islamic law and religion.

2. To publish reports that do not deride or humiliate Muslims.

3. To publish reports that do not contain pictures of any animate object.

The enforcer's duties relating to traders, artisans and farmers

Article 18

An enforcer is duty-bound to ensure that traders, artisans and farmers, when conducting their affairs and carrying out their functions, observe the following rules:

1. At the set times, to offer prayers in congregation in the mosque.

2. Pay the *zakat* [tax on an increase in flocks or herds], *ushr* [tax on harvest] and fulfil other financial obligations to those who are deserving at the appropriate time.

3. To conduct their affairs in accordance with the Hanafi school of law.

4. To avoid usury, hoarding, hiding defects in some items, cheating, selling people short in weight or measure, forcing people to buy something, injustice, swearing oaths and committing other un-Islamic actions in their dealings.

13 The Law on the Promotion of Virtue and Prevention of Vice, working translation

5. To abstain from selling or buying anything that is prohibited or unlawful in Islamic law, like wine, meat that is not allowed, blood, weapons, military ammunition and equipment, along with pictures of animate objects.

6. To avoid the use of pictures of any animate object when advertising some product.

7. To avoid selling or making use of any part of the human body, such as kidneys, livers, eyes and human hair.

The enforcer's duties with regard to sightseeing and recreation spots

Article 19

An enforcer is duty-bound to ensure that staff responsible for sightseeing and recreation spots observe the following rules:

1. To construct a mosque for offering prayers in congregation.

2. To ensure that staff and tourists observe congregational prayer.

The enforcer's duties with regard to passenger vehicles, lorries, motorcycles and other such vehicles

Article 20

An enforcer is duty-bound to ensure that staff and drivers of commercial vehicles observe the following rules:

1. Not to play music.

2. Not to use intoxicating substances or smuggle items.

3. Not to transport any woman who is not covered.

4. Not to allow women to sit or mingle with an unrelated man.

5. Not to transport any woman who is not in the company of an adult male who is a close relative and of sound mind.

6. That transport companies make a schedule that ensures that drivers and passengers are praying at the proper time.

The enforcer's duties with regard to public baths

Article 21

An enforcer is duty-bound to ensure that people using public baths and swimmers cover the required parts of the body.

The enforcer's duties with regard to individual wrongful acts

Article 22

An enforcer is duty-bound to prevent the following individual, wrongful acts:

1. Adultery, whether forced or consensual, whether hidden or in public. Similarly, temporary marriage is also not allowed.

2. Fornication.

3. Lesbianism.

14 The Law on the Promotion of Virtue and Prevention of Vice, working translation

4. Anal sex, even if it is with one's own wife.

5. Pedophilia.

6. Gambling, egg-fighting, *mardaki* [a betting game played with stones in southern Afghanistan and walnuts in eastern Afghanistan], *beday* [a game played in Kandahar, Helmand, Zabul and Loya Paktia with the bones of sheep and goats], playing with walnuts and other [gaming].

7. The creation of a platform or circumstances conducive to adultery, fornication, lesbianism, anal sex, pedophilia or gambling.

8. Making dogs, cocks, quails, pheasants or any other animals or birds fight with each other.

8. Wrongful use of tape recorders or radio; making pictures or videos of any animate object on computers or mobile phones, or any other such device.

10. The sound of a woman's voice or any music emanating from any gathering or from the home.

11. The use, buying and selling, storing or smuggling of any narcotics or liquor.

12. Revealing of parts of the body that are required to be concealed.

13. Women not covering themselves properly.

14. Not praying or delaying one's prayers.

15. Omitting mandatory and obligatory prayers.

16. Not praying in congregation.

17. Neglecting obligatory fasts.

18. Shaving one's beard or reducing it to less than the width of a fist.

19. Styling one's hair in an un-Islamic manner.

20. Befriending non-Muslims and assisting them; imitating them in one's appearance or character.

21. Observing Nawruz, Shab-e Yalda [festival marking the winter solstice], fireworks night and other festivals which are common among Muslims, but have no Islamic foundation.

22. Wearing and popularising crucifixes, neckties and other such un-Islamic symbols.

23. Implementing and popularising particular practises which are disapproved of and considered innovations [that which is newly introduced, is without precedent and contravenes the Quran or the tradition of the Prophet] in trusted books of Hanafi jurisprudence.

24. Disobeying one's parents.

25. Not respecting the rights of others.

26. Dealing harshly with orphans and those who have been wronged.

15 The Law on the Promotion of Virtue and Prevention of Vice, working translation

The enforcer's duties with regard to minorities living under an Islamic government, asylum-seekers, children and the mentally handicapped

Article 23

1. An enforcer is duty-bound to prevent minorities living under an Islamic government and asylum-seekers from open perpetration of wrongful acts.

2. If a child or a mentally handicapped person commits a wrongful act, then the enforcer is duty-bound to put an end to that wrongful act.

16 The Law on the Promotion of Virtue and Prevention of Vice, working translation

Chapter three

Punishments

Punishment administered by the enforcer

Article 24

1). A person who commits a wrongful act, in plain sight, is liable for punishment from the enforcer who, once he sets sight on both the sin and the perpetrator, should deal with it in the following manner:

1. Exhortation.

2. Reminding the person concerned of the displeasure of Allah that will ensue from such an act.

3. Threatening and punishing using strong words.

4. To punish the perpetrator with a fine.

5. To detain the perpetrator in a public prison from one to 24 hours.

6. To detain the perpetrator in a public prison for one to three days.

7. Any punishment that an enforcer considers appropriate, and which is not the exclusive prerogative of a court of law.

8. The enforcer is duty-bound, in the course of promoting virtue and prohibiting vice, to observe the various stages of punishment outlined in clause one of this article.

Rights of a director and commander with regard to punishment

Article 25

1. The directors of Promotion of Virtue and Prohibition of Vice on a provincial and city level have the right to deliver punishments as laid out in a) to g) of article 24, upon witnessing any such wrongful act.

2. The commanders of Promotion of Virtue and Prohibition of Vice on a district and department level have the right to deliver punishments as laid out in a) to g) of article 24, in consultation with the director, upon witnessing any such wrongful act.

3. In case the perpetrator, following implementation of clauses 1 and 2 of this article, does not mend his ways, then his case will be referred to a court of law.

Conditions under which a perpetrator is referred to the concerned court of law

Article 26

In the following circumstances, the enforcer will refer the perpetrator to the concerned court of law:

17 The Law on the Promotion of Virtue and Prevention of Vice, working translation

1. In case someone, without any valid excuse, repeatedly omits saying his daily obligatory and mandatory prayers.

2. In case someone, without any reasonable excuse, repeatedly omits joining in congregational prayers.

3. In case any community collectively omits saying the call to prayer or offering congregational prayers.

4. In case someone, without any valid excuse, does not fast during the holy month of fasting.

5. In case children are repeatedly disobedient to their parents.

6. In case anyone mistreats an orphan or misuses their property.

7. In case a person does not perform all the virtuous acts that are required of him or does not avoid all the iniquitous acts from which he should refrain.

An enforcer's duties with regard to his prisoners

Article 27

1. An enforcer is duty-bound to release any prisoner he has in his custody, immediately, once the prisoner's term has come to an end.

2. An enforcer is duty-bound to ensure and recommend that prisoners are able to offer their daily prayers, that their daily needs are met and that necessary facilities are provided to them.

18 The Law on the Promotion of Virtue and Prevention of Vice, working translation

Chapter four

Miscellaneous Injunctions

Ensuring good relations among the general public

Article 28

In order to achieve the following objectives, the Ministry is duty-bound to consult with religious scholars, with teachers in madrasas, schools and higher learning institutes and with pious and eminent individuals:

1. In working to promote virtue and eliminate vice.

2. In preventing the enemies of Islam from popularizing iniquitous behavior.

Monitoring and evaluation

Article 29

The Ministry is duty-bound to monitor the work of those delegated with the task of promotion of virtue, eliminating of vice and hearing of complaints.

Reporting

Article 30

1. Those who work in the Ministry are duty-bound to report to the Ministry on how they have discharged their duties and performed their functions.

2. The Ministry is duty-bound to submit reports to the office of the esteemed Commander of the Faithful, may Allah preserve him.

Training and education of enforcers and workers

Article 31

The Ministry is duty-bound, keeping in mind circumstances, to hold seminars aimed at educating and training for its enforcers and workers, to ensure that they are acquainted with the orders contained this law, as well as with other legal documents and with the effective principles and methods of the promotion of virtue and prohibition of vice, along with the hearing of complaints.

Seeking guidance

Article 32

In case an enforcer should come across a situation, concerning which he has not been made aware, either in this law or in other related legal documents, then he is duty-bound to inform the director about the situation, so that a higher authority could seek guidance and direction from the esteemed Amir al-Mu'minin, may Allah preserve him.

The Law on the Promotion of Virtue and Prevention of Vice, working translation

Obtaining assistance

Article 33

Through its provincial functionaries, the Ministry is duty-bound to share its method of conducting the promotion of virtue, prevention of vice and hearing of complaints with other provincial government functionaries, so that their assistance may be available.

Presenting methodology and procedure

Article 34

In order to implement the orders of this law in the best possible manner, the Ministry should compile its methodology and procedure and present it for approval in the presence of the esteemed Amir al-Mu'minin, may Allah preserve him.

Implementation

Article 35

This law will be implemented from the day of its publication. It should be published in the official circular. Other laws, which have not been approved or published by the esteemed Amir al-Mu'minin, may Allah preserve him, or those which differ from this law, are hereby annulled.

In the name of Allah, the Beneficent, the Merciful. Praise be to Allah, the Lord of the Worlds. Blessings and peace upon the foremost of the messengers, and on all his family and companions.

THE DECREE OF THE AMIR AL-MU'MININ, MAY ALLAH PRESERVE HIM, REGARDING THE IMPLEMENTATION OF THE PROPAGATION OF VIRTUE AND PREVENTION OF VICE LAW

Number: 1

Date: 3/1/1446 AH

Article 1

I hereby endorse the Propagation of Virtue and Prevention of Vice Law, composed of one preface, four sections and 35 articles.

Article 2

This law shall be enforced from the date the decree is signed and the text of the law shall be published in the Official Gazette.

Peace be upon you and the mercy of Allah and His blessings!

Amir al-Mu'minin [Commander of the Faithful] Sheikh al-Quran and Hadith Mawlawi Hibatullah Akhundzada

The Official Gazette

Date of publication: 25 Muharram 1446 Hijra lunar .10 Asad 1403 Hijra Solar [corresponds to 31 July 2024] Serial Number: 1452

The legal documents are published in this issue:

1. The Propagation of Virtue and Prevention of Vice Law.

2. The order of the Amir al-Mu'minin, May Allah preserve him, regarding the offering of the prayer.

Date of publication: 25 Muharram 1446 Hijra lunar

10 Asad 1403 Hijra Solar [corresponds to 31 July 2024] Serial Number: 1452

The legal documents are published in this issue: 1. The Propagation of Virtue and Prevention of vice Law. 2. The order of the Amir al-Mu'minin, May Allah preserve him, regarding the offering of the prayer. Copyright: Ministry of Justice. Production Manager: Mawlawi Muhammad Afzal (Ahmad) 0773262028. Deputy: Mawlawi Abdulhaq (Sediqqi) 0767680461. Manager: Muhammad Jan Rassouli. 0747627930. Website: www.moj.gov. af. Price of this issue (based on contract): 50 Afs. Print run: 6,000 copies. Number of pages, including cover: 114. Printing House: Baheer. Address: Ministry of Justice, Department of Publications and Public Information, District 6, west of Darul Aman Palace.

About The Afghanistan Analysts Network (AAN): AAN is an independent non-profit policy research organization. It aims to bring together the knowledge, experience and drive of a researchers, analysts and experts to better inform policy and to increase the understanding of Afghan realities. It is driven by engagement and curiosity and is committed to producing analysis on Afghanistan and its region, which is independent, of high quality and research-based. The ANN is committed to be bi-taraf but not bi-tafawut – impartial, but not indifferent. Since its establishment in 2009, AAN's publications have informed and influenced the work of Afghan and international policymakers, journalists, development workers and academics and others interested in Afghanistan and its region. AAN's analysts are regularly asked to speak at conferences and briefings around the world, and frequently appear as commentators in the media. AAN has a light institutional structure that includes an Executive Board with overall responsibility for AAN and its work, and a small team of analysts and researchers working from the AAN's office in Kabul. The Afghanistan Analysts Network is registered in Germany as an association (eingetragener Verein, e.V.) with registration number VR28652B, and as a non-profit research organization at the Ministry of Economy in Kabul under registration number 341, dated 17.6.1388. AAN's work is supported by an international advisory board and members. AIM AND PRIORITY AREAS. AAN's focus is on research and on producing high-quality, impartial analysis about Afghanistan and its region. AAN's aim is to provide solid ground for informed policy-making nationally and internationally, to ensure that Afghanistan stays on the international agenda and that lessons are learnt for future policy-making. We wish to contribute to fact-based, thoughtful and nuanced reporting and debate about Afghanistan among analysts, academics and the general public – in Afghanistan and internationally. AAN's research approach is conflict-sensitive, rights-based and with a focus on gender and marginalized groups. It focuses on eight priority areas crucial for sound policy-making on Afghanistan: War and Peace. This brings together AAN's reporting on the conflict in Afghanistan, its underlying causes and drivers, the various armed actors and how it affects Afghans in their everyday lives. It includes our reporting on how the war is fought with investigations into civilian casualties, detentions and the use of torture and analysis of military strategy. A deep and nuanced understanding of the conflict also informs our reporting on the various formal and informal attempts to end the war, establish a viable peace process and, eventually, peace. Political Landscape. This encompasses AAN's reporting on Afghanistan's major political events, including elections, the formation of cabinets and other appointments, the key political actors and their trajectories, and the many under-reported political trends. We believe a greater understanding of Afghanistan´s political dynamics can help reduce polarization, encourage politics that are neither violent nor exploitative, and inform thoughtful international policies in and beyond Afghanistan itself. Rights and Freedoms. Unless specifically stated otherwise, all material on this site was created, authored and/or prepared by AAN. AAN's material is licensed under a Creative Commons Attribution-NonCommercial-NoDerivatives 4.0 International (CC BY-NC-ND 4.0), unless stated otherwise. This means you are free to copy, distribute and transmit the work, provided that it is: (1) properly attributed to AAN, with a link to the original webpage; (2) used for non-commercial purposes only; (3) not changed in any way. In all other cases, you should contact AAN for prior permission at: info@afghanistan-analysts. org. The AAN logo is the trademark of the Afghanistan Analysts Network and cannot be used without prior written permission.

Notes and References

Summary

1. Daily Dawn newspaper, 2009.

2. The Fletcher School–al Nakhlah–Tufts University Journal of Academic and Social Research, 2018 VOL.1

3. Al Jazeera report (15 July 2014

4. Lt General V.K. Kapoor (Retd) in his analysis, (Pakistani Army Operations in North Waziristan. Land Forces, Issue 04, 2014

5. Sushant Sareen (Azm-e-Istehkam: China's wish is Pakistan's command, Jun 24, 2024

6. Manuel Lamela has noted (Pakistan's Inter-Services Intelligence and its ties with radical groups. Universidad de Navarra. https://www.unav.edu/en/web/global-affairs/detalle/-/blogs/pakistan-s-inter-services-intelligence-and-its-ties-with-radical-groups.

7. On 03 May 2011. https://www.bbc.co.uk/news/world-south-asia

8. Manuel Lamela (Pakistan's Inter-Services Intelligence and its ties with radical groups. Universidad de Navarra. https://www.unav.edu/en/web/global-affairs/detalle/-/blogs/pakistan-s-inter-services-intelligence-and-its-ties-with-radical-groups

9. Research Scholar at the JNU Special Centre for National Security Studies, Wankhede Rahul Bhojraj in one of his book review (The Defense Horizon Journal, 15 August, 2023

10. The Hindu newspaper on August 31, 2024

11. Expert and writer, Senior fellow at the Wilson Center, affiliated with the South Asia Institute, and a visiting fellow at the Hoover Institution at Stanford University, Nader Nadery in his analysis of Pakistan's interference in Afghanistan and its national security challenges (Unraveling Deception: Pakistan's Dilemma after Decades of Promoting Militancy in Afghanistan and beyond. Wilson center September 26, 2023

Chapter 1: The Pashtun Tahafuz Movement (PTM) and its Fight for Justice in Pakistan

1. The emergence of nonviolent nationalist movement among the tribes of Waziristan in Pakistan. Muhammad Irfan Mahsud. (Muhammad Irfan Mahsud (2024) The emergence of nonviolent nationalist movement among the tribes of Waziristan in Pakistan, Cogent Social Sciences, 10:1, 2333084, DOI: 10.1080/23311886.2024.2333084 © 2024 The Author(s). Published by Informa UK Limited, trading as Taylor & Francis Group. Published online: 02 Apr 2024.

2. Sana Hamid. The Crisis of Pashtun Tahaffuz Movement in Pakistan, Modern diplomacy June 25, 2023

3. Osama Ahmad in his article (Nonviolence: the most effective counter-terrorism tool-May 12, 2023

4. The Mehsud with a movement. The Friday Times. 03, 02, 2018

5. Seth Uzman and Snehal Shingavi. Solidarity with the Pashtun Tahafuz Movement

6. Zalmay Azad (Pashtun Tahafuz Movement's Great Disconnect: Zalmay Azad asks the existential question about PTM: why has it struggled to establish a meaningful connection with the broader Pashtun populace?), The Friday Times. September 05, 2023.

7. Shams, Shamil (2018-04-09). Deutsche Welle.

8. Manzoor Ahmad Pashteen (February 11, 2019. The New York Times.

9. Long march against Naqeeb killing reaches Peshawar". Daily Times. 01, 29, 2018

10. Pashtuns End Protest in Islamabad, Vow to Reconvene if Demands Not Met". Voice of America. 2018

11. Pakistani rights activist arrested on charges of sedition, protests threatened". Reuters. January 27, 2020.

12. Pakistan court grants bail to activists, drops sedition charges". Al Jazeera.

13. Manzoor Pashteen released from jail". Dawn. February 25, 2020.

14. Twenty-points National Action Plan (NAP) approved by Parliament, The News International, 24 December 2014

15. A perspective on Military Courts. Mohsin Raza Malik. 22 January, 2019

16. Dr. Muhammad Zubair, 28 January 2019

17. Military Courts in Pakistan: Will they return? What are the implications? D. Suba Chandran, National Institute of Advanced Studies (NIAS) Strategic Forecast, 11, December 2017.

18. Watchdog: Pakistan Military Courts; Disaster for Human Rights. Ayaz Gul. January 16, 2019

19. On 16 January 2019, International commission of jurists deeply criticised the illegal function of military courts in Pakistan.

20. On 12 January 2019, Dr. Mehdi Hasan, Chairperson of the Human Rights Commission of Pakistan (HRCP) expressed grave concern at the government's decision to table a bill in favour of extending the tenure of military courts, which were otherwise due to end their term, Press release of the Human Rights Commission of Pakistan (HRCP). 12 January 2019.

21. Dawn, 06 Mar, 2017

22. Amnesty international in its report, 27 March 2019

23. Pak Army's confession of enforced disappearances.19 May 2019, Rahim Baloch

24. General Ghafoor admitted in a Press conference on 29 April, 2019

25. Ibid

26. Imad Zafar. Asia Times, 17 September 2019

27. January 2018, Human Right Watch Report

28. Rights Movement in Pakistan Vows to Continue Its Protests, VOA News, May 13, 2018

29. Naqeebullah was killed in 'fake encounter', had no militant tendencies: police inquiry finds, Imtiaz Ali, Dawn newspaper, January 20, 2018

30. Impact of the Pashtun Tahafuz Movement on Pakistan. takshashila.org. S Ramachandran, 2018

31. Madiha Afzal (07 February 2020) interviewed leaders of PTM for her book in Lahore.

32. On 11 February 2019, in his New York Times article, PTM leader Manzoor Pashteen gave an account of his struggle for the recovery of kidnapped Pashtun activists by Pakistan's military establishment. The Military Says Pashtuns Are Traitors.

33. Ibid

34. The Print, 17 February 2020, the Print published yell of Gul Bukhari, a Pakistani human rights activist. Gul Bukhari complained that the ISI wing of the Pakistan embassy in the UK was sniffing for her home address in London.

35. Ibid

36. Journalist Aurang Zeb Khan Zalmay in his facebook comment criticised Pakistani agencies for their campaign against Pakistani human rights activists in Britain and Europe. 17-02-2020,

37. In his New York Times article, Jeffrey Gettleman reported that Gulalai Ismail had been advocating the rights of raped women, kidnapped and tortured Pashtuns, Punjabis and Balochs since years. New York Times, 19 September, 2019.

38. On 12 October 2018, Gulalai was arrested at Islamabad Airport by the Federal Investigation Agency (FIA) on her arrival from London and her name was put on the Exit Control List (ECL), which bans her from travelling outside the country. In February 2019, Gulalai was picked by security agencies at the Islamabad Press Club while she was attending a protest for the release of PTM activists, but her name was not on the list of people arrested and she went missing for 36 hours.

39. The CIVICUS analysis of her struggle to save lives of innocent women and children noted her pain and industrious struggle. Some newspapers also published stories about her zeal and plcukiness.

40. Journalist Daud Khattak, Foreign Policy, 30 April 2019

41. Ibid

42. Pakistan: Human rights ignored in the "war on terror". Pakistan Human rights ignored in the "war on terror", Refworld. www.refworld.org. Journalist, M. Ilyas Khan (Uncovering Pakistan's secret human rights abuses, M Ilyas Khan, BBC News, Dera Ismail Khan, 02 June 2019.

Chapter 2: The Pashtun Tahafuz Movement, Forced Disappearances and Violence in Khyber Pakhtunkhwa Province

1. Human Rights Commission of Pakistan report: "State of Human Rights"2018

2. Al Jazeera, April 2019

3. Dawn. 01 May 2019, Zahid Hussain article

4. Pakistan: Investigate North Waziristan Deaths: Uphold Rights of Region's Pashtun Population. Human Rights Watch, 30 May 2019.

5. - Charles Pierson in his Wall Street Journal, Pakistani Army. 31, 2014

6. Pakistan Declares War on Pashtun Nationalism: The Pakistani military is trying to sound the death knell of the Pashtun Tahaffuz Movement. By Kunwar Khuldune Shahid, the Diplomat--May 02, 2019

7. Pashtun Tahafuz Movement: The game changer for Pakistani politics, Jaibans Singh, June 2019 45. 14 January 2020, the News International

8. Ibid

9. Ibid

10. PTM is on a peaceful quest to free all Pakistanis from oppression: The Pakistani state's repeated attacks on us only strengthen our resolve. Mohsin Dawar. Al Jazeera, 6 Dec 2019.

11. PTM will continue pressurizing government for Pakhtuns' rights: Dawar, Syhoon New, 16 February, 2010

12. Friday Times, 22 February 2019, Senator Farhatullah Babar

13. 15 January 2020, General Ghafoor shamelessly humiliated the Pashtun nation that Pakistan army will butcher their children again.

Chapter 3: The Pashtun Tahafuz Movement and War Crimes in Waziristan

1. Twenty-points National Action Plan (NAP) approved by Parliament, The News International, 24 December 2014

2. A perspective on Military Courts. Mohsin Raza Malik. 22 January, 2019

3. Dr. Muhammad Zubair, 28 January 2019

4. Military Courts in Pakistan: Will they return? What are the implications? D. Suba Chandran, National Institute of Advanced Studies (NIAS) Strategic Forecast, 11, December 2017.

5. Watchdog: Pakistan's Military Courts 'Disaster' for Human Rights. Ayaz Gul. January 16, 2019

6. On 16 January 2019, International commission of jurists deeply criticised the illegal function of military courts in Pakistan.

7. On 12 January 2019, Dr. Mehdi Hasan, Chairperson of the Human Rights Commission of Pakistan (HRCP) expressed grave concern at the government's decision to table a bill in favour of extending the tenure of military courts, which were otherwise due to end their term, Press release of the Human Rights Commission of Pakistan (HRCP). 12 January 2019.

8. Dawn, 06 Mar, 2017

9. Amnesty international in its report, 27 March 2019

10. Rights Movement in Pakistan Vows to Continue Its Protests, VOA News, May 13, 2018

11. Naqeebullah was killed in 'fake encounter', had no militant tendencies: police inquiry finds, Imtiaz Ali, Dawn newspaper, January 20, 2018

12. Impact of the Pashtun Tahafuz Movement on Pakistan's. takshashila.org. S Ramachandran, 2018

13. Madiha Afzal (07 February 2020) interviewed leaders of PTM for her book in Lahore.

14. On 11 February 2019, in his New York Times article, PTM leader Manzoor Pashteen gave an accout of his struggle for the recovery of kinapped Pashtun activists by Pakistan's military establishment. The Military Says Pashtuns Are Traitors. We Just Want Our Rights: Pakistan's powerful military is trying to crush a nonviolent movement for civil rights. Manzoor Ahmad Pashteen. 11 February 2019.

15. Ibid

16. The Print, 17 February 2020, the Print published yell of Gul Bukhari, a Pakistani human rights activist. Gul Bukhari complained that the ISI wing of Pakistan embassy in UK was sniffing for her home address in London.

17. Ibid

18. On 17-02-2020, prominent journalist Aurang Zeb Khan Zalmay in his facebook comment criticised Pakistani agencies for their campaign against Pakistani human rights activists in Britain and Europe.

19. In his New York Times article, Jeffrey Gettleman reported that Gulalai Ismail had been advocating the rights of raped women, kidnapped and tortured Pashtuns, Punjabis and Balochs since years. New York Times, 19 September, 2019.

Chapter 4: The Military Establishment, Inter-Services Intelligence (ISI) and Tehrik-Taliban Pakistan (TTP)

1. The Taliban and Post-Taliban, Musa Khan Jalalza, Sang Meel Lahore, 2003

2. Nazim Rahim, Hashmat Ali and Muhammad Javed. Analysis of Social Impacts of Terrorism and Military Operations in Pakistan in Swat. Pakistan Languages and Humanities Review June 2019, Vol. 3, No. 1.

3. Asian Journal of Social Sciences and Humanities Vol. 3(3) August 2014

4. Operation Zarb-e-Azb, 2014 Dawn newspaper

5. Nuclear Jihad in Pakistan, Musa Khan Jalalzai, 2017

6. Ibid

7. Pakistan in the eye of Thunderstorm. Musa Khan Jalalzai, 2023, India

8. Ibid

9. The July 08, 2024, directive of the Shahbaz government

10. Journalist Syed Atiq ul Hassan (Friday Times, 12 September 2024

11. 30 January 2023, BBC report

12. India Today News Desk, 15 September 2023

13. Daily Beast, 13 July, 2017

14. The Dawn newspaper described the intelligence community as "our secret godfathers" in its 25 April, 1994 article.

15. 06 October 2016, (Inter-Services Intelligence. Wikipedia, the free encyclopedia

16. On February 25, 2014, Prime Minister Nawaz Sharif approved and published the National Internal Security Policy (2014-2018) and introduced a new mechanism to counter internal and external threats. Dawn newspaper.

Chapter 5: Military Courts, Fair Trials Violations, and Rough-Handling of Pashtun and Baloch Prisoners

1. The BBC reporter, M Ilyas Khan reported from Dera Ismail Khan the killings of thousands of people by the Pakistan army. M. Ilyas Khan also reported cases highlighted by the PTM, in which the army killed women and children with impunity.

2. M. Ilyas Khan (Uncovering Pakistan's secret human rights abuses 02 June 2019

3. News Intervention Bureau -May 6, 2024

4. News Intervention Bureau reported Pakistan's backlash in Quetta for brutal torture on Baloch Long Marchers on 23 December 2023.

5. Ibid

6. Asian Legal Resource Centre (Pakistan: Alternative Report to the Human Rights Committee under the International Covenant on Civil and Political Rights. Asian Legal Resource Centre, July 2016

7. 6th Amnesty International in its January 24, 2024

8. International law. Article 14 of the International Covenant on Civil and Political Rights (ICCPR), which Pakistan has ratified, guarantees the right to a trial before a competent, independent, and impartial tribunal established by law.

9. Masoom Sanyal and Mahika Suri in their well-written analysis (In Defence of Democracy: The Pakistani Supreme Court's Decision against Military Trials of Civilians-Nov 30, 2023.

10. 28 May 2024, Daily Dawn

11. International Commission of Jurists in its analysis (Military "justice" system: a glaring surrender of human rights. Issue: Independence of Judges and Lawyers, Analysis Brief, 2019

12. Dr. Muhammad Zubair, 28 January 2019

13. D. Suba Chandran (NIAS, 11, December 2017

14. Ayaz Gul (January 16, 2019

15. In its briefing paper, the ICJ documented serious fair trials violations in the operation of military courts, and warned that high number of convictions– more than 97 percent–based on " confessions without adequate safeguards against torture and ill treatment.

16. 12 January 2019, Dr. Mehdi Hasan, Chairperson of the Human Rights Commission of Pakistan (HRCP

17. Daily Dawn in its 06 March 2017

18. Amnesty international in its report (27 March 2019

19. Ibid

20. General Ghafoor Press conference on 29 April, 2019

21. Ibid

22. Sayed Irfan Raza in his Dawn (30 January 2019)

23. Asia Times, 17 September 2019. Imad Zafar

24. 22 May, 2020, OpIndia

Chapter 6: How do Militant Organizations Respond to Counterterrorism? Introducing the LIVE Typology, with Examples from Proscription in Pakistan. Muhammad Feyyaz and Brian J. Phillips

1. See the Anti-Terrorism Act of 1997. https://pakistancode.gov.pk/english/UY2FqaJw1-apaUY2Fqa-apaUY2Npappq-sg-jjjjjjjjjjjjj.

2. The U.K. government uses "proscription" to refer to the banning of groups "concerned in terrorism" (https://www.counterterrorism.police.uk/proscription/). The U.S. government only uses the term terrorist designation for the same idea. Proscription is often a broader phenomenon—the banning of any political group—while terrorist designation is usually seen as a specific type of proscription. Since 9/11, however, the terms have become synonymous in many contexts, since terrorism seems to be the main reason groups become proscribed.

3. Yasutaka Tominaga, Chia-yi Lee, and Mengting Lyu, "Introducing a New Dataset on Designated Terrorist Organizations (DTO)," Journal of Peace Research 59, no. 5 (2022): 756–66.

4. "Jaish-e-Mohammed," Chapter 6: Foreign terrorist organizations-Country Reports on terrorism 2011, US Department of State, available at https://2009-2017.state.gov/j/ct/rls/crt/2011/195553.htm#jem.

5. Milos Popovic, "The Perils of Weak Organization: Explaining Loyalty and Defection of Militant Organizations toward Pakistan," Studies in Conflict & Terrorism 38, no. 11 (2015), 919–37; Also read, Appendix D—Statement of Reasons—Jaish-E-Mohammad (JEM), Review of the listing of AQAP and the re-listing of six terrorist organisations 2011, https://www.aph.gov.au/Parliamentary_Business/ Committees/Joint/Completed_Inquiries/pjcis/AQAP_6_terrorist_orgs/report/index; James Mackenzie and Sanjeev Miglani, "Explainer: Jaish-e- Mohammad, the Pakistan-based militants, at heart of tension with India," Reuters, February 15, 2019, https://www.reuters.com/article/us-india-kashmir-group-explainer-idUSKCN1Q41IV.

6. According to the Global Terrorism Database, JeM carried out only 18 attacks between 2003 and 2007. Attacks then escalated for years, with more than 50 in 2018. See https://www.start.umd.edu/gtd/search/Results.aspx? expanded=no&casualties_type=b&casualties_

max=&dtp2=all&success=yes& perpetrator= 20233&ob=GTDID&od=
desc&page=2&count=100#results-table.

7. Rebecca H. Best and Simanti Lahiri, "Hard Choices, Soft Targets: Terror Proscription and Strategic Targeting Decisions of FTO," International Interactions 47, no. 6 (2021): 955–85; Erica Chenoweth and Laura Dugan, "The Canadian Way of Counterterrorism: Introducing the GATE-Canada Data Set," Canadian Foreign Policy Journal 22, no. 3 (2016): 316–30; Ursula E. Daxecker and Michael L. Hess, "Repression Hurts: Coercive Government Responses and the Demise of Terrorist Campaigns," British Journal of Political Science 43, no. 3 (2013): 559–77; Jenna Jordan, "When Heads Roll: Assessing the Effectiveness of Leadership Decapitation," Security Studies 18, no. 4 (2009): 719–55; Yasutaka Tominaga, "Killing Two Birds with One Stone? Examining the Diffusion Effect of Militant Leadership Decapitation," International Studies Quarterly 62, no. 1 (2018): 54–68.

8. Michael Kenney, From Pablo to Osama: Trafficking and Terrorist Networks, Government Bureaucracies, and Competitive Adaptation (University Park, PA: Penn State University Press, 2007).

9. Martha Crenshaw and Gary LaFree, Countering Terrorism (Washington, DC: Brookings Institution Press, 2017), especially chapter 6; Cynthia Lum, Leslie W. Kennedy, and Alison J. Sherley, "The Effectiveness of Counter-Terrorism Strategies: Campbell Systematic Review Summary," Campbell Systematic Reviews 2, no. 1 (2006): 1–50.

10. Gary LaFree and Joshua D. Freilich, "Government Policies for Counteracting Violent Extremism," Annual Review of Criminology 2 (2019): 383–404.

11. Patrick B. Johnston, "Does Decapitation Work? Assessing the Effectiveness of Leadership Targeting in Counterinsurgency Campaigns," International Security 36, no. 4 (2012): 47–79; Bryan C. Price, "Targeting Top Terrorists: How Leadership Decapitation Contributes to Counterterrorism," International Security 36, no. 4 (2012): 9–46.

12. Jenna Jordan, "Attacking the Leader, Missing the Mark: Why Terrorist Groups Survive Decapitation Strikes," International Security 38, no. 4 (2014): 7–38.

13. Victor Asal, Brian J. Phillips, and R. Karl Rethemeyer, Insurgent Terrorism: Intergroup Relationships and the Killing of Civilians (New York, NY: Oxford University Press, 2022); Brandt, Patrick T., Justin George, and Todd Sandler, "Why Concessions Should not be Made to Terrorist Kidnappers," European Journal of Political Economy 44 (2016): 41–52; Daxecker and Hess, "Repression Hurts"; James A. Piazza, "Repression and Terrorism: A Cross-national Empirical Analysis of Types of Repression and Domestic Terrorism," Terrorism and Political Violence 29, no. 1 (2017): 102–18; Sambuddha Ghatak and Aaron Gold, "Development, Discrimination, and Domestic Terrorism: Looking Beyond a Linear Relationship," Conflict Management and Peace Science 34, no. 6 (2017): 618–39.

14. Governments do not seem to indicate explicitly the goals behind terrorist designation. However, Audrey Cronin summarizes this advantage of terrorist lists: they bring "legal clarity to efforts to identify and prosecute members of terrorist organizations and those who support them. See Audrey Kurth Cronin, "The 'FTO List' and Congress: Sanctioning Designated Foreign Terrorist Organizations." Congressional Research Service, Library of Congress, 2003, page 7. On goals of counterterrorism more generally, See Crenshaw and LaFree, Countering Terrorism, especially pages 170–6.

15. These are among some of the advantages of terrorist designation discussed by Cronin (See above).

16. Best and Lahiri, "Hard Choices, Soft Targets"; Brian J. Phillips, "Foreign Terrorist Organization Designation, International Cooperation, and Terrorism," International Interactions 45, no. 2 (2019): 316–43; Mitchell Radtke and Hyeran Jo, "Fighting the Hydra: United Nations Sanctions and Rebel Groups," Journal of Peace Research 55, no. 6 (2018): 759–73; Yasutaka Tominaga, Chia-yi Lee, and Mengting Lyu, "Introducing a New Dataset on Designated Terrorist Organizations (DTO)," Journal of Peace Research 59, no. 5 (2022): 756–66.

17. Julia Palmiano Federer, "We do Negotiate with Terrorists: Navigating Liberal and Illiberal Norms in Peace Mediation," Critical Studies on Terrorism 12, no. 1 (2019): 19–39; Sophie Haspeslagh, "The 'Linguistic Ceasefire': Negotiating in an Age of Proscription," Security Dialogue 52, no. 4 (2021): 361–79.

18. Hyeran Jo, Brian J. Phillips, and Joshua Alley, "Can Blacklisting Reduce Terrorist Attacks?" The Power of Global Performance Indicators (2020): 271–99.

19. Lee Jarvis and Tim Legrand. Banning them, Securing Us?: Terrorism, Parliament and the Ritual of Proscription (Manchester University Press, 2020).

20. Michael Vasseur, Chad C. Serena, Colin P. Clarke, Irina A. Chindea, Erik E. Mueller, and Nathan Vest, Understanding and Reducing the Ability of Violent Nonstate Actors to Adapt to Change (Santa Monica, CA: RAND, 2022). See also Brian A. Jackson, John C. Baker, Kim Cragin, John Parachini, Horacio R. Trujillo, and Peter Chalk, Aptitude for Destruction. Volume 1. Organizational Learning in Terrorist Groups and its Implications for Combating Terrorism (Santa Monica, CA: Rand Corporation, 2005).

21. Mia Bloom, Dying to Kill: The Allure of Suicide Terror (Columbia University Press, 2005).

22. Lindsey A. O'Rourke, "What's Special about Female Suicide Terrorism?" Security Studies 18, no. 4 (2009): 681–718.

23. Mitchell Radtke and Hyeran Jo, "Fighting the Hydra: United Nations Sanctions and Rebel Groups," Journal of Peace Research 55, no. 6 (2018): 759–73. See also Jo, Phillips, and Alley, "Can Blacklisting Reduce Terrorist Attacks?"

24. Joshua Tschantret, "Repression, Opportunity, and Innovation: The Evolution of Terrorism in Xinjiang, China," Terrorism and Political Violence 30, no. 4 (2018): 569–88.

25. Kenney, From Pablo to Osama.

26. John Ishiyama, "Introduction to the Special Issue 'From Bullets to Ballots': The Transformation of Rebel Groups into Political Parties'," Democratization 23, no. 6 (2016): 969–71; Benjamin Acosta, "From Bombs to Ballots: When Militant Organizations Transition to Political Parties," The Journal of Politics 76, no. 3 (2014): 666–83; See also Leonard Weinberg, Ami Pedahzur, and Arie Perliger, Political Parties and Terrorist Groups, Vol. 10 (New York, NY: Routledge, 2008).

27. For example: Robert J. Art, and Louise Richardson, Democracy and Counterterrorism: Lessons from the Past (Washington, DC: US Institute of Peace Press, 2007); Erica Chenoweth, Richard English, Andreas Gofas, and Stathis N. Kalyvas, eds. The Oxford Handbook of Terrorism (New York, NY: Oxford University Press, 2019); Martha Crenshaw, ed. Terrorism in Context (University Park, PA: Penn State Press, 2010); Audrey Kurth Cronin, How Terrorism Ends: Understanding the Decline and Demise of Terrorist Campaigns (Princeton, NJ: Princeton University Press, 2009).

28. Hyeran Jo, and Catarina P. Thomson. "Legitimacy and Compliance with International Law: Access to Detainees in Civil Conflicts, 1991–2006," British Journal of Political Science 44, no. 2 (2014): 323–55; Hyeran Jo, Compliant Rebels (Cambridge, UK: Cambridge University Press, 2015).

29. Andrew H. Kydd and Barbara F. Walter, "The Strategies of Terrorism," International security 31, no. 1 (2006): 49–80.

30. Ethan Bueno De Mesquita, "Conciliation, Counterterrorism, and Patterns of Terrorist Violence," International Organization 59, no. 1 (2005): 145–76. But also See Jakana Thomas, "Rewarding Bad Behavior: How Governments Respond to Terrorism in Civil War," American Journal of Political Science 58, no. 4 (2014): 804–18.

31. Erica Chenoweth, "Terrorism and Democracy." Annual Review of Political Science 16 (2013): 355–378; Chia-yi Lee, "Democracy, Civil Liberties, and Hostage-Taking Terrorism," Journal of Peace Research 50, no. 2 (2013): 235–48; Robert A. Pape, "The Strategic Logic of Suicide Terrorism," American Political Science Review 97, no. 3 (2003): 343–61.

32. Chenoweth, "Terrorism and Democracy."

33. Victor Asal and R. Karl Rethemeyer, "The Nature of the Beast: Organizational Structures and the Lethality of Terrorist Attacks," The Journal of Politics 70,

no. 2 (2008): 437–49; Ido Levy, "Lethal Beliefs: Ideology and the Lethality of Terrorist Organizations," Terrorism and Political Violence 35, no. 4 (2023): 811–27; James A. Piazza, "Is Islamist Terrorism more Dangerous?: An Empirical Study of Group Ideology, Organization, and Goal Structure," Terrorism and Political Violence 21, no. 1 (2009): 62–88; Jessica Stern, Terror in the Name of God (New York: Ecco, 2003).

34. MarkJuergensmeyer, "Terror Mandated by God," Terrorism and Political Violence 9, no. 2 (1997): 16–23.

35. Michael C. Horowitz, "Nonstate Actors and the Diffusion of Innovations: The Case of Suicide Terrorism," International Organization 64, no. 1 (2010): 33–64.

36. Tricia Bacon, Why Terrorist Groups form International Alliances (Philadelphia, PA: University of Pennsylvania Press, 2018).

37. Mia Bloom, Dying the Kill: The Allure of Suicide Terror (New York: Columbia University Press, 2005).

38. Brian J. Phillips and Kevin T. Greene, "Where is Conflict Research? Western Bias in the Literature on Armed Violence," International Studies Review 24, no. 3 (2022): 1–25.

39. John Gerring, "What is a Case Study and What is it Good for?" American Political Science Review 98, no. 2 (2004): 341–54.

40. Lawrence Ziring, "Pakistan: A Political Perspective," Asian Survey, 15, no. 7 (1975): 629–44.

41. For a history of the evolution of anti-terrorism laws in Pakistan, read Shabana Fayyaz, "Responding to Terrorism: Pakistan's Anti-Terrorism Laws," Perspectives on Terrorism 2, no. 6 (2008): 10–9.

42. Christina Lamb, Waiting for Allah: Pakistan's Struggle for Democracy (New Delhi:Viking, 1991), 91; Luqman Saeed, S. H. Syed, and R. P. Martin, "Historical Patterns of Terrorism in Pakistan", Defense & Security Analysis 30, no. 3 (2014): 209–29.

43. Saeed, Syed and Martin, "Historical Patterns of Terrorism in Pakistan."

44. S. Vali Nasr, "Islam, the State and the Rise of Sectarian Militancy in Pakistan," in Nationalism Without a Nation, ed. C. Jaffrelot (London: Zed Books, 2002), 85–114.

45. Hassan Abbas, "The Black-Turbaned Brigade: The Rise of TNSM in Pakistan," Terrorism Monitor 4 (2006): 1–4.

46. Christophe Jaffrelot, The Pakistan Paradox: Instability and Resilience (Haryana: Random House, 2015).

47. South Asia Terrorism Portal, "Sipah-e-Sahaba Pakistan." http://www.satp.org/ satporgtp/ countries/pakistan/terroristoutfits/Ssp.htm.

48. Abdul Sayed and Amira Jadoon, Lashkar-e-Jhangvi's Role in the Afghanistan-Pakistan Militant Infrastructure: Current Trends in Islamist Ideology (Washington, DC: Hudson Institute, 2023).

49. See note 43 above.

50. Muhammad Feyyaz, "Religion, Ethnicity, Social Organizations and Terrorists' Behavior—A Case of Taliban Movement in Pakistan," Behavioral Sciences of Terrorism and Political Aggression 8, no. 2 (2016). 111–34.

51. Hassan Abbas, "A profile of Tehrik-i-Taliban Pakistan," CTC Sentinel 1, no. 2 (2008): 1–4.

52. Muhammad Feyyaz, "Facets of Religious Violence in Pakistan," Counter Terrorist Trend and Analysis 5, no. 2 (2013): 9–13; Muhammad Feyyaz, "Terrorism Can and Should be Defined. But How?" Strategic Analysis 43, no. 4 (2019): 310–27; Milos Popovic, "The Perils of Weak Organization."

53. Popovic, "The Perils of Weak Organization."

54. For a comprehensive account of Pakistan's war against terrorism, read Muhammad Feyyaz, "Countering Terrorism in Pakistan: Challenges, Conundrum and Resolution," in Non-Western Response to Terrorism, ed. M. J. Boyle (Manchester, UK: Manchester University Press, 2019).

55. To understand why these groups generally stayed loyal to the state, read C. Christine Fair, "Lashkar-e-Taiba and the Pakistani State," Survival 53, no. 4 (2011): 29–52; Popovic, "The Perils of Weak Organization."

56. Samina Yasmeen, Jihad and Dawah (London: Hurst, 2017), 46–50.

57. Amira Jadoon, The Evolution and Potential Resurgence of Tehrik e Taliban Pakistan (Washington DC: USIP, 2021); Asfandyar Mir, After the Taliban's Takeover: Pakistan's TTP Problem (Washington DC: USIP, 2022).

58. According to the latest listing, 78 Organizations have been proscribed by the Pakistani Ministry of Interior since 1997. Available at https://nacta.gov.pk/wp-content/uploads/2018/12/Proscribed-OrganizationsEng-3.pdf.

59. Lamb, Waiting for Allah; Pervez Hoodbhoy, Pakistan Origins, Identity and Future (Lahore: Folio Books, 2023).

60. Read foot notes 64–68, The Anti-Terrorism Act 1997, https://punjabcode.punjab.gov.pk/ uploads/articles/the-anti-terrorism-act-1997-pdf.pdf.

61. Following the United States and other countries, Pakistan started a comparable proscription regime in the early 2000s. As other scholarship suggests, the framework of "terrorism" had not been used as frequently to describe oppositional violence in earlier decades. Lisa Stampnitzky, Disciplining Terror: How Experts Invented "Terrorism" (Cambridge, UK, 2013), 51–3; Muhammad Feyyaz and Sadaf Husnain Bari, "Understanding India and Pakistan's Intriguing Terrorism Discourses," Critical Studies on Terrorism (2024: Online ahead of print).

62. Salahuddin Haider and Nilofar Suhrawardy, "Musharraf Bans Key Militant Groups," Arab News, January 13, 2002.

63. Kalbe Ali and Munawer Azeem, "Ludhianvi Hopeful of ASWJ's 'Unbanning,'" Dawn, March 29, 2017, https://www.dawn.com/news/1323522/ludhianvi-hopeful-of-aswjs-unbanning.

64. See note 48 above.

65. Syed Shoaib Hasan, "Pakistan Bans Ahle Sunnah Wal Jamaat Islamist Group," BBC News, March 9, 2012.

66. Ibid.

67. Tariq Butt, "Inconsequential Proscription: TLP Contesting Elections as it is Registered with ECP," The News International, July 15, 2021.

68. Tahir Sherani, "Govt revokes TLP's Proscribed Status," Dawn, November 7, 2021, https://www.dawn.com/news/1656594.

69. For details, read United Nations Security Council: Hafiz Muhammad Saeed, https://www.un.org/securitycouncil/   sanctions/1267/aq_sanctions_list/summaries/individual/hafiz-muhammad-saeed.

70. Yashwant Raj, UN rejects Hafiz Saeed's appeal to remove name from list of banned terrorists: Sources, Hindustan Times, March 7, 2019. In early 2018, Pakistan announced plans to take over the entire infrastructure of JuD and its charities, e.g., FIF, present in over 100 cities of Pakistan. JuD termed the government move illegal and resolved, "We will not keep silent. We will fight a legal battle." The government subsequently proscribed it and all affiliated organizations in 2019.

71. Waqar Gillani, "Finding relief in Jihad," TNS, January 25, 2015, http://tns.thenews.com.pk/jamaat-ud-dawa-finding-relief-in-jihad-through-falah-e-insaniat-foundation/; Ayaz Gul, "Pakistan Moves to Ban Charities Linked to Hafiz Saeed," VOA, February 12, 2018, https://www.voanews.com/a/pakistan-moves-ban-charities-linked-hafiz-saeed/4250654.html.

72. Asif Shahzad, "Exclusive—Pakistan Plans Takeover of Charities run by Islamist Figure U.S. has Targeted," Reuters, January1, 2018.

73. Sutirtho Patranobis, "China blocks India's Move to Ban Jaish chief Masood Azhar, Again," Hindustan Times, October 2, 2016.

74. For listing, See UNSC-Mohammad Azhar Masood Alvi, https://www.un.org/securitycouncil/ content/mohammad-masood-azhar-alvi.

75. Animesh Roul, "Pakistan's Lashkar-e-Taiba Chooses between Kashmir and the Global Jihad," Terrorism Focus 6, no. 3 (2009).

76. Shakeel Karar, "Banned ASWJ Chief Ahmed Ludhianvi Removed from Fourth Schedule," DAWN, June 28, 2018.

77. International Crisis Group (ICG), Pakistan's Jihadist Heartland: Southern Punjab (Brussels, , Belgium, 2016), 6.

78. Al Rashid Trust: UN security council, available at https://www.un.org/securitycouncil/ sanctions/1267/aq_sanctions_list/summaries/ entity/al-rashid-trust.

79. Harkat-ul-Mujahideen. South Asia Terrorism Portal.

80. "Special Analysis," Defense Intelligence Agency, January 14, 2002, https://www.dia.mil/FOIA/FOIA-Electronic-Reading-Room/FileId/161399/.

81. Riaz Masroor, "How is the Death of Indian Army Colonel Major...?" BBC Urdu, Srinagar, September 14, 2023, https://www.bbc.com/urdu/articles/cgezpv7qqeno.

82. India revokes Kashmir's special status, Al Jazeera, September 4, 2019; Saral Sharma, "The Political Impact of India's Removal of Jammu & Kashmir's Special Status," South Asian Voices, August 19, 2019.

83. See note 80 above.

84. Pakistan's counter-extremism challenge and policy recourse, PIPS, Webinar, June 2021, https://www.pakpips.com/web/wp-content/uploads/2021/06/Full-webinar-report_for-website.pdf.

85. Naimat Khan, "Sindhi, Baloch 'Separatists' Forming Ties in Sindh, Pakistani Officials Say," Arab News, July 13, 2020; Safdar Sial and Ahmed Ali, "Overview of Security in 2020: Critical Challenges and Recommendations," in Pakistan Security Report 2020 (Islamabad: PIPS, 2021), 35.

86. Popovic, "The Perils of Weak Organization"; Mackenzie and Miglani, "Explainer."

87. See note 53 above.

88. Roul, "Pakistan's Lashkar-e-Taiba Chooses Between Kashmir and the Global Jihad."

89. See note 53 above.

90. Zia Khan, "Militant Group's Resurgence: Dreaded Jaish Looks to Rise Again," Express Tribune, August 19, 2011.

91. Abid Hussain, "Pakistan Removed from Global 'Terrorism' Financing List," Al Jazeera, October 21, 2022.

92. Lamb, Waiting for Allah.

93. See note 4 above.

94. Khan, "Militant Group's Resurgence."

95. "Treasury Targets Pakistan-Based Terrorist Organisations Lashkar-e-Tayyiba and Jaish-e-Mohammed," Press release, U.S. Treasury Department, November 4, 2010.

96. Pepe Escobar, "Anatomy of a 'Terrorist' NGO," Asia Times, October 26, 2001.

97. Ibid.

98. See note 80 above.

99. International Crisis Group (ICG), Pakistan's Jihadist Heartland, 6.

100. "India Sponsoring Terrorism in Pakistan alleges Rehman Malik," Hindustan Times, September 23, 2009; David Wright-Neville, Dictionary of Terrorism (Cambridge, UK: Polity Press, 2010), 48; Asad Kharal, "Foreign Intelligence Services Bankrolling Terror: Report," Express Tribune, September 2, 2012; Balochistan: Giving the People a Chance (Lahore: Human Rights Commission of Pakistan, 2013), 21.

101. Gary LaFree, Laura Dugan, and Raven Korte, "The Impact of British Counterterrorist Strategies on Political Violence in Northern Ireland: Comparing Deterrence and Backlash Models," Criminology 47, no. 1 (2009): 17–45.

102. Feyyaz and Bari, "Understanding India and Pakistan's Intriguing Terrorism Discourses": Online ahead of print; Nikita Saxena, "Good Faith, Bad Faith," Caravan, May 15, 2019, https://caravanmagazine.in/religion/elections-2019-hindu-terror-islamic-sikh-terrorism-mac-narendra-modi.

103. Benjamin Acosta, "Reconceptualizing Resistance Organizations and Outcomes: Introducing the Revolutionary and Militant Organizations Dataset (REVMOD)," Journal of Peace Research 56, no. 5 (2019): 724–34; Dongfang Hou, Khusrav Gaibulloev, and Todd Sandler, "Introducing Extended Data on Terrorist Groups (EDTG), 1970 to 2016," Journal of Conflict Resolution 64, no. 1 (2020): 199–225; Iris Malone, "Unmasking Militants: Organizational Trends in Armed Groups, 1970–2012," International Studies Quarterly 66, no. 3 (2022): 1–12.

104. Yasutaka Tominaga, Chia-yi Lee, and Mengting Lyu, "Introducing a New Dataset on Designated Terrorist Organizations (DTO)," Journal of Peace Research 59, no. 5 (2022): 756–66.

105. See for example: Voice of America, "Ban on Islamic Organization Draws Mixed Reactions in India," September 30, 2022, https://www.voanews.com/a/ban-on-islamic-organization-draws-mixed-reactions-in-india/6771344.html.

Chapter 7: The Emergence of Nonviolent Nationalist Movement among the Tribes of Waziristan in Pakistan. Muhammad Irfan Mahsud

1. Until 2018, the Federally Administered Tribal Areas (FATA) was a semi-autonomous tribal region within the Pakistan federal system. Located in northwestern Pakistan, FATA consisted of seven Tribal Agencies (Bajaur, Mohmand, Khyber, Orakzai, Kurram, North Waziristan and South Waziristan) and six Frontier Regions (Bannu, Dera Ismail Khan, Kohat, Lakki

Marwat, Peshawar, Tank). In 2018, the FATA were merged within the bigger state of Khyber Pakhtunkhwa. For greater clarity, the name "erstwhile FATA" is kept throughout the note rather than a reference to a given territory within Khyber Pakhtunkhwa.

2   Primary occupations in Waziristan are agriculture, pastoralism, mining, forestry and foreign remittances from the workers based in Gulf States. See Ahmed (Citation2004). The rise of conflict in the post 2003-2004 period damaged the already fragile economic structure in Waziristan (Haider & Jameel, Citation2017).

3   The Jirga system is a Pashtun tribal tradition. Local life is ruled by a council of elders that is particularly active in conflict-settlements.

4.   The Mahsud represent one of the most important tribal group in South Waziristan.

5   Waziristan was divided by the British rulers for administrative purpose. On the ground, there is no ethnic, linguistic or social distinctions to support the division of Waziristan in two parts.

6   "Under the FCR, an innocent individual can be imprisoned for the crimes of their kin, the government can displace entire villages without compensation, explanation, or warning, and individuals can languish behind bars for up to three years without any charges being filed" Akins (Citation2020).

7   Muhammad Qayyum, tribal elder, interview, South Waziristan, 06 December 2019.

8   Naeem Khan, lawyer, interview, District Tank, 15 December 2019.

9   Muhammad Azam, a PTM activist, interview, District Tank, 17 December 2019.

10   Schools are still active (M.S. Khan, Citation2018).

11   Ishtiaq Mehsud, journalist in Waziristan, interview, District Dera Isamil Khan, 01 December 2019.

12   This input is based on the agglomeration of different interviews.

13   The Pashtun minority is not the sole group that feel un- or under- represented within the political system of Pakistan.

14   The traditional Mazari hat is now nicknamed the "Pashteen hat".

15   Ishtiaq Mehsud, journalist in Waziristan, interview, District Dera Isamil Khan, 04 December 2019.

16   The ANP was also a partner of the Pakistan People's Party in the central government led by Yousef Raza Gillani.

17   Ali Khan, former ANP activist now member of PTM, interview, District Dera Ismail Khan, 03 December 19.

18 Shaherullah, university student, interview, District Bannu, 07 December 2019.

19 Permit cards were issued by the government to the Mahsuds so that they can enter their area. Without a permit card, one was not allowed to access his area.

20 Muhammad Qayyum, tribal elder, interview, South Waziristan, 06 December 2019.

21 Naseer Noreen, professor in University of Peshawar, interview, District Peshawar, 02 January 2020.

22 Naseer Noreen, professor in University of Peshawar, interview, District Peshawar, 02 January 2020.

23 Soharab Khan, researcher student and a PTM activist, interview, North Waziristan, 23 December 2019.

24 Ishtiaq Mehsud, journalist in Waziristan, interview, District Dera Isamil Khan, 04 December 2019.

25 Ibid.

26 Sohail Muhammad, one of the PTM's main leaders, interview, District Dera Isamil Khan, 04 December 2019.

27 Muhammad Khalil, retired bureaucrat at the top level, interview, South Waziristan, 21 December 2019.

28 Shaherullah, university student, interview, District Bannu, 07 December 2019.

References

Abbas, H. (2008). A profile of Tehrik-i-Taliban Pakistan. Military Academy West Point NY Combating Terrorism Center. Google Scholar

Abbas, H. (2009). Defining the Punjabi Taliban network. CTC Sentinel, 2(4), 1–15. Google Scholar

Abbas, H. (2010). Militancy in Pakistan's borderlands: Implications for the nation and for Afghan policy. Century Foundation. Google Scholar

Abbas, H. (2014). The Taliban revival: violence and extremism on the Pakistan-Afghanistan frontier. Yale University Press. Google Scholar

Ahmed, A. S. (2004). Resistance and control in Pakistan (2nd ed.). Routledge. View Google Scholar

Ahmed, R. Q., & Khan, R. (2022). The rise of peripheral nationalism in Pakistan and the Pashtun Tahafuz movement. Asian Ethnicity, 23(2), 215–229. https://doi.org/10.1080/14631369.2020.1785840. View Web of Science °Google Scholar

Akhtar, A. S. (2021). The war of terror in praetorian Pakistan: The emergence and struggle of the Pashtun Tahaffuz movement. Journal of Contemporary Asia,

51(3), 516–529. https://doi.org/10.1080/00472336.2020.1809008. View Web of Science °Google Scholar

Akins, H. (2020). FATA and the frontier crimes regulation in Pakistan: The enduring legacy of British colonialism. The Howard H. Baker Jr Center for Public Policy Brief. November 2017; 5:17, 27 April 2020. Google Scholar

Ali, I. (2018). Naqeebullah was killed in 'fake encounter', had no militant tendencies: Police inquiry finds. Daily Dawn. 20 January. https://www.dawn.com/news/1384163. Google Scholar

Arsalan, A. (2018). Pashtun protestors hold out for concrete assurances. The Express Tribune, Pakistan. 09 February. https://tribune.com.pk/story/1630115/1-pashtun-protesters-hold-concrete-assurances/.Google Scholar

Arshad, A. (2010). Militancy and socio-economic problems: A case study of Pakistan. National Institute of Pakistan Studies (NIPS). Google Scholar

Aslam, W., & Neads, A. (2021). Renegotiating societal-military relations in Pakistan: the case of the Pashtun Tahafuz Movement. Democratization, 28(2), 265–284. https://doi.org/10.1080/13510347.2020.1816965. View Web of Science °Google Scholar

Baloch, S. M., & Bugti, R. (2018). Return from a Pakistan Dungeon. The Diplomat, Washington D. C. USA. 05 November. https://thediplomat.com/2018/11/return-from-a-pakistan-dungeon/. Google Scholar

Banerjee, M. (2000). The Pathan unarmed: Opposition & memory in the North West Frontier. School of American Research Press. Google Scholar

Barfield, T. (2022). Afghanistan: A cultural and political history. Princeton University Press.View Google Scholar

Beattie, H. (2019). Empire and tribe in the Afghan frontier region: Custom, conflict and British strategy in Waziristan until 1947. Bloomsbury Publishing. View Google Scholar

Borchgrevink, K. (2010). Beyond borders: Diversity and transnational links in Afghan religious education. PRIO paper. PRIO. Google Scholar

Buechler, S. M. (1995). New social movement theories. The Sociological Quarterly, 36(3), 441–464. https://doi.org/10.1111/j.1533-8525.1995.tb00447.xView Web of Science °Google Scholar

Caron, J., & Khan, S. (2022). Writing war, and the politics of poetic conversation. Critical Asian Studies, 54(2), 149–170. https://doi.org/10.1080/14672715.2022.2030776.View Web of Science °Google Scholar

Chughtai, M. W. (2013). The impact of rising terrorism and military operations on socio economic culture of federally administered tribal areas (FATA) of Pakistan. A Journal of Peace and Development, 3(1), 18–32. Google Scholar

Dawar, A. I. (2021). Are you a spy? On the inconveniences of conventional methodology in terror wrap ethnography. Qualitative Research Journal, 21(1), 29–39. https://doi.org/10.1108/QRJ-11-2019-0091. View Web of Science °Google Scholar

European Asylum Report Office. (2019). Pakistan security situation country of origin information report. Google Scholar

Fozia, S., & Khan, S. (2017). Reform process in the federally administered tribal areas and the future of frontier crimes regulation (FCR): A local perspective. Punjab University. Google Scholar

Gandhi, R. (2008). Ghaffar Khan, nonviolent badshah of the Pakhtuns. Penguin Books India. Google Scholar

Haider, B., & Jameel, S. (2017). Geneses, causes, and ramification of militancy in FATA in the post 9/11 scenario. Google Scholar

Hameed, N. (2015). Struggling IDPS of North Waziristan in the wake of operation Zarb-e-Azb. NDU Journal, 29(1), 95–116. Google Scholar

Haroon, S. (2007). Frontier of faith: Islam in the Indo-Afghan borderland. Google Scholar

Haroon, S. (2008). The rise of Deobandi Islam in the north-west frontier province and its implications in colonial India and Pakistan 1914–19961. Journal of the Royal Asiatic Society, 18(1), 47–70.View Google Scholar

Haroon, S. (2012). 3. Religious revivalism across the Durand line. In S. Bashir & R. D. Crews (Eds.), Under the drones (pp. 45–59). Harvard University Press. View Google Scholar

Hopkins, B. D. (2009). Jihad on the frontier: A history of religious revolt on the north-west frontier, 1800–1947. History Compass, 7(6), 1459–1469. https://doi.org/10.1111/j.1478-0542.2009.00640.x. View Google Scholar

Hopkins, B. D. (2015). The frontier crimes regulation and frontier governmentality. The Journal of Asian Studies, 74(2), 369–389. https://doi.org/10.1017/S0021911815000030. View Web of Science °Google Scholar

Hopkins, B. D. (2020). Ruling the savage periphery: Frontier governance and the making of the modern state. Harvard University Press.View Google Scholar

Hopkins, B. D., & Marsden, M. (2012). Fragments of the Afghan frontier. Google Scholar

Hussain, Z. (2008). Frontline Pakistan: the struggle with militant Islam. Columbia University Press. Google Scholar

Jafri, Q. (2021). The Pashtun protection movement (PTM) in Pakistan. International Center on Nonviolent Conflict. Google Scholar

Jan, M. A. (2010). Contested and contextual identities: Ethnicity, religion and identity among the Pakhtuns of Malakand, Pakistan [Diss.]. University of York. Google Scholar

Johnston, P. B., & Sarbahi, A. K. (2016). The impact of US drone strikes on terrorism in Pakistan. International Studies Quarterly, 60(2), 203–219. https://doi.org/10.1093/isq/sqv004View Web of Science °Google Scholar

Jones, R. (2009). Geopolitical boundary narratives, the global war on terror and border fencing in India. Transactions of the Institute of British Geographers, 34(3), 290–304. https://doi.org/10.1111/j.1475-5661.2009.00350.xView Web of Science °Google Scholar

Khaliq, F. (2022). KP protests denounce resurgence of violence. Daily Dawn, Pakistan. 12 October. https://www.dawn.com/news/1714569 Google Scholar

Khan, A. (2018). Bacha Khan: The legacy of hope and perseverance. In Partition of India (pp. 223–233). Routledge.View Google Scholar

Khan, M. S. (2018). Bacha Khan's vision of alternative education. Abdul Wali Khan University. Google Scholar

Khan, Z., & Shah, Z. A. (2021). Pashtun community Indigenous resilience to changing socio-cultural and political challenges. In The Routledge International Handbook of Indigenous Resilience (pp. 121–133). Routledge.View Google Scholar

Leake, E. (2017). The defiant border: The Afghan-Pakistan borderlands in the era of decolonization, 1936–65. Cambridge University Press.View Google Scholar

Mahsud, M. I. (2019). Religious militancy and tribal transformation in Pakistan: A case study of Mahsud Tribe in South Waziristan Agency [Unpublished PhD dissertation]. University of Peshawar. Google Scholar

Mahsud, M. I., Naseer, N., & Fatima, M. (2023). Colonial governance system in Pakistan: A case study of South Waziristan, Erstwhile FATA. Lex localis - Journal of Local Self-Government, 21(2), 421–439. https://doi.org/10.4335/21.2.421-439(2023)View Web of Science °Google Scholar

Makki, M., & Akash, S. A. (2022). Building community resilience to violent extremism through community-based youth organizations: A case of post-conflict North Waziristan, Pakistan. Sustainability, 14(15), 9768. https://doi.org/10.3390/su14159768viewView Web of Science °Google Scholar

Mallick, A. (2020). From partisan universal to concrete universal? The Pashtun Tahaffuz movement in Pakistan. Antipode, 52(6), 1774–1793. https://doi.org/10.1111/anti.12661View Web of Science °Google Scholar

Markey, D. S. (2013). No exit from Pakistan: America's tortured relationship with Islamabad. Cambridge University Press.View Google Scholar

McAdam, D., McCarthy, J. D., & Zald, M. N. (1988). Social movements. In. N. J. Smelser (Ed.). Handbook of sociology (pp. 695–737). Sage Publications. Google Scholar

Mughal, M. A. Z. (2020). Ethnicity, marginalization, and politics: Saraiki identity and the quest for a new Southern Punjab province in Pakistan. Asian Journal of Political Science, 28(3), 294–311. https://doi.org/10.1080/02185377.2020.1814360View Web of Science °Google Scholar

Muraviev, A. D. (2022). Russia's views on and initial responses to the 2021 strategic retake of Afghanistan by the Taliban. Journal of Asian Security and International Affairs, 9(3), 424–445. https://doi.org/10.1177/23477970221133145View Web of Science °Google Scholar

Nichols, R. (2013). The frontier crimes regulation. Oxford University Press. Google Scholar

Omrani, B. (2009). The Durand line: History and problems of the Afghan-Pakistan border. Asian Affairs, 40(2), 177–195. https://doi.org/10.1080/03068370902871508 viewView Google Scholar

Oxford Analytica. (2018). Pakistan's Pashtun movement faces struggle to survive. Emerald Expert Briefings oxan-db. Google Scholar

Oztig, L. I. (2020). Pakistan's border policies and security dynamics along the Pakistan–Afghanistan border. Journal of Borderlands Studies, 35(2), 211–226. https://doi.org/10.1080/08865655.2018.1545598 View Web of Science °Google Scholar

Phongpaichit, P., & Baker, C. (1999). Theories of social movements and their relevance for Thailand. Position Paper for Social Movements in Thailand. Project. Google Scholar

PTM Europe Holds Protests Against Pakistan. (2018). Khyber Institute of research and strategic studies. 24 October. https://khyberinstitute.wordpress.com/2018/10/24/ptm-europe-holds-protests-against-pakistan/. Google Scholar

Qaiser, A. (2016). Between the tailors and politicians: Pakistan military's internal battlefronts. CDA Institute. https://cdainstitute.ca/between-traitors-and-politicians-pakistan-military-s-internal-battlefronts-part-2/. Google Scholar

Qazi, S. H. (2011). Rebels of the frontier: origins, organization, and recruitment of the Pakistani Taliban. Small Wars & Insurgencies, 22(4), 574–602. https://doi.org/10.1080/09592318.2011.601865View Google Scholar

Rashid, A. (2010). Taliban: militant Islam, oil and fundamentalism in Central Asia. Yale University Press. Google Scholar

Rubin, B. R., & Armstrong, A. (2003). Regional issues in the reconstruction of Afghanistan. World Policy Journal, 20(1), 31–40. https://doi.org/10.1215/07402775-2003-2008View Web of Science °Google Scholar

Saddique, K., & Xiumei, L. (2019). Pashtun Tahafuz Movement restoring or destroying Pashtoon's pride; social media and international media coverage. European Academic Research, VII(1), 727–728. Google Scholar

Schetter, C. (2013). The Durand line. The Afghan-Pakistani border region between Pashtunistan, Tribalistan and Talibanistan. Internationales Asienforum, 44(1–2), 47–70. Google Scholar

Sen, A., & Avci, Ö. (2016). Why social movements occur: Theories of social movements. Journal of Knowledge Economy and Knowledge Management, 11(1), 125–130. Google Scholar

Shah, A. R. (2020). The rise of the Pashtun Protection Movement (PTM): Polemics and conspiracy theories. Asian Affairs, 51(2), 265–285. https://doi.org/10.1080/03068374.2020.1752568View Web of Science °Google Scholar

Shah, S. W. A. (1999). Ethnicity, Islam and nationalism. Muslim Politics in the North-West Frontier Province. Google Scholar

Smith, J. (2005). The case for asymmetry in Canadian federalism. Institute of Intergovernmental Relations, School of Policy Studies, Queen's University. Google Scholar

Spain, J. W. (1961). The Pathan borderlands. Middle East Journal, 15(2), 165–177. Web of Science °Google Scholar

Tarlton, C. D. (1965). Symmetry and asymmetry as elements of federalism: A theoretical speculation. The Journal of Politics, 27(4), 861–874. https://doi.org/10.2307/2128123View Web of Science °Google Scholar

Threlkeld, E., & Easterly, G. (2021). Afghanistan-Pakistan ties and future stability in Afghanistan. United States Institute of Peace. Google Scholar

Two PTM leaders make it to the NA. (2018).The News. 29 July. https://www.the-news.com.pk/print/347687-two-ptm-leaders-make-it-to-na. Google Scholar

Waseem, A. (2018). National Assembly green-lights Fata-KP merger by passing 'historic' bill. Daily Dawn, Pakistan. 25 May. https://www.dawn.com/news/1409710 Google Scholar

Welton, M. (1993). Social revolutionary learning: The new social movements as learning sites. Adult Education Quarterly, 43(3), 152–164. https://doi.org/10.1177/0741713693043003002View Web of Science °Google Scholar

Chapter 8: Still under Sanctions, Still Unrecognized: A Dossier of Reports on Afghanistan, International Relations and aid ahead of Doha III. AAN Team 09 Jun 2024

References

An earlier dossier, published on 14 May 2023, The Afghan Economy since the Taleban Took Power: A dossier of reports on economic calamity, state finances and consequences for households, took a wide look at the economy, both at the household and macro-economic levels. It also included reports on international aid to Afghanistan, which inevitably deal also with (non-) recognition and sanctions. Revisions: This article was last updated on 11 Jun 2024

Chapter 9: The Taliban War against Women and Children in Afghanistan and

1. Imam Abdul Aziz of Red Mosque Islamabad, in his recent interview with a local journal (Quran orders to become terrorists, SAMVADA-25 August 2021) communicated that the Holy Quran had ordained Muslims to become terrorists against enemies of Allah.

2. No nation can rise to the height of glory unless to seek the support of women in building a nation." Father of the Nation, Mohammed Ali Jinnah warned while speaking to the Muslim Union of Aligarh University on10 March 1944.

3. 2020, the World Economic Forum report. The Report and an interactive data platform are available at http://reports.weforum.org/global-gender-gap-report-2020/dataexplorer.

4. Women's Rights are Human Rights, United Nations Report, 2014

5. the US State Department (Country Reports on Human Rights Practices for 2021 United States Department of State. Bureau of Democracy, Human Rights and Labour-04 January, 2021

6. On 15 July 2022; a woman named Koratul Aeen Baloch was tortured to death by her husband in front of her four children in Sindh province (MM News)

7. September 2021, Asian development Bank report

8. Ibid

9. Domestic Violence against Women: Empirical Evidence from Pakistan. Ashraf, S. Abrar-ul-haq, M. and Ashraf, S, 2017, Universiti Putra Malaysia Press Social Science and Humanities homepage:http://www.pertanika.upm.edu.my/

10. 20 July 2021, Noor Moqadam, a 27 years old girl was killed by her living-partner in a house in Islamabad. The murder caused nationwide revulsion and prompted demands for more to be done to ensure women's safety. CNN News Bulletin.

11. 09 September 2021, Dawn

12. Daily Times reported (News Desk, February 03, 2021

13. CNN report, 20 July 2021

14. The beheading of a diplomat's daughter shows how badly Pakistan is failing its women. Sophia CNN News, 09 Aug 2021

15. Human Rights Watch (HRW) in its 2022 report painted a bleak picture of civil liberties in Pakistan

16. Pakistan Events of 2021. Human Rights Watch

17. Ibid

18. Daily the Nation in its 23 November 2022 news report

19. The Holy Quran has strictly prohibited sex without marriage. In this report, I have already quoted verse from the Holy Quran (Chapter-17: Verse-32): "And do not approach unlawful sexual intercourse. Indeed, it is ever an immorality and is evil as a way."

20. Aurat Foundation-Pakistan-2021

21. Barrister in the Supreme Court of Pakistan and Legal Consultant of the Ministry of Interior in Pakistan, and a former Deputy Attorney General, Muhammad Arif Choudhry told me: (27 November 2022

22. Mr. Miftahuddin Haroon of Wintworth Solicitors Paddington London, is an Islamic scholar.

23. Senior journalist of Jang newspaper, Mr. Akhtar Jaffery

Bibliography

A Pilot Study on: Honour Killings' in Pakistan and Compliance of Law By: Maliha Zia Lari. Published under Legislative Watch Programme for Women's Empowerment Aurat Foundation. 2011.

Ashraf, S.1, Abrar-ul-haq, M. and Ashraf, S.Domestic Violence against Women: Empirical Evidence from Pakistan. Social Science and Humanity Journal-2017. http://www.pertanika.upm.edu.my/

Ali, Kalbe (5 March 2020). "Jamia Hafsa students claim responsibility for defacing feminist mural in Islamabad". Dawn newspaper

Aurat Foundation: The Politics of our Lives: The Rising Her Voice in Pakistan Experience.

Country Reports on Human Rights Practices for 2021 United States Department of State • Bureau of Democracy, Human Rights and Labor

Education and Inequality Discerning the Foundation of Citizenry. Lead researcher and author: Amjad Nazeer, IDRAC. Muhammad Asad Khan, IDRAC, Azhar Sharif, IDRAC, Field research coordinators: Sultan Mahmood. Saqib Khadim. Institute of Development Research and Corresponding Capabilities Human Rights Commission of Pakistan. 2019.

Forced Marriages and Inheritance. Deprivation in Pakistan. A Research Study Exploring Substantive and Structural Gaps in the Implementation of Prevention of Anti-Women Practices [Criminal Law Amendment] Act, 2011, in Six Select Districts of Pakistan. Researched and Written by: Sarah Zaman. Published under Gender Based Violence Policy Research, & Capacity Building Programme.

Gender-based violence in Pakistan: a scoping study. Publishing place: Islamabad. Publishing year: 2011

Hasan, Shazia (4 March 2020). "'Aurat March seeks to join people for cause of gender justice'". Dawn newspaper

Honor Killing: Tackling an Abhorrent Crime against Pakistani Women: Challenges, Hopes and Obstacles. Dr. Sajid Jamil. Dr. Naseem Akhter and Shumaila Rafiq, Al-Qamar, Volume 4, Issue 1 (January-March 2021).

Islamabad's Women's Day march was met with violent opposition from conservative agitators. Global Voices. 13 March 2020.

Khan, Ayesha; Jawed, Asiya; Qidwai, Komal (2 September 2021). Women and protest politics in Pakistan.

Lahore, Sabrina Toppa, in (8 March 2019). "Women take to the streets of Pakistan to rewrite their place in society". the Guardian.

Mahmood, Aisha (4 March 2020). "Extremist mob vandalises mural of two women painted by Aurat March organizers". Business Recorder.

State of Human Rights in 2021. 2022 Human Rights Commission of Pakistan

The Shadow Pandemic: Violence against Women in Pakistan during COVID-19 Lockdown. Malik Mamoon Munir. Malik Haroon Munir. Ume Rubaca. Journal of International Women's Studies, Volume 22Issue 5 Article 15. 2021. https://vc.bridgew.edu/jiws/vol22/iss5/15

Women Access to Justice in Pakistan. Extrapolating Abuses and Barriers. Competitive Educational Research Journal (CERJ), ISSN (Print): 2709-9784, ISSN (Online): 2709-9792. Volume 3 Issue 2. https://cerjournal.com

Violence against Women & Girls in the Times of Covid-19 Pandemic: A Rapid Analysis of the Quantitative Data from 25 districts from all 4 Provinces and Gilgit-Baltistan, 14 case studies & interviews of 6 key officials from women machineries and office of the ombudspersons, sexual harassment at workplace. Annual Report on VAWG. January – December 2020.

Violence against Women in Pakistan: Causes, Consequences and the Way Forward. M. Rafique Wassan, Abdul Razaque Channa, Syed Faisal Hyder Shah. International Research Journal of Arts and Humanities (IRJAH) Vol.49, No. 49, 2021 ISSN: 1016-9342.

Yasin, Aamir (7 March 2020). Opponents of Aurat Azadi March are oblivious to the suffering of women. Daw, newspaper

Bibliography

Ahady Anwar-ul-Haq. 1991. Conflict in post-soviet-occupation Afghanistan. Journal of Contemporary Asia, Vol. 21, No. 4

Abbas, Hassan 2015. Pakistan's Drift into Extremism: Allah, the Army, and America's War Terror. Abingdon: Routledge.

Afzal, Madiha 2018. Pakistan under Siege: Extremism, Society, and the State. Washington, DC: Brookings Institution Press.

Ahmed, Shamila Kouser, 2012, July. The Impact of the "War on Terror": On Birmingham's Pakistani / Kashmiri Muslims' Perceptions of the State, the Police and Islamic Identities. (Doctoral Thesis, University of Birmingham, Birmingham, United Kingdom). http://etheses.bham.ac.uk/id/eprint/3635

Ali, Murad, 2012. The Politics of Development Aid: The Allocation and Delivery of Aid from the United States of America to Pakistan. Doctoral Thesis, Massey University, Palmerston North, New Zealand. URL: http://hdl. handle.net/10179/3418

Ahmed, Khaled. 2016, Sleepwalking to Surrender: Dealing with Terrorism in Pakistan. Haryana: Viking. Ataöv, Türkkaya (2018): Kashmir and Neighbors: Tale, Terror, Truce.

Abingdon: Routledge. Barfield, Thomas. 1996. 'The Afghan Morass', Current History, Vol. 95, No. 597.

Andrew, Christopher M. and Jeremy Noakes. 1987. Intelligence and International Relations, 1900-1945. Exeter: Exeter University Press,

Ashman, Harold Lowell. 2009. Intelligence and Foreign Policy: A Functional Analysis. Salt Lake City: Ashman, 1974. Association of the Bar of the City of New York, Committee on Civil Rights The Central Intelligence Agency: Oversight and Accountability. New York,

Abshire, David. 2001, "Making the Pieces Fit: America Needs a Comprehensive National Security Strategy." American Legion Magazine,

Ackerman, Wystan M. 1998, "Encryption: A 21st Century National Security Dilemma." International Review of Law, Computers & Technology.

Andersen, Per, Richard Morris, David Amaral, Tim Bliss, & John O'Keefe 2006. The Hippocampus Book, Oxford: University Press.

Anderson, Alan Ross, & Nuel D. Belnap, Jr. 1975 Entailment: The Logic of Relevance and Necessity, Princeton University Press, Princeton.

Anderson, John R. (1983) The Architecture of Cognition, Cambridge, MA: Harvard University Press.

Anderson, John R., & Gordon H. Bower,1973 Human Associative Memory, Washington, DC: Winston.

Anderson, John R., & Gordon H. Bower, 1980 Human Associative Memory: A Brief Edition, Hillsdale, NJ: Erlbaum.

Anderson, John R., & Lebiere, C. 1998. The atomic components of thought, Mahwah, NJ: Erlbaum.

Adams, Thomas K. "Future Warfare and the Decline of Human Decisionmaking." Parameters, Winter 2001/2002, v. 31, no. 4

Adler, Emanual. "Executive Command and Control in Foreign Policy: The CIA's Covert Activities," Orbis, fall 1979, v. 23, no. 3

Agrell, Wilhelm. Sweden and the Dilemmas of Neutral Intelligence Liaison. Journal of Strategic Studies, August 2006, v. 29, no. 4

Aid, Matthew M. "All Glory is Fleeting: SIGINT and the Fight against International Terrorism." Intelligence and National Security, Winter 2003, v. 18, no. 4

Ast, Scott Alan. Managing Security Overseas: Protecting Employees and Assets in Volatile Regions Boca Raton; FL: CRC Press, 2010.

Ataov, Türkkaya 2018: Kashmir and Neighbors: Tale, Terror, Truce. (Routledge Revivals). Abingdon: Routledge.

Afghanistan Analyst Network (Osman, B.) 18 October 2019, The Islamic State in 'Khorasan': How it began and where it stands now in Nangarhar, 27 July 2016, https://www.afghanistan-analysts.org/the-islamic-state-inkhorasan-how-it-began-and-where-it-stands-now-in-nangarhar/,

Amnesty International, Pakistan: Enduring Enforced Disappearances, 27 March 2019,https://www.amnesty.org/en/latest/research/2019/03/pakistan-enduring-enforceddisappearances/, accessed 15 July 2019

Azam, M., Javaid, U, 2017, The sources of Militancy in Pakistan, in: Journal of the Research Society of Pakistan, Volume No. 54, Issue No. 2 http://pu.edu.pk/images/journal/history/PDF-FILES/13-Paper_54_2_17.pdf, accessed 24 July 2019.

Baloch, H., Peace Talks, ISKP and TTP--The Future in Question, 6 May 2019, ITCT (Islamic Theology of Counter Terrorism), https://www.itct.org.uk/wp-content/uploads/2019/05/Peace-Talks-ISKP-andTTP.

Bell, Paul M. P. 2007, Pakistan's Madrassas – Weapons of Mass Instruction? (Master's Thesis, Naval Postgraduate School, Monterey, United States). URL: http://hdl.handle.net/10945/3653

Bennett, John T. 2014, Bend but Don't Break: Why Obama's Targeted-Killing Program Challenges Policy and Legal Boundaries but Rarely Breaches them. (Master's Thesis, Johns Hopkins University, Baltimore, United States). http://jhir.library.jhu.edu/handle/1774.2/37221

Badalic, Vasja, 2019 The War against Civilians: Victims of the "War on Terror" in Afghanistan and Pakistan.(Palgrave Studies in Victims and Victimology). Cham: Palgrave Macmillan / Springer Nature. DOI: https://doi.org/10.

Bergen, Peter L.; Rothenberg, Daniel (Ed.) 2015, Drone Wars: Transforming Conflict, Law, and Policy. New York: Cambridge University Press.

Bergen, Peter L.; Tiedemann, Katherine (Eds.), 2013, Talibanistan: Negotiating the Borders between Terror, Politics, and Religion. Oxford: Oxford University Press. Brooke-Smith, Robin (2013): S

Bayly, C. A. 1996, Empire and Information: Intelligence Gathering and Social Communication in India: 1780-1880. NY: Cambridge University press,.

Bazan, Elizabeth B. 2008. The Foreign Intelligence Surveillance Act: Overview and Modifications. New York: Nova Science Publishers,

Bailey, David, 1997, A Computational Model of Embodiment in the Acquisition of Action Verbs, Doctoral dissertation, Computer Science Division, EECS Department, University of California, Berkeley.

Baillie, Penny, 2002 The Synthesis of Emotions in Artificial Intelligence, PhD Dissertation, University of Southern Queensland.

Baker, Mark C. 2003 Lexical Categories: Verbs, Nouns, and Adjectives, Cambridge University Press, Cambridge.

Baldwin, J.F. 1986 Automated fuzzy and probabilistic inference, Fuzzy Sets and Systems, vol 18,

Ballard, Dana H., Mary M. Hayhoe, Polly K. Pook, & Rajesh P. N. Rao 1997 Deictic codes for the embodiment of cognition, Behavioral and Brain Sciences 20, 723-767.

Bar Hillel, Yehoshua, 1954 Logical Syntax and Semantics, Language 30, 230-237.

Beck, Melvin. 1984. Secret Contenders: The Myth of Cold War Counterintelligence. New York, NY: Sheridan Square Publications,

Beichman, Arnold. 1984. "The U.S. Intelligence Establishment and Its Discontents." IN Dennis L. Bark (ed.) To Promote Peace: U.S. Foreign Policy in the Mid-1980s. Stanford, CA: Hoover Institution Press, Stanford University,

Bazai, Fida Muhammad, 2016 Pakistan's Responses to the United States' Demands in the War against the Taliban and Al-Qaeda. (Doctoral Thesis, University of Glasgow, Glasgow, United Kingdom). http://encore.lib.gla.ac.uk/iii/encore/record/C-Rb3258590

Bell, Paul M. P. (2007, March): Pakistan's Madrassas – Weapons of Mass Instruction? (Master's Thesis, Naval Postgraduate School, Monterey, United States). URL: http://hdl.handle.net/10945/3653

Bennett, John T. 2014 Bend but Don't Break: Why Obama's Targeted-Killing Program Challenges Policy and Legal Boundaries but Rarely Breaches them. (Master's Thesis, Johns Hopkins University, Baltimore, United States). http://jhir.library.jhu.edu/handle/1774.2/37221

Bhattacharya, Sandhya S. 2008 The Global Impact of Terror: 9/11 and the India-Pakistan Conflict. (Doctoral Thesis, Pennsylvania State University, State College, United States https://etda.libraries.psu. edu/catalog/7900

Barrett, David M. "Glimpses of a Hidden History: Sen. Richard Russell, Congress, and Oversight of the CIA." International Journal of Intelligence and Counterintelligence, Fall 1998, v. 11, no. 3, p. 271-298.

Barry James A. "Managing the Covert Political Action: Guideposts from Just War Theory." Studies in Intelligence, 1992, v. 36, no. 5 https://www.cia.gov/library/center-for-the-study-of-intelligence/kentcsi/docs/v36i3a05p_0001.htm

Barry, James A. Bridging the Intelligence-Policy Divide. Studies in Intelligence, 1994, v. 37, no. 5. https://www.cia.gov/library/center-for-the-study-of-intelligence/kentcsi/docs/v37i3a02p_0001.htm

Basile, James F. Congressional Assertiveness, Executive Authority and the Intelligence Oversight Act: A New Threat to the Separation of Powers. Notre Dame Law Review, 1989, v. 64, no. 4

Beres, Louis Rene. On Assassination, Preemption, and Counterterrorism: The View from International Law." International Journal of Intelligence and Counterintelligence, Winter 2008, v. 21, no. 4

Bhattacharya, Sandhya S. 2008, The Global Impact of Terror: 9/11 and the India-Pakistan Conflict. (Doctoral Thesis, Pennsylvania State University, State College, United States). https://etda.libraries.psu. edu/catalog/7900

Clarke, Ryan 2011, Crime–Terror Nexus in South Asia: States, Security and Non-State Actors. (Asian Security Studies). Abingdon: Routledge.

Coll, Steve, 2018 Directorate S: The C.I.A. and America's Secret Wars in Afghanistan and Pakistan. New York: Penguin Press.

Dorronsoro, Gilles. 2012. 'The transformation of the Afghanistan-Pakistan border', in under the drones: Modern lives in the Afghanistan-Pakistan Borderlands. Harvard University Press

Cassirer, Ernst,1942 Zur Logik der Kulturwissenschaften, translated by S. G. Lofts as The Logic of the Cultural Sciences, Yale University Press, New Haven.

Cattell, R. G. G., & Douglas K. Barry, eds. 1997, The Object Database Standard, ODMG 2.0, Morgan Kaufmann, San Francisco, CA.

Ceccato, Silvio. 1961 Linguistic Analysis and Programming for Mechanical Translation, Gordon and Breach, New York.

Ceccato, Silvio,1964 Automatic translation of languages, Information Storage and Retrieval 2:3, 105-158.

Chafe, Wallace L. 1970 Meaning and the Structure of Language, University of Chicago Press, Chicago.

Chamberlin, Don, 1996 Using the New DB2, Morgan Kaufmann Publishers, San Francisco.

Cruickshank, Paul, 2013, Al Qaeda. (5 Vols.). (Critical Concepts in Political Science). Abingdon: Routledge.

Canfield, Robert L. 1992. 'Restructuring in Greater Central Asia: Changing Political Configurations', Asian Survey, Vol. 32, No. 10.

Drumbl, Mark A. 2002. 'The Taliban's 'other' crimes', Third World Quarterly, No. 23.

Daily Times, Police service-challenges and reforms, 6 October 2018,https://dailytimes.com.pk/306595/police-service-challenges-and-reforms/,

Daily Times, Reforming the judicial system, 8 March 2019,https://dailytimes.com.pk/362536/reforming-the-judicial-system/, accessed 17 October 2019

Dawn, 2009: Southern Punjab extremism battle between haves and have-nots, 21 May 2011 https://www.dawn.com/news/630651, accessed 21 July 2019

David, G.J. 2009. Ideas as Weapons: Influence and Perception in Modern Warfare. Washington, DC: Potomac Books,

DCAF Intelligence Working Group, Intelligence Practice and Democratic Oversight – a Practitioner's View. DCAF, Occasional paper no. 3. August 2003.

Dehaene, Stanislas, 2014 Consciousness and the Brain, New York: Viking.

DeJong, Gerald F.1979 Prediction and substantiation, Cognitive Science, vol. 3,

DeJong, Gerald F. 1982 An overview of the FRUMP system, in W. G. Lehnert & M. H. Ringle, eds., Strategies for Natual Language Processing, Erlbaum, Hillsdale, NJ,

Deledalle, Gerard, 1990 Charles S. Peirce, Phénoménologue et Sémioticien, translated as Charles S. Peirce, An Intellectual Biography, Amsterdam: John Benjamins.

de Moor, Aldo, Wilfried Lex, & Bernhard Ganter, eds. 2003 Conceptual Structures for Knowledge Creation and Communication, LNAI 2746, Berlin: Springer.

Deng, Li, & Dong Yu, 2014 Deep Learning: Methods and Applications, Foundations and Trends in Signal Processing.

Dennet, Daniel C. 1987 The Intentional Stance, MIT Press, Cambridge.

Dennet, Daniel C. 1995 Darwin's Dangerous Idea: Evolution and the Meanings of Life, Simon & Schuster, New York.

Dennet, Daniel C. 1996 Kinds of Minds, New York: Basic Books.

Dearth, Douglas H. 1992, Strategic Intelligence and National Security: A Selected Bibliography. Carlisle Barracks, PA: U.S. Army War College Library, http://handle.dtic.mil/100.2/ADA256389

Dearth, Douglas H. and R. Thomas Goodden. 1995. Strategic Intelligence: Theory and Application. 2nd ed. Carlisle Barracks, PA: U.S. Army War College Library

Der Derian, James. 1992. Antidiplomacy: Spies, Terror, Speed and War. Cambridge, MA: Blackwell,

Diamond, John. 2008.The CIA and the Culture of Failure: U.S. Intelligence from the End of the Cold War to the Invasion of Iraq. Stanford, CA: Stanford Security Series,

Dawn, Military courts cease to function today, 31 March 2019,https://www.dawn.com/news/1472947, accessed 3 July 2019

Dawn, Military Courts part of National Action Plan: PM Nawaz, 30 December 2014https://www.dawn.com/news/1154046, accessed 20 July 2019

Diplomat, July 2019,The, Taking Stock of Pakistan's Counterterrorism Efforts, 4 Years After the Army Public School Attack, 21 December 2018, https://thediplomat.com/2018/12/taking-stock-of-pakistanscounterterrorism-efforts-4-years-after-the-army-public-school-attack/,

Economic Times (The), US asks Pakistan to act against Haqqani network, other terror groups, 27 February 2018, https://m.economictimes.com/news/defence/us-asks-pak-to-act-against-haqqaninetwork-other-terror-groups/articleshow/63096010.cms, accessed 17 June 2019

Express Tribune, The Army launches Operation Radd-ul-Fasaad against terrorists across the country,22 February 2017, https://tribune.com.pk/story/1335805/army-launches-country-wide-operationterrorists/, accessed 30 July 2019

Einstein, Albert, 1921 The Meaning of Relativity, Princeton University Press, Princeton, NJ, fifth edition, 1956.

Einstein, A., H. A. Lorentz, H. Weyl, & H. Minkowski, 1923 The Principle of Relativity, Dover Publications, New York.

Einstein, Albert, 1944 Remarks on Bertrand Russell's Theory of Knowledge, in P. A. Schilpp, ed., The Philosophy of Bertrand Russell, Library of Living Philosophers.

Eklund, Peter W., Gerard Ellis, & G. Mann, eds. 1996 Conceptual Structures: Knowledge Representation as Interlingua, LNAI 1115, Berlin: Springer,

Express Tribune (The), Blast hits Hazara community's shoe market in Quetta, 6 August 2019, https://tribune.com.pk/story/2029583/1-least-two-martyred-13-injured-quetta-market-blast/

Elahi, N. 2019 Terrorism in Pakistan: The Tehreek-e-Taliban Pakistan (TTP) and the Challenge to Security. London: I.B. Tauris.

Fair, C. Christine 2014 fighting to the End: The Pakistan Army's Way of War. Oxford: Oxford University Press.

Fair, C. Christine 2018 In their Own Words: Understanding Lashkar-e-Tayyaba. London: Hurst.

Farwell, James P. 2011 The Pakistan Cauldron: Conspiracy, Assassination & Instability. Dulles: Potomac Books.

Feldman, J. A. 1981. A connectionist model of visual memory. In Hinton, G. E. and Anderson, J. A., editors, Parallel Models of Associative Memory, chapter 2. Erlbaum, Hillsdale, NJ.

Fukushima, K. 1975. Cognitron: A self-organizing multilayered neural network. Biological Cybernetics, 20:121–136.

Feigenbaum, Edward A., & Pamela McCorduck, 1983. The Fifth Generation, Addison-Wesley, Reading, MA. Brain and Language 89, 385-392.

Feldman, Jerome A. 2006 From Molecule to Metaphor: A Neural Theory of Language, MIT Press, Cambridge, MA.

Feldman, Jerome, & Srinivas Narayanan,2004 Embodied meaning in a neural theory of language, Brain and Language 89, 385-392.

Feldman, Jerome, Ellen Dodge, & John Bryant,2009. Embodied construction grammar, in B. Heine & H. Narrog, eds., The Oxford Handbook of Linguistic Analysis, Oxford: University Press.

Fellbaum, Christiane, 1998. WordNet: An Electronic Lexical Database, MIT Press, Cambridge, MA.

Feynman, Richard, 1965 The Character of Physical Law, Cambridge, MA: MIT Press.

Glatzer, Bernt. 2002. 'Centre and Periphery in Afghanistan: New Identities in a Broken State', Sociologus, winter issue.

Goodson, Larry. 1998. 'The Fragmentation of Culture in Afghanistan', Alif: Journal of Comparative Poetics, No. 18, Post-Colonial Discourse in South Asia.

Goodson, Larry P. 1998 'Periodicity and intensity in the Afghan War', Central Asian Survey, Vol. 17, No. 3.

Goudarzi, Hadi. 1999. 'Conflict in Afghanistan: Ethnicity and Religion', Ethnic Studies Report, Vol. XVII, No. 1.

Harpviken, Kristian Berg. 1997. 'Transcending nationalism: the emergence of non-state military formations in Afghanistan', Journal of Peace Research, Vol. 34, No. 3.

Haqqani, Husain, 2018 Reimagining Pakistan: Transforming a Dysfunctional Nuclear State. Noida: HarperCollins India.

Hayes, Louis D. 2016 The Islamic State in the Post-Modern World: The Political Experience of Pakistan. Abingdon: Routledge.

Hiro, Dilip, 2012 Apocalyptic Realm: Jihadists in South Asia. New Haven: Yale University Press.

Hussain, Rizwan, 2005 Pakistan and the Emergence of Islamic Militancy in Afghanistan. Aldershot: Ashgate.

Hinsley, F.H. and Richard Langhorn. 1985, Diplomacy and Intelligence during the Second World War: Essays in Honour of F.H. Hinsley. Cambridge, NY: Cambridge University Press

Hitchcock, Walter T. 1991, The Intelligence Revolution: A Historical Perspective: Proceedings of the Thirteenth Military History Symposium, U.S. Air Force Academy, Colorado Springs, Colorado, October 12-14, 1988. Washington, DC: U.S. Office of Air Force History,

Haaparanta Leila, 1994, Charles Peirce and the Drawings of the Mind, in Histoire Épistémologie Langage 16:1, 35-52.

Harris, Kathryn E. 2015, Asymmetric Strategies and Asymmetric Threats: A Structural-Realist Critique of Drone Strikes in Pakistan, 2004-2014. (Master's Thesis, Virginia Polytechnic Institute and State University, Blacksburg, United States).http://hdl.handle.net/10919/64516

Hoyt, Melanie Raeann, 2014, Decembe. A Game of Drones: Comparing the U.S. Aerial Assassination Campaign in Yemen and Pakistan. (Master's Thesis, Angelo State University, San Angelo, United States).http://hdl. handle. net/2346.1/30273

Hubbard, Austen, 2016, A Study on the Relationship between Security and Prosperity in Pakistan. (Master's Thesis, Angelo State University, San Angelo, United States). URL: http://hdl.handle.net/2346.1/30604

Hussain, Syed Ejaz, 2010, Terrorism in Pakistan: Incident Patterns, Terrorists' Characteristics, and the Impact of Terrorist Arrests on Terrorism. (Doctoral Thesis, University of Pennsylvania, Philadelphia, United States). https://repository.upenn.edu/edissertations/136

Hoffman, Bruce. Lessons of 9/11. Santa Monica, CA: RAND, 2002. http://www.rand.org/pubs/testimonies/CT201/index.html

Hussain, Safdar, and Muhammad Ijaz Latif. 2012. 'Issues and Challenges in Pakistan-Afghanistan Relations after 9/11', South Asian Studies, Vol. 27, No. 1.

Hussain, Shabir, and Syed Abdul Siraj. 2018. 'Coverage of Taliban conflict in the Pak–Afghan press: A comparative analysis', International Communication Gazette.

ICG. 2014. 'Resetting Pakistan's Relations with Afghanistan', International Crisis Group.

Iqbal, Khalid. 2015. 'Natural Allies: TurkeyPakistan-Afghanistan', Defence Journal, Vol. 18. No. 8.

Inderfurth, Karl F. and Loch K. Johnson. 1988, Decisions of the Highest Order: Perspectives on the National Security Council. Pacific Grove, California: Brooks/Cole,.

Ibrahimi, S. Yaqub. 2017. 'The Taliban's Islamic Emirate of Afghanistan (1996–2001): 'War-Making and State-Making' as an Insurgency Strategy', Small Wars & Insurgencies, Vol. 28, No. 6.

Intelligence Services and Democracy. Geneva, Switzerland: Geneva Centre for Democratic Control of Armed Forces, 2002.

Iran: Intelligence Failure or Policy Stalemate? Washington, DC: Georgetown University, Institute for the Study of Diplomacy, 2005. http://www12.georgetown.edu/sfs/isd/Iran_WG_Report.pdf

Jinnah Institute. 2013. 'Sources of Tension in Afghanistan & Pakistan: Perspectives from the Region

Johnson, Thomas H. and M. Chris Mason. 2008. 'No Sign until the Burst of Fire: Understanding the Pakistan-Afghanistan Frontier', International Security, Vol. 32, No. 4.

Jaffrelot, Christophe (Ed.), 2016, Pakistan at the Crossroads: Domestic Dynamics and External Pressures.

(Religion, Culture, and Public Life). New York: Columbia University Press.

Jamal, Arif, 2009, Shadow War: The Untold Story of Jihad in Kashmir. New York: Melville House.

Jan, Faizullah, 2015, The Muslim Extremist Discourse: Constructing Us versus Them. Lanham: Lexington Books.

Jalalzai Musa Khan. May 2018, Pakistan: Living with a Nuclear Monkey, Vij Books India Pvt Ltd, Darya Ganj New Delhi, India,

Judah, Tim. 2002. 'The Taliban Papers', Survival, Vol. 44, No. 1.

Jaffrelot, Christophe, 2016, Pakistan at the Crossroads: Domestic Dynamics and External Pressures. New York: Columbia University Press.

Jalalzai Musa Khan, 22 September, 2015. The Prospect of Nuclear Jihad in Pakistan: The Armed Forces, Islamic State, and the Threat of Chemical and Biological Terrorism. Algora Publishing, Riverside, New York, USA. ISBN-10: 1628941650. ISBN-13: 978-1628941654.

Jan, Faizullah, 2015, The Muslim Extremist Discourse: Constructing Us versus Them. Lanham: Lexington Books.

Kalia, Ravi, 2016, Pakistan's Political Labyrinths: Military, Society and Terror. Abingdon: Routledge.

Kapur, S. Paul, 2017, Jihad as Grand Strategy: Islamist Militancy, National Security, and the Pakistani State. New York: Oxford University Press.

Khalilzad, Zalmay. 1996. 'Afghanistan in 1995: Civil War and a Mini-Great Game', Asian Survey, Vol. 36, No. 2.

Khan, Ijaz. 1998. 'Afghanistan: A geopolitical study', Central Asian Survey, Vol. 17, No. 3.

Magnus, Ralph H. 1998. 'Afghanistan in 1997: The War Moves North', Asian Survey, Vol. 38, No.2.

Maley, William. 1997. 'The Dynamics of Regime Transition in Afghanistan', Central Asian Survey, Vol. 16, No. 2.

Malik, Iftikhar Haider, 2005, Jihad, Hindutva and the Taliban: South Asia at the Crossroads. Karachi: Oxford University Press.

Malik, Jamal, 2008, Madrasas in South Asia: Teaching Terror? (Routledge Contemporary South Asia Series, Vol. 4). Abingdon: Routledge.

Murphy, Eamon, 2013, The Making of Terrorism in Pakistan: Historical and Social Roots of Extremism. (Routledge Critical Terrorism Studies). Abingdon: Routledge.

Murphy, Eamon, 2019, Islam and Sectarian Violence in Pakistan: The Terror Within. Abingdon: Routledge.

Maloney, Sean M. 2015. 'Army of darkness: The jihadist training system in Pakistan and Afghanistan, 1996-2001', Small Wars & Insurgencies, Vol. 26, No. 3.

Mukhopadhyay, Dipali. 2012. 'The Slide from Withdrawal to War: The UN Secretary General's Failed Effort in Afghanistan, 1992', International Negotiation, Vol. 17, No. 3.

Nester, William, 2012, Hearts, Minds, and Hydras: Fighting Terrorism in Afghanistan, Pakistan, America, and Beyond – Dilemmas and Lessons. Dulles: Potomac Books.

Nielsen, Thomas Galasz; Syed, Mahroona Hussain; Vestenskov, David, 2015, Counterinsurgency and Counterterrorism: Sharing Experiences in Afghanistan and Pakistan. Copenhagen: Royal Danish Defence College.

Ollapally, Deepa M. (2008): The Politics of Extremism in South Asia. Cambridge: Cambridge University Press.

Odom, William E. 2003, Fixing Intelligence: For a More Secure America. New Haven: Yale University Press, 2003.

Odom, William E. 2004, Fixing Intelligence: For a More Secure America. 2nd ed.New Haven, CT: Yale University Press, 2004.

Odom, William E. et al. 1997, Modernizing Intelligence: Structure and Change for the 21st Century. Fairfax, VA: National Institute for Public Policy,

Olmsted, Kathryn S. 1996, Challenging the Secret Government: The PostWatergate Investigation of the CIA and FBI. Chapel Hill: University of North Carolina Press,

Olmsted, Kathryn Signe. 1993, Challenging the Secret Government: Congress and the Press Investigate the Intelligence Community, 1974-76. Dissertation. Davis, CA: University of California, Davis.

Pande, Aparna, 2018, Routledge Handbook of Contemporary Pakistan. Abingdon: Routledge.

Rais, Rasul Bakhsh. 2000. 'Afghanistan: A Forgotten Cold War Tragedy', Ethnic Studies Report, Vol. XVIII, No. 2.

Rieck, Andreas. 1997. 'Afghanistan's Taliban: An Islamic Revolution of the Pashtuns' in Orient, Vol. 38, No. 1.

Roy, Olivier. 1992. 'Political elites in Afghanistan: rentier state building, rentier state wrecking', International Journal of Middle East Studies, No. 24.

Rashid, Ahmed, 2008, Descent into Chaos: The United States and the Failure of Nation Building in Pakistan, Afghanistan, and Central Asia. New York: Viking.

Rashid, Ahmed, 2012, Pakistan on the Brink: The Future of America, Pakistan, and Afghanistan. New York: Viking.

Riedel, Bruce, 2011, Deadly Embrace: Pakistan, America, and the Future of the Global Jihad. Washington, DC: The Brookings Institution Press.

Riedel, Bruce, 2013, Avoiding Armageddon: America, India, and Pakistan to the Brink and Back. (Brookings Focus Books). Washington, DC: Brookings Institution Press.

Rubin, Barnett R. 2000. 'The Political Economy of War and Peace in Afghanistan', World Development, Vol. 28, No. 10.

Rubin, Barnett R. 1999. Afghanistan under the Taliban', Current History, Vol. 98, No. 625.

Rubin, Barnett R. 1994. Afghanistan in 1993: abandoned but surviving'Asian Survey, Vol. 34, No. 2.

Schmidt, John R. 2011, the Unraveling: Pakistan in the Age of Jihad. New York: Farrar, Straus and Giroux.

Shah, Sikander Ahmed, 2015, International Law and Drone Strikes in Pakistan: The Legal and Socio-Political Aspects. Routledge Research in the Law of Armed Conflict

191

Sharma, Surinder Kumar; Behera, Anshuman, 2014, Militant Groups in South Asia. New Delhi: Pentagon Press.

Sheikh, Mona Kanwal, 2016, Guardians of God: Inside the Religious Mind of the Pakistani Taliban. New Delhi: Oxford University Press.

Saikal, Amin. 1996. 'The UN and Afghanistan: A Case of Failed Peacemaking Intervention', International Peacekeeping, Vol. 3, No. 1.

Shahrani, M. Nazif. 2002. 'War, Factionalism, and the State in Afghanistan', American Anthropologist, Vol. 104, No. 3.

Schneider, Erich B. 2013, Balancing the Trinity: U.S. Approaches to Marginalizing Islamic Militancy in Pakistan. Master's Thesis, Naval Postgraduate School, Monterey, United States. http://hdl.handle. net/10945/39008

Shabab, Asma (2012, May): Marketing the Beard: The Use of Propaganda in the Attempt to Talibanize Pakistan. Master's Thesis, University of Southern California, Los Angeles, United States. http://digitallibrary.usc. edu/cdm/ref/collection/p15799coll3/id/38217

Shah, Abid Hussain, 2007,The Volatile Situation of Balochistan – Options to Bring it into Streamline. Master's Thesis, Naval Postgraduate School, Monterey, United States. http://hdl.handle.net/10945/10280

Siddique, Osman, 2013, Rational Irrationality: Analysis of Pakistan's Seemingly Irrational Double Game in Afghanistan. Master Thesis, University of Oslo, Oslo, Norway. https://www.duo.uio.no/ handle/10852/37342

Shahrani, M. Nazif. 2001. 'Resisting the Taliban and Talibanism in Afghanistan: Legacies of a Century of Internal Colonialism and Cold War Politics in a Buffer State', Perceptions: Journal of International Affairs, Vol. 5, No. 4.

Shahrani, M. Nazif. 2000. 'The Taliban Enigma: Person-Centered Politics & Extremism in Afghanistan', ISIM Newsletter, Vol. 6.

Tankel, Stephen, 2013, Storming the World Stage: The Story of Lashkar-e-Taiba. Oxford: Oxford University Press.

Topich, William J. 2018, Pakistan: The Taliban, Al Qaeda, and the Rise of Terrorism. Praeger Security International. Santa Barbara: Praeger.

Tripathy, Amulya K.; Pandit, D. Santishree; Kunjur, Roshni, 2016, Understanding Post 9/11 Cross-Border Terrorism in South Asia: U.S. and other Nations' Perceptions. New Delhi: Ess Ess Publications.

Tarzi, Shah M. 1993. 'Afghanistan in 1992: A Hobbesian State of Nature', Asian Survey, Vol. 33, No. 2.

Verkaaik, Oskar, 2004, Migrants and Militants: Fun and Urban Violence in Pakistan.Princeton Studies in Muslim Politics. Princeton: Princeton University Press.

Vandenbroucke, Lucien S. Perilous Options: Special Operations as an Instrument of U.S. Foreign Policy. New York: Oxford University Press,

Violia, Marc Anthony. 1993. A Spy's Résumé: Confessions of a Maverick Intelligence Professional and Misadventure Capitalist. Lanham, MD: Scarecrow Press

Volkman, Ernest. 1989. Secret Intelligence. New York: Doubleday,

Von Hassell, Agostino. 2006. Alliance of Enemies: The Untold Story of the Secret American and German Collaboration to End World War II. New York: Thomas Dunne Books,

Williams, Brian Glyn. 2014. 'Afghanistan after the Soviets: From jihad to tribalism', Small Wars & Insurgencies, Volume 25, Issue 5-6.

Webel, Charles; Tomass, Mark, 2017, Assessing the War on Terror: Western and Middle Eastern Perspectives. Contemporary Terrorism Studies. Abingdon: Routledge.

Woods, Chris, 2015, Sudden Justice: America's Secret Drone Wars. London: Hurst.

Yasmeen, Samina, 2017, Jihad and Dawah: Evolving Narratives of Lashkar-e-Taiba and Jamat ud Dawah. London: Hurst.

Yusuf, Moeed, 2008, Insurgency and Counterinsurgency in South Asia: Through a Peacebuilding Lens. Washington, DC: United States Institute of Peace Press.

Zaidi, Syed Manzar Abbas, 2016, Terrorism Prosecution in Pakistan. USIP Peaceworks, No. 113 https://www.usip.org/publications/2016/04/terrorism-prosecution-pakistan

Zaidi, Syed Manzar Abbas, 2016, Reconstituting Local Order in Pakistan: Emergent ISIS and Locally Constituted Shariah Courts in Pakistan. (Brookings Local Orders Paper Series, Paper 4). https://www. brookings.edu/research/reconstituting-local-order-in-pakistan-emergent-isis-and-locally-constitutedshariah-courts-in-pakistan

Index

About the Author

Musa Khan Jalalzai is a journalist and research scholar. He has written extensively on Afghanistan, terrorism, nuclear and biological terrorism, human trafficking, drug trafficking, and intelligence research and analysis. He was an Executive Editor of the Daily Outlook Afghanistan from 2005-2011, and a permanent contributor in Pakistan's daily *The Post*, *Daily Times*, and *The Nation*, *Weekly the Nation*, (London). However, in 2004, US Library of Congress in its report for South Asia mentioned him as the biggest and prolific writer. He received Masters in English literature, Diploma in Geospatial Intelligence, University of Maryland, Washington DC, certificate in Surveillance Law from the University of Stanford, USA, and diploma in Counter terrorism from Pennsylvania State University, California, the United States.

Mr. Imal Katswal graduated from the Faculty of Law and Political Science, Kabul University, 1995. He is living in Europe since 2004. From 2009 to 2014, he worked as an official translator in the Office of the Commissioner for Refugees in Belgium. Imal Katswal, is an active member of PTM in Douai, France who contributed his professional experience, intellectual tips-off and ideas to make PTM members vigilant and updated. He worked and supported Pashtuns right movements in Belgium from 2009-2013, before shifting to France. However, he participated in PTM protests and rallies in Europe to draw the attention of international community towards the forced disappearances and torture of its workers and leaders by the agencies. Currently, he lives in France.